The Nobility of
the *Election* of Bayeux,
1463-1666

The Nobility of
the *Election* of Bayeux,
1463-1666

Continuity through Change

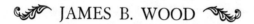 JAMES B. WOOD

PRINCETON UNIVERSITY PRESS
PRINCETON, NEW JERSEY

Copyright © 1980 by Princeton University Press
Published by Princeton University Press, Princeton, New Jersey
In the United Kingdom: Princeton University Press, Guildford, Surrey

All Rights Reserved

Library of Congress Cataloging in Publication Data will be
found on the last printed page of this book
Publication of this book has been aided by a grant from
The Andrew W. Mellon Foundation

This book has been composed in linotype Granjon

Clothbound editions of Princeton University Press books are printed
on acid-free paper, and binding materials are chosen for
strength and durability.

Printed in the United States of America by Princeton University
Press, Princeton, New Jersey

TO MARGI

CONTENTS

vii

ᥫᩣ LIST OF TABLES ᥫᩣ

ᏽᎦ LIST OF FIGURES ᏽᏎ

xi

✒ ACKNOWLEDGMENTS ✑

THE IDEA for this book came in 1968, when I had just begun my graduate study at Emory University. I was struck then, as now, by how little is known about the early modern French nobility. For reasons that were at first hard to identify, I found most treatments of the nobility unconvincing. This book represents my attempt to produce a more convincing interpretation of that nobility.

Several institutions and foundations provided financial assistance and scholarly resources for this project, including Emory University, Williams College, the Ford Foundation, the American Council of Learned Societies, and the Andrew W. Mellon Foundation, whose grant assisted the publication of this work. The librarians of Emory University and Williams College Libraries as well as the archivists and staffs of the Bibliothèque nationale, the Archives nationales, the Bibliothèque municipale de Rouen, the Archives départementales de la Seine-Maritime and the Archives départementales de Calvados provided invaluable help in locating the primary and secondary sources on which this book rests.

I also owe a debt of gratitude to the many people who assisted and encouraged me in this work. First of all, my thanks to Professors Robert A. Smith and Rondo Cameron of Emory University, for their careful reading of a much earlier version of this manuscript. My colleagues at Williams College, in particular Professors Robert G. L. Waite, Francis Oakley, Gordon Winston, and David Rice, contributed a great deal by their criticisms. Professors Miriam U. Chrisman of the University of Massachusetts, John J. Hurt of the University of Delaware, Robert M. Kingdon of the University of Wisconsin, and William A. Weary of Amherst College (whose own work in this area should soon be in print) provided many thoughtful suggestions, and, at critical moments, the positive reinforcement and encouragement from relatively objective observers that all developing historians need. My thanks go also to Ms. Jocelyn Shaw, who typed the initial draft of the book, and Ms. Georgia Swift, who retyped much of the manuscript before it went to press.

Special thanks go to Professor J. Russell Major of Emory University, my dissertation director, whose continued interest in my career and work since I received my degree has been most appreciated.

Finally, the greatest debt of gratitude belongs to my wife, Margi, whose love and intellectual comradeship sustained me and guided my steps every inch of the way. I dedicate this book to her.

The Nobility of
the *Election* of Bayeux,
1463-1666

A HISTORICAL PROBLEM:
THE EARLY MODERN NOBILITY

THIS WORK reconstructs the socioeconomic history of an entire provincial nobility over a period of two centuries. The reader will not encounter here the detailed history of a few great noble families or a tightly restricted portion of officialdom. What will be uncovered, instead, are the social and economic structures and changes that characterized all the nobles, poor as well as prosperous, obscure as well as notable, who lived in the *élection* (a tax district) of Bayeux, in Lower Normandy, between the mid-fifteenth and mid-seventeenth centuries.

This approach to the study of the nobility combines the methods of quantitative social history with a local historical perspective. Its strength lies in the fact that its conclusions are based on solid, cumulatively corroborating evidence of the collective experience of an entire local nobility. Generalizations about the economic and social life of this area's nobility, therefore, can be made a great deal more confidently than if this work relied on a small number of isolated, unrepresentative individual cases, as most previous work on the early modern nobility has.

Although interesting as a local study, its findings have broad significance for more general historical interpretations of the nobility and, indeed, of early modern France. My goal has been to test accepted theories and to provide materials for the construction of new generalizations. Therefore, this introduction concentrates on the general historical and historiographical background against which the experience of the

Bayeux nobility will take on a significance that transcends its own particular history. Current theories about the early modern nobility will be examined critically and the inadequacies of current research explored. It will be shown how the present work addresses itself to these weaknesses in our knowledge of the early modern nobility, and how its conclusions will suggest revisions that need to be made in accepted interpretations of the role of the French nobility in the sixteenth and early seventeenth centuries.

Historians have long been aware of the important position the nobility occupied in early modern French society. From feudal times to the Revolution, it was one of the most important propertied groups in France and had a higher social status and prestige than any other group in French society. Its landholdings and social status, combined with training in the use of arms, enabled it to dominate local life in most of rural France in the sixteenth and seventeenth centuries. In addition to dominating local life both socially and economically, the nobility also played an influential role in regional and national political life. Military commands were a noble preserve, and almost all important royal posts were filled by nobles, many of them newly ennobled. Nobles controlled the Parlements and other royal courts, dominated most provincial assemblies, and were active participants in Assemblies of Notables and in meetings of the Estates General. The officers of state and the monarchs' most influential advisors were drawn almost exclusively from their ranks. They played a leading and sometimes dominant role in the social disorders, rebellions, and civil wars of the sixteenth and seventeenth centuries, forcing French monarchs to spend much of their resources and energy in pacifying, buying off, or defeating important sections of the nobility. The importance of the nobility is further demonstrated by the attention that social commentators and theorists at that time gave to it in their analyses of French society and politics.[1] Modern historians have inherited this interest, and conclusions about the condition of the nobility and the origins of its behavior are an integral part of all explanations of the historical development of prerevolutionary France.

The origin of the Wars of Religion, for instance, is one of the most important questions historians of the early modern era must attempt to answer. The nobility helped to spread Calvinism in France and came to dominate its leadership. Their military prowess enabled the Huguenot minority to avoid extermination by the Catholic majority and to establish, at least temporarily, an officially recognized position within the French state. In addressing themselves to the question of why so many nobles converted to Calvinism, historians must directly confront the problem of whether religious change in the sixteenth century was caused by deep-rooted social and economic change, or was primarily the result of powerful religious beliefs and ideologies. An explanation of the role the nobility played in the spread of Protestantism and in the Wars of Religion, in other words, helps to shed light on the nature of the Reformation itself.

The establishment of an absolute monarchy in France is another historical development for which an understanding of the nobility's role is of paramount importance. Nobles were active, both collectively and as individuals, in promoting and opposing the growth of royal power. Thus an understanding of the origins of the nobility's political behavior is essential for an understanding of the pace of political change in France in the sixteenth and seventeenth centuries. And the significance we attach to these political developments depends to a great extent on the conclusions we draw about the way the rise of a more centralized French state affected the nobility's wealth, power, and influence.

To paint in even broader strokes, the importance attached to the period of the sixteenth and seventeenth centuries in the evolution of the modern world also depends to some degree on our assessment of the fate of the nobility. While most historians would readily admit that the nobility played an integral part in historical developments during that era, more often than not they characterize that role as a swan song. Many historians believe that modernization as it first began in Europe was fundamentally antithetical to the interests of the nobility, and that the development of modern institutions could only have occurred in conjunction with the destruction or displacement of the nobility's position and influence in society and government. Many interpretations of modern France, therefore, depend on the assumption that the destruction of the nobility as a class in the eighteenth century must have been preceded by its decline in the sixteenth and seventeenth centuries. So our view of the causes and timing of the emergence of modern France is also intertwined with our conception of the history and fate of the French nobility in an earlier period.

Given the importance of the nobility in society and the prominent role it is assigned in most interpretations of the sixteenth and seventeenth centuries, one would assume that historians have spent a great deal of time investigating it. In fact, there is no more neglected field in pre-eighteenth-century French social history. With a single exception, there are no substantive studies of the nobility of this era. The exception, Jean-Pierre Labatut's study of the upper nobility of France in the seventeenth century, concentrates only on the handful of great noble families at the pinnacle of French society.[2] There are, of course, colorful and suggestive studies of individual noblemen or noble families, and bits and pieces about the local nobility surface in every regional or urban study that emerges from the *sixième section* of the Ecole pratique des hautes études.[3] But we know almost nothing about those nobles who, while making up the vast majority of their class, never were individually notable enough to attract the interest of historians. While students of eighteenth-century France have Robert Forster's work on the nobility of Toulouse and Jean Meyer's magisterial study of the Breton nobility, Katherine Fedden's 1934 recreation of the social milieu of that renowned Norman gentleman, Gilles Picot, sieur of Gouberville, still remains the

6

most interesting and thought-provoking work on the nobility of the earlier period.[4]

Historians, however, have not permitted the lack of concrete studies of the nobility to deter them from making sweeping conclusions about their condition in the early modern period. Since the beginning of this century they have been confident that the French nobility underwent an economic and social decline in the sixteenth and early seventeenth centuries. This viewpoint portrays the nobility of that period as the loser in a long postfeudal struggle against the market forces of capitalism and the political forces of the monarchy. The classic statement of this thesis came from Lucien Romier in 1922. The first half of the sixteenth century, he wrote, witnessed a drastic decline in the real value of noblemen's incomes. By 1560 widespread impoverishment was forcing nobles to sell their lands and fiefs, and "in certain localities entire groups of gentlemen were dispossessed." Their lands and fiefs were acquired by an increasing number of merchants and officials, who formed a new "noble" class.[5]

Other historians soon added to this description of the decline of the nobility. Gaston Roupnel and Henri Drouot, for example, described similar fates for the Burgundian nobility, and Paul Raveau traced the widespread dispossession of nobles in Upper Poitou.[6] In a more general, but very influential work, Pierre de Vaissière, though characterizing the first half of the sixteenth century as a golden age for nobles, agreed that by the end of the century many impoverished country nobles had sold or were in the process of selling their property to rich merchants and lawyers.[7] And although four or five decades have passed since these men wrote, the theory of noble crisis and decline still has widespread currency among historians.[8] In a book published as recently as 1969, for example, Davis Bitton described a crisis of the nobility that departed in no significant respect from Romier's earlier formulation.[9]

Much of the continued attractiveness of this theory stems from its usefulness in causal explanations. If the concept of a declining nobility is accepted, then much of the social and political conflict of early modern France can be explained as a product of a kind of class struggle between a rising bourgeoisie and an economically declining nobility. A belief in a declining nobility is also important for those who wish to see the emergence of the unified modern state as the central theme of French history. Since in this view a strong state and a strong nobility were inherently incompatible, the foundering of the nobility in the sixteenth century was a necessary condition for the triumph of the state and its social agents and allies—the merchants, lawyers, and bureaucrats—in the seventeenth century.

The notion that the nobility was seriously weakened in the sixteenth and early seventeenth centuries proved to be so useful that for a long time historians rarely examined it too closely. A careful reexamination of their work, however, leads inescapably to the conclusion that the vast generalizations that have been made about the nobility really rest on very weak foundations. Although the decline of the nobility is often advanced as an indisputable fact, the only concrete evidence of decline cited in these works consists of isolated examples of the sale of fiefs to the bourgeoisie. Romier, for example, asserted that "this poverty of the nobility stands out from the facts and witnesses." But, close examination reveals that his case rests on two examples: the sale of only nineteen seigneuries in the area of Lyons at an unspecified time during the sixteenth century and the repossession and sale by the crown in 1531 of the Constable Bourbon's lands, when thirty-seven of forty seigneuries were purchased by commoners.[10] The appropriateness of the latter example at least is open to question, since most of the constable's lands were later granted to Louise of Savoy, and he had been deprived of them for political reasons not forced to sell by financial exigencies. Other works that have advanced a thesis of noble decline, those of de Vaissière or Bitton, for example, rest almost entirely on literary sources and deal with a narrow and selective group of individual perceptions rather than direct evidence of noble decline.[11]

In recent years this interpretation has been increasingly

8

questioned, but even when it was in vogue it did not remain completely unchallenged. De Vaissière's work, for example, which was pessimistic in terms of the fate of the provincial nobility during the seventeenth century, attempted to show that the first two-thirds of the sixteenth century was a time of great prosperity for nobles.[12] As early as 1964, J. Russell Major suggested that the nobility as a class might actually have improved its economic and political position in the sixteenth and early seventeenth centuries.[13] Much recent research has stressed the continued power and prosperity of the nobility in the period immediately following its supposed demise. Jean-Pierre Labatut, for example, emphasized the great wealth and prestige of the upper nobility of France in the seventeenth century.[14] Jean Meyer, Mohamed El Kordi, and Robert Forster outlined the economic, social, and political dominance by the nobility in the eighteenth century of, respectively, Brittany, the Norman Bessin, and the diocese of Toulouse.[15] During the same period nobles continued to monopolize positions in the royal council, the Parlements, the army, and the church.[16] How could the nobility be so prosperous in the eighteenth century if it had been in such economic trouble in the sixteenth and seventeenth centuries? How did the nobility manage to dominate French government and society until the very end of the old regime if it had been so seriously weakened in the sixteenth century? The fact that historians of the eighteenth century have discovered few effects of a previous, and no evidence of a continuing decline of the nobility raises the possibility that such a decline never took place.

The progress of this major historical revision, however, has been very slow. For even if serious questions have been raised about the adequacy of the concept of the decline of the nobility, the research that would enable a more convincing interpretation to be advanced has not been done. Attacks on the older view of the nobility have focused primarily on its lack of solid evidence and its own internal contradictions, rather than presenting fresh and positive evidence to the contrary. Despite their suspicion of the old view, historians have not yet

9

shown that the nobility as a whole or any significant part of it experienced relatively stable or prosperous socioeconomic fortunes during the Renaissance. To do this, studies that follow changes in the incomes, landholdings, and social composition of large numbers of nobles over long periods are needed. This study is designed to begin the process of filling this enormous gap in the social history of early modern France by providing the type of concrete evidence on which a new and much more positive evaluation of the history of the French nobility can be based.

There are several problems that any study must address if progress is to be made in resolving the debate over the status of the early modern French nobility. The first is to find an adequate definition of noble status and of the nobility as a social group.[17] The second is to measure the impact of changes in the membership of the nobility over time, uncover the relationship of different groups of nobles to one another, and analyze the relationship of the class as a whole to the rest of society. The economic condition of the nobility is a third vital area of concern. A fourth, and final, concern is the problem of systematically demonstrating the connection between social and economic change and the political and religious activity of nobles. Almost every assessment of the historical role of the early modern nobility has revolved around finding answers in one or more of these areas. This section addresses itself to the problem of finding an adequate definition of the nobility as a social group. The following section shows how these other areas have been handled in the past and indicates the way in which this work undertakes a different and more productive approach to them.

Confusion about the meaning of noble status and the identity of the nobility as a social group can be traced directly back to the sixteenth and seventeenth centuries. The meaning of "noble" and "the nobility" was the topic of intense debate during that period, a situation that was not helped by an outpouring of inconsistent and frequently contradictory royal proclamations. Debate centered on such topics as whether or not the nobility of individuals should be based on birth or merit, whether membership in the nobility should be defined customarily or legally, what sort of activities should be reserved for or forbidden to nobles, and how extensive the crown's rights to define and regulate the conditions of noble status should be.[18] Much of this debate was frivolous, but the existence of many competing ideas about noble status and the identity of the nobility as a social group has led to confusion among modern historians. When some historians refer to the nobility they mean the rural *gentilhomme* class, while others mean the *grands seigneurs*, or upper nobility. Some historians refer specifically to a *noblesse de fonction*, that is, officials ennobled by their position. The nobility has also been described as a landowning class, a military class, an ethnic group, and a political order or estate. The problem is that most of these categories either leave out large numbers of those who could legitimately claim to be noble, or are not based on any characteristic unique to the nobility and therefore do not really differentiate nobles from commoners.

The nobility has traditionally been portrayed, for example, as a seigneurial class of rent-receiving rural landlords.[19] But while this description fits many, indeed the great majority of nobles, it does not fit all nobles or unambiguously set them off from commoners. Some nobles owned little or no land; many, even if they enjoyed landed income, possessed no fief or seigneury. Some nobles worked their holdings with their own hands while others never even set foot on their vast holdings.[20] Many commoners were also landowners and possessed fiefs and seigneuries.[21] Furthermore, nobles who held office or royal favor received wages and pensions in addition to landed income.[22] Many of the richest men in the kingdom, as well as some of its paupers, were nobles.[23] It would be difficult to argue that the nobility of the sixteenth and seventeenth centuries constituted any kind of unitary economic group.

The nobility has also been described as a military class.[24] By the sixteenth century, however, a majority of soldiers were commoners, and only a minority of the nobility fulfilled regular military functions.[25] Many nobles were magistrates or financial officers.[26] A few even engaged in wholesale trade or industry.[27] Many nobles performed no visible function at all. Therefore the nobility was not restricted to any single function or occupation.

The eighteenth century developed a racialist theory of the myth that the nobility could trace its lineage back to the original race of Frankish conquerors.[28] But, in fact, the nobility did not differ ethnically from other Frenchmen; they intermarried with both commoners and recently ennobled families. While the theory of *race* is of overwhelming importance for understanding noble mentalities it cannot be used as the basis for an objective description of the nobility as a social group.

It is also true that the nobility was one of the three estates represented in the political constitution of France. But while the Second Estate was reserved exclusively for nobles, many members of the First Estate were also nobles. Furthermore, some nobles sat with the Third Estate in the Estates General. Noble status, therefore, was something that transcended the estate system. The three estates corresponded to the political divisions in French society. But the order of nobles was much more than simply the Second Estate in the political constitution of early modern France.[29]

Given the diversity of noble types, it should be clear that their legal standing as nobles was the only characteristic that simultaneously was shared by all nobles without exception and clearly divided nobles from commoners. The nobility, in other words, was what Pierre Goubert refers to as an *ordre juridique*, a special legal status which was both personal and transmissable through the male line.[30] The distinction between noble and commoner was probably the most fundamental division in early modern society, and from this distinction flowed the many legal or social privileges enjoyed by nobles. It is difficult to specify any unitary system of privileges and duties associated with noble status, but, in general, nobles were allowed to initiate legal cases directly at a higher court, they enjoyed tax exemptions of various kinds, and they took precedence over, or even excluded commoners, in a variety of social situations and activities (the right of precedence in processions, the right to hunt, the possession of a privileged place in church are examples).[31]

Many French nobles would have disagreed, of course, that the defining characteristic of the nobility was legal standing as a noble. Despite the fact that, juridically speaking, all nobles were the same, and that the nobility as a group was simply the aggregate of individuals who shared that noble status, some groups of nobles were of the opinion that other groups that claimed to be noble were not noble at all, or were certainly not as noble as themselves. Representatives or apologists of what historians have called the *noblesse de race, noblesse d'extraction*, or *noblesse d'épée*, for example, considered *anoblis* and nobles holding offices as bourgeois.[32] Many nobles did not clearly distinguish between being a noble legally and being accepted as being noble by other nobles.[33] But when historians follow suit and argue that new nobles were only quasi-nobles, or that it took three generations of nobility to remove all stain of a nonnoble background, they are confusing status and snobbery with legal reality.

Noble subgroups' exclusive definitions of what it meant to be noble ignore what all nobles held in common—legal standing as nobles—in order to emphasize what Pierre Goubert has called *les querelles d'ancienneté*, or internal squabbles of the nobility.[34] For despite the fact that the actual rights and exemptions enjoyed by the nobility varied from one locality to another, there were definite legal proofs of nobility, which were common to all of France, and, as we shall see in the next chapter, the membership of the nobility in certain areas was regulated by fairly effective periodic official investigation.[35] Within the boundaries of the well-articulated official mechanisms for regulating nobility, nobleness was simply a matter of legally establishing prior noble status, or, for new families, proving their status had been legally attained. Old nobles simply had to prove that their families had been living nobly according to local standards and had habitually used the correct local title of nobility. New nobles had in addition to show their letters of nobility. Only legal documents were acceptable, and proof of three or four generations, or one hundred years, of noble standing was enough to remove all doubts about one's origin.[36]

Acceptance of the fact that the early modern nobility was an *ordre juridique*, and that personal legal standing was the only criterion that set off all nobles from all commoners does not mean that the existence and importance of differences among nobles should be ignored. Within this legal category coexisted many different subgroups with different economic, occupational, and cultural characteristics. But what they all had in common was that they were nobles, not that they had a certain range of income or performed similar functions. In the sixteenth and seventeenth centuries this legal standing, by itself, was as important as economic standing or vocation. It is, moreover, the only way the score of different noble subgroups that have been identified can be compounded into a single group.[37] This approach sacrifices the idea of a monolithic nobility based on certain economic, functional, or even intellectual criteria, for, after all, such groups were only subgroups of the legal order of the nobility. The sooner the preconception of a homogeneous nobility is thrown out of contemporary early modern French historiography the better, for it only obscures the originality and complexity of old regime society.

The advantage of using a legal definition of the nobility is that it makes it possible to avoid many of the practical and conceptual errors that have hampered previous attempts to study the nobility. The legal definition is clear and comprehensive and was used consistently by royal authorities in their efforts to regulate claims to noble privileges. By casting the widest possible net, moreover, and studying all nobles, no significant group or number of individuals who legitimately claimed to enjoy the perquisites of noble status is omitted. In the past it was literally impossible to determine how large the nobility of any area was because historians disagreed over who could be considered "really" noble. And since no one knew how large the class was, it was hard to say anything sensible about the dimensions and impact of social mobility or the incidence of poverty. Consequently, accurate and systematic measures of the degree of social and economic change that affected the nobility during the sixteenth and early seventeenth centuries were never possible. The first part of this study will use periodic official investigations of the order of nobles to establish the size of the Bayeux nobility and identify the changes that took place in its membership over time, so that the *relative* importance of social continuity and change within it can accurately be assessed.

Once the general social and quantitative contours of the nobility are established, this work then analyzes the social relations between different types of nobles. Historians have placed a great deal of emphasis on the development of internal social divisions along quasi-class lines within the nobility during the sixteenth and early seventeenth centuries.[38] This conclusion is based almost entirely on literary evidence: the hostile social attitudes toward *anoblis* expressed by some *noblesse de race* in memoirs, pamphlets, and petitions to the Estates General has been assumed to reflect hard, underlying social realities. Without denying that such attitudes may in fact have existed, we will trace the relative size and importance of the principal noble constituencies through time, measuring in particular the degree to which new types of nobles were successfully assimilated into the older parts of the nobility, rather than simply deducing the nature of relations among different groups of nobles from literary sources. A close study of marriage patterns, social mobility, and the occupations or functional profiles of the nobility will enable us to draw some overall conclusions, set in the context of social evolution among the nobility of this area of Normandy, about the strengths and weaknesses of the nobility as a whole, its relations to other social groups, and its ability to adapt to changing social conditions in the sixteenth and seventeenth centuries.

In the end, however, much of the debate over the nobility centers on the very important question of their economic health as a class. Previous attempts to answer this question have failed because they adopted a piecemeal approach—the financial and economic health of the nobility as a whole or of large parts of it was inferred from a few scattered examples of noble indebtedness or the sale and transfer of a few estates to the bourgeoisie. Quite apart from the problem of developing meaningful time series from such inadequate sources, little or no attempt was made to determine whether the information gleaned from these individual cases was truly representative of economic conditions among the nobility as a whole. The approach adopted in this work—to reconstruct the income levels and landownership patterns of an entire provincial nobility at periodic intervals—avoids both these problems. It allows us to distinguish an individual aberration from a general pattern, and to make significant comparisons across time.

Furthermore, the unit that most historians have used in measuring changes in noble landholdings—the fief or seigneury—has rarely been described in any detail, despite the fact that fiefs were the principal form of noble property. This work tries to give an accurate picture not just of general trends in noble landownership, but also, on a fairly basic level, of the nobility's economic assets and the extent of typical noble properties.

Finally, though examples of indebted or poverty-stricken nobles crowd every page that has ever been written about the nobility of this era, no attempt has ever been made to determine the actual incidence and amount of indebtedness among nobles over any extensive period, that is, to assess the relative importance of poverty and bankruptcy as an everyday reality for the nobility as a whole. This study attempts systematically to reconstruct the incidence and importance of indebtedness among a sizable group of nobles and thereby establish the social identities of both debtor nobles and their creditors.

After reconstructing and analyzing the population and social composition of the Bayeux nobility—its occupational profiles and life styles, social mobility and integration, marriage patterns, landownership, income distribution, and indebtedness—my study then addresses itself to the fundamental problem: the connection between social and economic change and the nobility's political and religious behavior. Many attempts have been made to explain the nobility's refusal to serve and obey the crown at crucial moments in French history and its willingness to join and lead rebellions of various kinds. Extensive noble participation in the Huguenot movement, for example, is often seen as a response to worsening economic conditions in the mid-sixteenth century, rather than simply a mass religious conversion. Noble opposition to the crown in the late sixteenth and early seventeenth centuries has usually been viewed as the last desperate attempt of an increasingly impoverished and weakened class to rescue its political and economic fortunes by reversing the rising tide of monarchical power. More examples could be given, but the common thread running through almost all explanations of the nobility's actions and attitudes during that era is a fairly straightforward socioeconomic determinism: nobles become testy and then rebel because they are losing their lands; nobles challenge the crown because its agents push nobles from positions of authority and threaten their political dominance; impoverished nobles convert to Calvinism because they hope that rebellion will force the crown to restore them to their former condition, and so on. Such statements rest, ultimately, upon essentially quantitative concepts of socioeconomic conditions and trends among nobles, and a conclusion about the nobility's inability, as a social group, to react to changing times in a manner that would ensure its success and survival. To be valid, these quantitative notions about the changing fortunes of large groups of nobles need to reflect accurately the actual conditions of the time.

This work approaches the problem of the socioeconomic roots of noble behavior in two ways. First, it tries to assess the relative number and socioeconomic profile of those nobles who engaged in collective acts of civil disobedience or joined the Huguenot movement. These results can then be used to check the accuracy, for this area at least, of conventional historical explanations of the socioeconomic foundations of such behavior among the nobility. Second, reconstructing the facts of social structure and social change among the Bayeux nobility makes it possible to develop a much clearer picture of stratification patterns among the nobility than ever before. This clearer and more factually grounded picture of the social and economic actualities in noble life can then be used to put our understanding of the influence of the socioeconomic dimension on the individual and collective behavior of nobles on a sounder and more realistic basis.

Besides demonstrating that many historical generalizations that have been made about the social and economic position of the nobility in the sixteenth and seventeenth centuries are without foundation, we will also advocate a major shift in the perspective from which the French nobility has been viewed in the past. By accepting an inclusive rather than exclusive viewpoint, and by following the fortunes of the nobility as a whole rather than some section of it, over time, we can demonstrate the manner in which social change sometimes operated to preserve, rather than undermine, the strength of an old-regime elite. Although the cast underwent some changes over time, we will argue that the position of the nobility as a class probably improved during the sixteenth and seventeenth centuries. Acceptance of this conclusion, however, depends upon recognition of the fact that some processes that traditionally have been viewed as threats to the nobility actually helped to buttress and even increase its strength as a class. Social mobility, for example, will be viewed as beneficial rather than threatening, since infusions of new blood and property helped to preserve rather than to undermine the position of the class as a whole.

As an *ordre juridique*, the nobility continued to exist until its legal foundation was destroyed by the Revolution. The decisive element in any judgment about its importance in society should therefore be the changes in the aggregate wealth and influence of the legal order of the nobility as a whole rather than the health of any one of its constituent parts. The net effect of the triumphs and tragedies of its individual families and subgroups, this work will argue, may have been to leave the position of the nobility as a whole relatively unchanged or even improved. For in the *élection* of Bayeux, at least, in the sixteenth and seventeenth centuries, social change led to the preservation and enhancement, not the decline, of the social and economic power of the nobility.

I will also show that most of the socially determinative explanations of the religious and political behavior of nobles do not fit the actual historical experience of the Bayeux nobility. The origin of the Protestant movement among the nobility of the *élection* of Bayeux did not conform to any clear socioeconomic pattern. All types of nobles, rich and poor, old and new, *noblesse d'épée* and venal officeholder alike, converted to Calvinism and were active in the Huguenot movement, and the social and economic profiles of Protestant nobles were virtually the same as those of the *politiques* and the ardent Catholics. Nor did any clear common social or economic characteristics motivate nobles who participated in other collective acts of civil disobedience, such as the refusal to serve, despite the levying of heavy fines, at the siege of Amiens in 1597. The most satisfactory explanation of noble actions, it will be suggested, may lie less with any simple set of social determinants, than in the conflicting appeals of religious and political ideology, and personal and family loyalties.

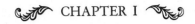

DEFINING THE NOBILITY:
THE *RECHERCHES*

THE DIFFICULTIES of finding adequate sources for social history in a prestatistical era like the sixteenth and early seventeenth centuries are well known. Comprehensive socioeconomic information was hardly ever systematically collected, and the few surviving sources are scattered and difficult to interpret. In the case of the nobility of the *élection* of Bayeux, however, this general rule does not apply. Starting in the middle of the fifteenth century, in response to the fiscal needs of the crown, royal officials began to conduct periodic *recherches*, or investigations of the nobility, in Lower Normandy. During the course of these *recherches* the crown adopted a clear legalistic definition of noble status, and over time the *recherches* developed into an effective institutional means of controlling membership in the nobility. The surviving records of these periodic inspections of noble credentials make it possible to study the changing social dimensions of the entire Bayeux nobility over a period of more than two centuries.

Since these investigations played an important part in shaping, and are the main source of information on, the membership of the Bayeux nobility, an understanding of how they were conducted and of their overall effectiveness is important. This chapter therefore will examine the structure, procedures, and standards of the noble *recherches* in some detail. It will show how this institution defined and regulated noble status in Lower Normandy from the mid-fifteenth to the mid-seventeenth century and analyze the cumulative effect of the *recherches* on the Bayeux nobility as a whole.

The *élection* of Bayeux belonged to the Lower Norman *généralité* (provincial administrative unit) of Caen. It contained 225 parishes, organized in nine sergeantries varying in size from 9 to 50 parishes, and covered an area of approximately 1,000 square kilometers.[1] Triangular in shape, the *élection*'s northern boundary ran for fifty kilometers along the English Channel between the Veys estuary and the mouth of the Seulles river, a coast made famous by the D-Day landings in 1944. The western boundary ran southward for some fifty-five kilometers, roughly paralleling the course of the Vire river, while the eastern boundary, following the Seulles much of the way, was about sixty kilometers long.

Like most of the rest of Lower Normandy, the *élection* of

Figure I.1 The *Election* of Bayeux and Lower Normandy

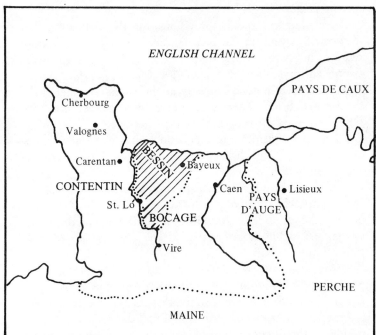

Bayeux was predominantly agricultural. Its northern half belonged to the rich Norman Bessin, now famous for its Isigny butter, while the southern half merged into the less prosperous Bocage.[2] In 1713 the entire area supported 22,620 hearths (*feux*), or somewhere between 80,000 and 100,000 inhabitants.[3] Bayeux, with approximately 6,000 inhabitants in the first half of the seventeenth century, was the only major city in the *élection*.[4] Neither unusually prosperous nor unusually stagnant during this period, Bayeux was nevertheless an important secondary administrative center, being the seat of a *vicomté* and a diocese as well as of the *élection*.[5] Like the rest of Lower Normandy, the area of the *élection* was free of the direct influence of any of the great urban centers, such as Paris, Rouen, or Lyons. The nearest major city, which lay thirty kilometers to the east, was Caen, the seat of the *généralité* and *bailliage* (bailiwick), and an important regional commercial center.

There were no special provisions for the nobles of the *élection* of Bayeux in the Norman customary laws. Like the rest of the Norman nobility, they had the right to wear swords and style themselves as *écuyer* or *noble homme*.[6] Their legal cases were initiated directly at the *bailliage* rather than the *vicomté* level.[7] They were exempted from the *taille*.[8] In return for these privileges, they were required to live nobly and not pursue demeaning occupations such as manual labor or retail trade.[9] They had to follow the strict Norman law of succession which excluded women and guaranteed at least two-thirds of the inheritance, with right of *préciput* (the privilege of first choice among fiefs), to the eldest son.[10] If fiefholders, they were liable for all the customary feudal dues and obligations including attendance at the *ban* and *arrière-ban* musters and military service.[11]

Since Normandy was the most heavily taxed province in France, and nobility brought exemption from the *taille*, regulation of the noble status of individuals in this area had been a constant concern of the crown and its local agents since the middle of the fifteenth century. As early as 1461, in the aftermath of the reconquest of the province from the English, and in response to widespread complaints about the usurpation of noble status, and therefore tax exemption, Louis XI had ordered a "general reformation" of the nobility of Normandy. This *recherche* was carried out in the nine *élections* of Lower Normandy under the direction of Raymond de Montfaut, bourgeois of Rouen and *directeur général des monnaies* in Normandy.[12] In each *élection* lists were compiled of "persons who have been certified to be noble and extracted from noble line and certified to be such by the *élus* [heads of an *élection*] and officers for the *aides* and similarly by other persons of the locality and for this cause not to be subject to the *taille*."[13] Lists were also kept of "other persons who claim to be nobles because of their wives, mothers, and noble fiefs which they have acquired, who otherwise would have to be subject to the *taille* according to their wealth,"[14] persons, that is, "who have not been found to be nobles, to be subject to the *taille* by the report of officers and others."[15]

Between 1461 and 1463, Montfaut certified a total of 1,024 individual male family heads as nobles in Lower Normandy, while rejecting 301 claims to noble status.[16] Even before Montfaut's commission had finished its work Louis XI was deluged with complaints from those who felt that they had been unfairly treated by the *recherche*.[17] For some time the custom in Normandy had been that a commoner who possessed a noble fief without challenge for forty years could claim noble status.[18] Many whose nobility was challenged by Montfaut apparently belonged to this category of "people who claim to be nobles because of their wives, mothers, and noble fiefs which they have acquired, who otherwise would have to be subject to the *taille*," persons, in other words, whose ancestors had paid the *taille*, but who possessed a fief and had been living nobly for several generations.[19]

Louis XI's response to these protests was to halt Montfaut's *recherche* before it reached Upper Normandy and to agree not to take official notice of the results of the commission's work in Lower Normandy.[20] But protests flared up again in

1470 when, as a fiscal measure, Louis attempted to require many of those who in 1463 had claimed prescriptive noble status according to Norman custom, to pay a *franc-fief* tax (levied on commoners who held fiefs) on their fiefs. The Norman Estates remonstrated that this was contrary to the laws and customs of Normandy dating back to the original Norman charter.[21] A compromise was reached between crown and province, which was embodied in the November 5, 1470 *charte des francs-fiefs*, a royal edict that, recognizing Norman practice, officially ennobled all commoners who had possessed noble fiefs for forty years in return for a collective payment of 47,250 livres tournois.[22]

In typical Renaissance fashion, the Normans had been allowed to buy official recognition of a time-honored customary local practice. During 1470-71 royal commissioners of *francs-fiefs et nouveaux acquêts* certified all the families who came under the provisions of the edict, and later decisions of the Chambre des Comptes confirmed the right to nobility of any family who possessed a letter of certification from the commissioners or could prove that they had been in possession of a noble fief in 1470.[23] The *charte des francs-fiefs* was periodically renewed by the crown until 1569. At that time it was abolished by Charles IX while the general practice of acquiring nobility through possession of a fief was also outlawed by article 258 of the 1579 Ordinance of Orleans, which stipulated that "*roturiers* and nonnobles buying noble fiefs will not for this be ennobled nor put in the rank and degree of nobles, whatever the revenue and value of the fiefs they have acquired may be."[24]

The *charte des francs-fiefs* of 1470 marked the beginning of the end of an era for the Norman nobility. Their outraged reaction to the crown's attempt to regulate noble status for royal fiscal purposes forced the crown to certify retrospectively the local practice of customary prescription of noble status. But by purchasing official recognition of such past actions, the nobility also recognized that the crown now had the right to demand official certification by letters patent of a previously unquestioned method of becoming noble.[25] And once its right to certify even the oldest of customary methods of ennoblement was established, it took the crown less than a century to take the next logical step and legally abolish customary prescription of noble status altogether. As far as Normandy was concerned, the retrospective ennoblement of fiefholders that the crown agreed to in 1470 marked the end of the period in which such prescriptions were legally acceptable.

Montfaut's *recherche* of 1461-1463 also marked the beginning of a new era of constant royal regulation of noble status in Lower Normandy. For Montfaut's much maligned investigation was only the first of a whole series of similar *recherches* undertaken by royal officials in Lower Normandy over the next two centuries: in 1523, 1540, 1555, 1576, 1598, 1624, 1634, 1641, 1655, and 1666.[26] The 1598 and 1666 *recherches*, like that of 1463, covered all of Lower Normandy.

For the *élection* of Bayeux, copies have survived of the 1463, 1523, 1540, 1598, 1624, and 1666 *recherches*.[27] Norman antiquarians and genealogists have used these documents since the seventeenth century, but they have not been systematically exploited. Yet for the *élection* of Bayeux, the rest of Lower Normandy, and even other parts of France, such documents form the foundation of any quantitative study of the nobility. Those for a single locality like the *élection* of Bayeux can be combined to give a clear picture of the mechanisms that evolved to regulate noble status, the basis on which judgments about nobility were made, and the social contours and dimensions of the provincial nobility of Lower Normandy between the mid-fifteenth and mid-seventeenth centuries.

Recherches for false nobles were fiscal devices intended to discover illegal usurpers of noble status and return them to the tax rolls. The 1540 *recherche* of nobles by the *élus* of the *élection* of Bayeux, for example, was directed at "noble persons engaged in acts derogating to nobility or those who abused the said privilege."[28] The review of the exemptions and privileges of the nobility in 1598 was part of a general *règlement des tailles*.[29] The 1666 "investigation of usurpers of the title of nobility," a brainchild of Colbert, was also undertaken in order to return false nobles to the *taille* rolls.[30] Since the *recherches* were undertaken for fiscal reasons and were often part of a general reformation of the *taille* rolls, the officials who directed them were drawn from the ranks of the crown's fiscal administration. Raymond de Montfaut, director of the first "general reformation" of nobles, it will be recalled, was a bourgeois of Rouen and *directeur général des monnaies* in Normandy, an office he had held under the English and been maintained in by Louis XI.[31] The 1523 *recherche* was undertaken by the officers of the *élection*,[32] while the 1540 *recherche* was directed by Guillaume Prud'homme, sieur of Fontenay-en-Brye and counselor for finances, with the local king's attorney and the *élus*.[33] The 1598 *recherche*, the first after Montfaut's to cover all of Lower Normandy, was directed by Jean-Jacques de Mesmes, chevalier, sieur of Roissy, a Parisian who was, successively, counselor at the Paris Parlement (1583), *maître des requestes* (1594), *conseiller d'Etat* (1600), *des finances* and *des dépêches* (1613), and finally "doyen des tous les conseils" (1642).[34] Roissy was assisted by Jacques de Croixmare, seigneur of Saint Just and of Bosrots, counselor in the Cour des Aides at Rouen, from a native Rouennais family ennobled in 1370, and Michel de Repichon, seigneur d'Avenay, a 1587 *anoblis* who, starting out as secretary to Louis de Bourbon, prince of Conde, became a *receveur général des finances* (1574) and by 1598 royal counselor and *trésorier général de France* at the Bureau des finances at Caen.[35] The 1624 *recherche* was directed by Mathieu Paris, intendant for the *généralité* of Caen, assisted by the officials of the Bureau des finances at Caen,[36] while Guy Chamillart, director of the 1666 *recherche*, was also the intendant in the *généralité* of Caen, son of an advocate at the Paris Parlement and father of the more well known. Michel Chamillart, *secrétaire d'Etat de la guerre*.[37]

While all the *recherche* commissions shared the common goal of discovering taxable mountebanks, their methods of operation differed. The 1540 *recherche* was conducted as a *chevaunché*, or visitation. In each parish the list of the exempted was examined and a *procès-verbal* held to determine the authenticity of the nobility of those families who claimed tax exemptions as nobles.[38] In 1598 Roissy and his assistants traveled from one *chef-lieu* to the next, acting as a court to which the noble family heads of each *élection* had to submit proofs of their nobility. The commission arrived in the *élection* of Bayeux in late February 1599, and held hearings throughout the month of March, though many Bayeux nobles had previously appeared at the hearings held in neighboring St. Lô in December 1598, and January 1599.[39] Chamillart in 1666 held his *procès-verbal* in the city of Bayeux, where he established a residence, and was assisted by a panel of four local gentlemen from extremely old families, one of whom, Michel Suhard, sieur of Loucelles, was also the king's advocate at Bayeux.[40]

The *recherche* commissions had access to local parish, notary, and assize records and to *taille* rolls—all of which could be used to identify persons who had previously claimed tax exemptions as nobles or had used the quality of *écuyer* or *noble homme* in their legal records and contracts.[41] In addition, the commissioners could refer to earlier investigations of individuals whose exemptions had been challenged by the local officials or contested by the parish in which they lived. In the *élection* of Bayeux alone, between 1460 and 1620, the Cour des Aides issued more than one hundred individual *arrêts* (decrees), unrelated to the *recherches*, confirming the nobility of local families.[42] All of these cases involved long legal proceedings, some lasting for several generations. Finally, investigators had access to the records of previous *recherche* commissions. The records of the 1540 proceedings in the *élection* of Bayeux, for example, contain many references to the 1523 *recherche*,[43] and Roissy in 1598 made many references to Montfaut's 1463 *recherche*.[44] The 1624 commission referred back to 1523 and 1540,[45] and Chamillart in 1666 used Mont-faut extensively and referred to the *recherches* of 1576 and 1598.[46]

Given the kinds of records that the various *recherche* commissions were able to use, especially records of previous litigations, the *taille* rolls, and the decisions from previous *recherches*, it seems extremely unlikely that any person who had claimed tax exemption or contracted as a noble could easily have escaped the scrutiny of the *recherche* commission. But in addition to the official records, there is plentiful evidence that the commissioners also paid attention to the opinions and rumors produced by local witnesses and informers. Montfaut's decisions were based in part on the testimony of people who were not officials,[47] while during the 1523 *recherche*, for example, the commissioners heard oral testimony from Pierre Picot, *curé* of Russy, that his mother, Anne de Tour, aged seventy-two was the daughter of a nobleman and should be taken off the tax roll.[48] In 1540, a Nicolas Reviers produced an affidavit from the vicar of his parish church stating that he had viewed a martyrology that mentioned many past foundations made by nobles with the name of Reviers.[49] The king's attorney in 1540 noted about Alonce and Thomas du Chastel, who had produced proofs going back to 1353, that the "rumor of this locality is that the said du Chastel are not nobles and that their commencement and origin is from one of them who lived at the castle of Neuilly as a servant of the bishop of Bayeux."[50] In 1598 the instructions to Roissy stipulated that announcements of the forthcoming *recherche* be read in every parish by the local priests so that complaints about abuses of the *taille* could more easily be gathered.[51] In 1624 a clerk noted on the genealogy of Jesse de Riuray the accusation that "there has been a Pierre de Riuray who was a sergeant."[52] Chamillart, it should be recalled, was assisted by four local gentlemen and offered informers two shillings out of every pound of fines levied on the false nobles they denounced.[53] The Lambert, Philippes, and du Chastel families, who were indisputably noble, denounced families with the same surnames who were attempting to claim descent from them.[54] Clerks noted on the dossier of a Jean de Royville that "Semilly Potier promises papers to prove his *dérogeance* [derogation]."[55] The Poilley family were described as having "wanted to graft themselves on the family of the baron of Poilley, in Britanny, who does not recognize them."[56] The usurpation of Jean Petit-Coeur, it was observed, "is notorious in the province."[57] The Le Breton were said to "have a great deal of temerity to maintain that they are of noble quality and to produce a long descent of noble ancestors in the place of their birth where everyone is aware of their common extraction."[58]

To prove its nobility a family had to present to the commissioners a genealogy that showed its male filiation and to provide documents that indicated the links between generations and identified the individuals in each generation as nobles. Proof of at least four degrees, or successive generations of noble descent in the male line, the presenter himself counting as one degree, had to be produced because "in Normandy . . . the title is never secure until the fourth degree, it being required of those who claim they are nobles that they have justified, by authentic letters that their father, grandfather and great-grandfather have always lived nobly without exercising vile and mechanical acts nor contributed to the *tailles* and other subsidies."[59]

Although no one was required to prove more than four degrees of nobility, a family that did so was usually certified as being of the ancient nobility. In 1666, for example, it was ordered that "those who have borne the title of *noble homme* . . . , *écuyer*, and *chevalier* since the year 1560, with possession of fiefs, employs, and services, and without any trace of *roture* before the said year 1560, shall be reputed *nobles de race* and maintained as such."[60] New nobles, of course, who had not yet been noble for four generations, had to prove that the foundation of their nobility had been attained legally.

To establish their nobility, each family head presented the

recherche commission with documents that were supposed to prove that each generation indicated in their genealogy had indeed been noble. The number of documents demanded as proof for each degree varied. In 1540, 1598, and 1624, one original document, if it contained all the names in a particular degree, was considered sufficient, though usually more than one was submitted.[61] In 1666, Chamillart required at least three documents for each degree.[62] To be suitable as proof a document had to be an original record of a legally recognized transaction or agreement in which an individual was clearly identified as an *écuyer* or *noble homme*. The most common kinds of documents used were succession papers, marriage contracts, *aveux* (acknowlegment of a lord by a vassal), rent contracts, bills of sale, acts of tutelage, certifications of military service, inquiries by local officials, *arrêts* from the Cour des Aides, genealogies certified in preceding *recherches*, and, for recently ennobled nobles, letters of ennoblement with proof of their registration at the sovereign courts.[63]

Each family's presentation was checked to make sure that the genealogy satisfactorily established the male filiation and that the documents that accompanied each degree identified the individuals in that degree as nobles. The commissioners made certain that none of a family's direct ascendants in the male line had paid the *taille* or been inscribed on the tax rolls as a nonnoble. Family claims were cross-checked against the work of the commission in other *élections* and against a file of the previous *recherches*.[64] If the documents submitted by a family, taken together, showed that they had lived and been accepted as nobles for the requisite number of generations or more, copies were made of all the appropriate documents, the originals returned to the family in question, and that family recorded in the register of nobles.

The presentations of the Gallon and d'Escageul families, in 1540, are good examples of the kind of presentations that fulfilled all the requirements of the *recherches*. The Gallon family produced a genealogy with several very ancient letters and documents [*escriptures*] and among others one from the year 1015 how one named Guillaume Gallon was entitled *écuyer*. And by other documents up to the number of sixteen it appears sufficiently, by marriage contracts, *aveux, partages*, and otherwise that the predecessors of the said Gallon were noble persons holding a noble fief seated at Fontenay le Pesnel which passed directly in line of succession for 200 years until the father of the said Richard and Jean called Gallon. All their predecessors, degree by degree had held the said fief and another fief called the fief of Banville near Thorigny. By which production it appears and is sufficiently justified that the said Gallon are *nobles d'ancienneté*.[65]

The d'Escageul

have produced their genealogy with eighteen pieces of writing [*descriptures*] examined by the *procureur du roy*. The first, dated with the year 1246, makes mention of Messire Richard d'Escageul, *chevallier*, sieur of la Ramée. By this and by the other documents it appears and is duly verified the said d'Escageul to be *nobles d'ancienneté* because of their predecessors named in their said genealogy and from whom they are derived and descended as it is justified degree by degree. And until the present holding the said fief of la Ramée and the said fief of Sully which came into their line because of *damoiselle* Isabeau de Sully married to one of the said sieurs of la Ramée, and therefore the said sieurs of la Ramée and Sully at present.[66]

A major complaint of the *recherche* commissioners, and a frequent reason for challenging a family's presentation, was simply that a family's genealogy was so confused or their proofs so insufficient that it was impossible to determine whether their claims were warranted. Few nobles had the advantage of François le Bret, sieur of Val, who arranged for a cousin who was an attorney at the Cour des Aides to prepare his genealogy for the 1666 *recherche*.[67] More common were cases like Richard de Grimouville, sieur of Septvents, who in 1540 produced a fancy booklet with a prologue and five chapters but, unfortunately, "no justification nor genealogical order. . . . So that one cannot know or understand the said Grimouville's derivation without [further] production and clarification."[68] Jacques le Bonnet, "so-called" sieur of Aagy, was condemned in 1540 because his genealogy was so confused and contradictory that his predecessors were shown "descended by marriage from their own sister."![69] Jacques and Richard Pothier, though eventually maintained in 1540, represent another variation. Claiming descent from a Noel Pothier, ennobled by the *charte des francs-fiefs* in 1470, their initial presentation included Noel's letter of ennoblement and an attestation of military service from 1454, but they "produced no genealogy nor justified by written document nor otherwise that they are descended from the said Noel."[70]

Sometimes the genealogy was clear enough, but the accompanying documents did not prove the connections between the generations identified by the genealogy. Jean de Grandval, for example, produced in 1540 a genealogy and fifteen notary records dating back to 1336 to prove his nobility, "but it is not shown nor verified by the said production that those named in the genealogy were derived not descended the one from the other nor that the said Jean at present was descended nor possessed a right of succession to anything."[71] Jean Guerente was challenged in 1540 despite the fact that he produced thirty-eight pieces of evidence dating back to 1361 in each of which the principals were styled *écuyer*, because it was not "verified by the said production that they are descended the one from the other."[72] In 1666, when the commissioners condemned the Le Breton family to pay the *taille*, one of the main points against them in the charge of usurpation was that their genealogy showed them to be descended from a younger son of another, but legitimately noble, Le Breton family who had never been married.[73]

32

Occasionally the proofs provided by a family were so weak that they were summarily condemned. A typical example is the 1540 condemnation of Laurens and Gilles le Senescal, who

> produced a genealogy by which they explain that in the region of Brittany, near the city of de Penes there formerly was a gentleman named Allain le Senescal, sieur of Fontaines from whom was descended Georges, from this Georges, Jean, from his Jean Georges, Guillaume, and Pierre, father of the said Laurens and Gilles. This Pierre, younger son of the said Jean came to live in the parish of Surrain, *vicomté* of Bayeux. But the said le Senescal have not produced nor shown a single piece of writing that makes mention of them or their predecessors as well as in the year 1523 their said father did not produce their genealogy nor claim that they were nobles. Because of which the said Senescal will not be permitted to enjoy the privilege of nobility.[74]

Varied reasons were advanced to explain the lack of a suitable presentation. One of the most common was that the person who was supposed to present the genealogy and proofs was unable to do so because he was a minor. Another was that the required documents were unattainable. For example, in 1540, Jean de la Haye "notified the commission in writing that he is underage and that he does not yet have the administration of his property. And that he is the natural and legitimized son of the deceased Pierre de la Haye, *écuyer*, and of *damoiselle* Margueritte Gygnel and also that his father was from the house of Beaumont in Brittany, a noble and very ancient house, but he does not have the documents to prove this because of his being underaged and asks to be excused."[75] François d'Arragon, also condemned in 1540, testified that "he was fifteen years old when his father died and that presently he is only twenty years old and that he does not have certain knowledge of his extraction because he is not furnished with information of the nobility of his predecessors and the *aînes* [elder branch] had always lived and are now living in the

bailliage of Cotentin. He intends to use what will be pro-
cured by his said relatives before the *élus* in the *bailliage* of
Cotentin and to that end has requested and asked for time."[76]

Guillaume de Hudebert was condemned in 1540 because he
gave the commissioners only a "copy of an attestation by Jean
Heudey, *élu* at Alençon which says that the said Hudebert has
duly presented a genealogy to the *élu* at Alençon with documents, and the copies of the documents along with the said
genealogy were retained by the *procureur du roy* in the *élection* of Alençon. Nevertheless, the said Hudebert at the time
he made his production in this *élection* was in possession of
the said originals; therefore he cannot be excused that he did
not produce them given he lives in this *élection*."[77]

If a commission found fault with some part of a family's
documentary proof, they almost always gave them the opportunity to produce additional evidence. In 1540, for example,
the king's attorney threatened to prosecute Noel le Moigne if
he did not "otherwise show and justify" his filiation.[78] Pierre
Helyes, sieur of Luserne, and his cousins Jean and Nicolas,
were given time in 1540 to produce additional proof of their
great-grandfather's 1461 *ennoblement* which they successfully
did.[79] Members of the Tallevast family were requested in
1540 to produce additional verification of their nobility and
in 1624 to "justify more amply" or be condemned.[80] In 1598
it was noted that the Frolet family, ennobled in 1543, would
be maintained when they produced proof that they had reacquired the hypothetical rent that had previously been set up
to soften the blow of their removal from the *taille* role in the
parish of La Vacquerie,[81] while Philippe Courtelais took the
opportunity that Roissy gave him to be styled *ancienne noblesse* by providing additional evidence of the filial link to
his father, Pierre Courtelais.[82] In 1624 the Messager and Du
Fay families were also ordered to "justify more amply" if
they wanted to continue to enjoy their tax exemptions as
nobles,[83] and there are many instances of families providing
additional proofs (sometimes to no avail) in 1666.[84]

The time allowed to produce additional evidence varied.

Montfaut's 1463 *recherche* only vaguely notes that those who were condemned as nonnobles "have had the time to verify their nobility."[85] In 1598 Antoine Forestier, sieur of Carelettes, was given three weeks to justify that he had married a descendant of the family of Joan of Arc (which by special provision carried ennoblement), which he did by producing his marriage contract.[86] But the Estampes family was given a month,[87] and Charles le Mercier, a lieutenant for the *bailliage* in the *vicomté* of Bayeux, who was involved in a suit for his nobility which had gone all the way to the Grand Conseil, was given a three-month extension to rid himself of the suit and get his affairs in order.[88] Only when a family was unable to produce the additional documents required within the given time or when their documentation was outweighed by counterproofs produced by the commission, were they finally condemned, fined, and put back on the tax rolls.

Table I.1 shows the types of decisions handed down in five of the six *recherches* that took place in the *élection* of Bayeux.

TABLE I.1

Decisions on the Noble Status of Family Heads Appearing
before the *Recherche* Commissions

| | Percentage of family heads | | | | |
	1463	*1540*	*1598*	*1624*	*1666*
Permanently condemned	6.2	1.6	1.4	3.2	6.0
Condemned but later maintained	8.0		.9	2.2	3.8
Required additional proofs		13.7	3.2	4.3	
Maintained without challenge	85.8	84.7	94.5	90.3	90.2
Total	100.0	100.0	100.0	100.0	100.0
Total number of decisions	225	314	567	536	630

35

On the average, one out of every ten family heads claiming to be noble was seriously challenged, and between 1 and 6 percent of all those who had enjoyed or attempted to gain tax exemptions as nobles since the previous *recherche* were permanently put back on the *taille* roll. These results and the numerous protests and recriminations of those who were condemned as false nobles by the different *recherches* indicate that, if anything, the commissioners probably erred on the side of harshness.

Those who were rejected by the commissions as false nobles or usurpers fell into four general categories. The first group was composed of individuals who could properly claim noble ancestry but who (either themselves or one of their direct ascendants) had engaged in some profession or occupation considered incompatible with nobility. The *recherches* systematically weeded out individuals and families who had been notaries and sergeants, or who had engaged themselves as manual laborers or *fermiers*.[89] It was always possible to obtain letters in relief of *dérogeance* and to be reestablished as a noble, but the number of families who managed to rehabilitate themselves in this manner was small. Many *dérogés* pleaded no contest, or even renounced the quality of *écuyer* in an attempt to avoid a fine.[90] Often impoverished, some *dérogés* seem to have been treated with pity by the commissioners: Jacques Courtelais, for example, a carpenter, was released "without tax, given his poverty," in 1666.[91]

Bastards and legitimized children formed a second category of people consistently rejected by the *recherches*. Although they were legitimately of noble blood, bastards, or individual branches of families who claimed descent from a bastard, were always condemned as nonnoble.[92] And while the legitimized son of a noble might enjoy noble privileges during his lifetime, if his letters of legitimation did not also ennoble his posterity, his descendants, while of noble blood, were usually condemned. Bertrin de Leaupartie, for example, was the legitimized son of Jacques Maillard, *écuyer*, sieur of Leaupartie. But his son Guillaume Leaupartie was condemned in 1598, and Guillaume's grandsons were condemned in 1666 because "their letters of legitimation do not bring ennoblement and are not *for his posterity born and to be born*."[93] Like the *dérogés*, bastards were often poor and sometimes renounced their pretensions without a struggle.[94]

A third group rejected by the *recherches* included those who for reasons of personal vanity, in an effort to gain notoriety, or in ignorance of the actual legal requirements, insisted on styling themselves as *écuyer* even though it was obvious that there was no objective basis for their claim. These fringe elements were often poverty-stricken old soldiers like Eustache Thezart, "poor," a veteran of eight campaigns, who renounced his claim to nobility in 1666,[95] or Jean Monnier, who had served "*longtemps*," possessed "nothing," and acquiesced without protest in his condemnation.[96] Some marginal families of this type appeared before successive *recherche* commissions only to be condemned time after time. For five generations members of the d'Arragon family attempted to claim nobility, only to be condemned in 1540, 1598, and 1624, and the Senescal family whose 1540 condemnation was cited above, were still unsuccessfully trying to establish their claim to nobility as late as 1624.[97]

The fourth and largest group was composed of individuals and families who, over the course of several generations, attempted to usurp noble status by concealment and fraud. It was chiefly at this group of offenders, who often had the advantage of sizable incomes and distinguished official posts, that the *recherches* were aimed. Derogating nobles, after all, were not accused of usurping their nobility, but of not living up to it. Bastards and legitimized nobles were at least the blood offspring of genuine nobles, even if they had no legal claim to the status of nobility itself. Poor or desperate elements on the fringes of the nobility who insisted on styling themselves nobles, or stubbornly pressed obviously spurious claims in *recherche* after *recherche*, could easily be detected and were as much objects of pity or derision as serious threats to the public order. These marginal nobles were also the victims of

37

the *recherches,* but the commissioners were much more interested in uncovering those substantial commoners who had managed to usurp noble status and remove themselves from the tax rolls and were now involved in the process of covering their tracks by whatever means necessary.

Such usurpers attempted to use a wide variety of illegal methods to establish their nobility. They smoked documents and changed seals to make them appear older,[98] forged dates and signatures,[99] and produced completely counterfeit *arrêts,* inquiries, and letters patent.[100] They tried to substitute the documents of, or claim descent from, legitimate noble families with surnames similar to their own.[101] Some attempted to claim descent from distant relatives who may have received bona-fide letters of ennoblement but were not their direct ascendants. Others claimed descent from nonexistent persons or from ascendants who had previously been convicted of usurpation and put back on the *taille* roll.[102] Some were accused of arranging with relatives who held posts at the Cour des Aides to receive spurious, but seemingly official, confirmations of their alleged nobility, or false letters of rehabilitation.[103] Others were accused of making sub-rosa accommodations with their neighbors so they would not be informed on.[104] Many officeholders tried to usurp noble status under the cover of their official positions or conspired with minor officials to cover up their true origins.[105] Three specific examples from the 1666 *recherche* of families who were uncovered and rejected as usurpers and false nobles will give a good indication of what was involved.

Jean Petit-Coeur, sieur of Saint-Vaast, a resident of Bayeux and grand master of waters and forests in the *vicomté* of Bayeux, was condemned as a usurper in 1666 because his grandfather, Pierre Petit-Coeur, a physician who liked to style himself *écuyer,* had been included in the 1576 *recherche* among the nonnobles living in Bayeux.[106] Pierre's son, also named Pierre, an *élu* in the *élection* of Bayeux, had continued the usurpation, and Jean, the *condamné,* could produce only copies rather than the original documents themselves, to prove the link between his grandfather and great-grandfather.[107] The commission admitted that the Petit-Coeur had been living nobly since 1576; in addition to holding an office, for example, Jean had served at the siege of Bordeaux in 1616 and as a lieutenant in the light cavalry in 1630, and in 1666 his sons were all serving in the army.[108] Nevertheless, the commissioners concluded that his family had clearly usurped the quality of *écuyer* because they could not satisfactorily prove the foundation of their nobility, had never received letters of ennoblement nor held an ennobling office, and their usurpation was "notorious in the province."[109]

The grandfather of Pierre Godefroy, sieur of la Gouberdiere, Laurens Godefroy, his second cousin, and two other relatives who were officeholders but did not reside in the *élection*, were in 1666 accused of having taken advantage of a 1566 fire in Pierre's house to usurp noble status. Claiming that his documents had been consumed in the flames, Pierre had arranged with a relative who was an advocate at the Parlement of Rouen to have letters issued confirming his nobility. These letters, however, were based solely on the testimony of neighbors whom he coerced into testifying that before the fire his family had always styled themselves *écuyer* and been accepted as nobles.[110]

Philippe, Thomas, and Pierre Le Breton were accused of using a false marriage contract and *aveux* to graft themselves onto the noble family Le Breton de la Bretonniere, even though their ancestors had always paid the *taille* in the parish of Bricqueville.[111] They had succeeded in obtaining letters in relief of *dérogeance*, which were nullified at the beginning of the seventeenth century.[112] They "accommodated themselves with all the parties who could have opposed them"[113] and "had adroitly taken advantage of the conformity of their name with that of the sieurs Le Breton whose predecessors were noble in order to claim that they were of their family."[114] They were also accused of using smoke and ink to make borrowed documents appear older.[115] The Le Breton of course protested that the commission was persecuting them at the behest of their personal enemies,[116] but the commission concluded that they "had a great deal of temerity to claim the quality of noble and to produce a long descent of noble ancestors in the place of their birth where everyone knows of their *roturier* extraction by the imposition to the *taille* of their father and grandfather and all their blood relatives."[117]

Although it is not possible to identify the social origins of every one of these false nobles, it is clear that most had roots in the bourgeoisie or officeholder class. Some apparently came from wealthy peasant stock, but more were simply bourgeois from Bayeux or Caen, or came from the ranks of the medical or legal professions. The majority were minor financial officials—investigators, assessors, receivers of the *taille*, controllers of the domain, *monnayeurs*, presidents, lieutenant generals, and *élus* in one of the Lower Norman *élections*.

There is some irony in the fact that many of the *recherches'* victims were servants of the very same fiscal institutions that were carrying out the *recherches*. The chief problem was that minor officials often attempted illicitly to turn their temporary right to the personal title of *écuyer* and certain fiscal privileges into permanent noble status in order to ennoble their descendants. While this tactic may have often been successful over the short run, the *recherches* periodically rejected the dubious credentials of such people and returned them to the tax rolls. It is interesting that, as we shall see in chapter three, most bona-fide new nobles came from exactly the same strata of society as these false nobles. The chief difference between successful new nobles and the false nobles was that the bona-fide new nobles almost always had received or purchased valid letters of ennoblement from the king. In accepting, from among a group of people with nearly identical backgrounds, only those who had gone through the minimum official routine necessary to establish a new noble, and rejecting those who had not, the *recherches* were a powerful force for turning the monarchy's theoretical claim to sole control of the creation of new nobles into a practical and accepted reality.

Despite the appearance of strong cases against them, some of the families whom the *recherches* condemned as usurpers of noble status were able to appeal adverse decisions to the Cour des Aides or, during the 1666 *recherche*, directly to the king's council. A family could often get an adverse decision reversed if they had the resources to appeal the case, had lived nobly for several generations or served in the military, or had made themselves useful as officials. The Petit-Coeur, Godefroy, and Le Breton, for example, who were used as examples of usurpers in the preceding section, were all eventually maintained as nobles by the king.[118]

Because the commissioners' adverse decisions were sometimes overturned, and because the commissioners depended on the assistance of local officials, some historians have questioned the reliability of the *recherches* and the integrity and fairness of the commissioners. Edmond Esmonin's low opinion of the *recherches*, which appeared in his classic study of the *taille* in Normandy, for example, has often been cited as definitive evidence of the unsatisfactory nature of the *recherches*.[119] But Esmonin's unfavorable comments were directed at the entire *grand recherche* of Colbert, which covered many parts of France and many years; he considered Chamillart's 1666 *recherche* of the *généralité* of Caen, which included the *élection* of Bayeux, to have been one of the most successful.[120] Jean Meyer, who used part of the *grand recherche* of 1666 in his study of the Breton nobility, also concluded that most of the charges brought against the *recherche* were unfounded.[121]

An examination of the records of the various *recherches* that covered the *élection* of Bayeux indicates rather severe requirements for proofs. Although a complete record of the deliberations of any single *recherche* has not survived, the marginal notations, the critical comments on documents used as proofs, and the number of adverse decisions, taken together, indicate a careful, thorough, and even stringent adversary proceeding. This is not to suggest that every family was subjected to intense scrutiny, but even the greatest and most ancient local families were required to go through the procedure, and the commissioners were diligent in discovering what they considered faults and omissions in proofs, in requiring additional proofs, and in presenting counterproofs. The commissioners cannot be blamed for the fact that the crown overruled some of their decisions and maintained some usurpers in the nobility. And in any case, as we shall see in the next chapter, the total number of such successful usurpations was quite small. Despite the purely fiscal motives that lay behind the search for false nobles, the *recherches* did play an effective part in regulating noble membership and reinforcing the underlying legalistic nature of noble status. Between the end of the Hundred Years' War and the beginning of the personal rule of Louis XIV, the nobility of the *élection* of Bayeux moved from a situation in which their status was defined in a purely customary way, depending essentially upon the unchallenged adoption of a noble way of life over several generations, to a situation in which they were forced practically every generation to defend their nobility anew, on ever narrowing juridical grounds, to the financial officers of the crown.

CHAPTER II

THE MEMBERSHIP OF THE NOBILITY:
SIZE AND SOCIAL MOBILITY

CHANGES in the size and composition of any social group are determined by the interplay between population changes within the group itself and the operation of social mobility across the social or legal boundaries that separate the group from other social groups. The relative degree of stability or continuity that characterizes the makeup of a group is directly related to the rates at which these twin processes of population change and social mobility take place. The French nobility, some historians maintain, was, demographically speaking, a dying class. Its members died out faster than they reproduced, and as a group stood in danger of eventual biological extinction if losses were not somehow made up through social mobility.[1] And indeed, as historians like to point out, at the same time that the old nobility was slowly becoming extinct, many new families were entering the nobility through one of the processes of ennoblement open to commoners during the old regime.[2] This widespread ennoblement enabled the nobility to maintain its numbers, for as old families inevitably disappeared, new families took their place.[3] But social mobility also led to changes over time in the composition of the class as a whole; as the number of genuinely old families decreased and the number of upwardly mobile, relatively new nobles increased, the membership of the nobility as a whole changed in a direction that was sure to cause anxiety among long-established noble lines.

The sixteenth and early seventeenth centuries supposedly witnessed a particularly dramatic episode of this sociological ver-

43

sion of the changing of the guard. On the one hand, it is said, the disappearance of the old feudal nobility, weakened by economic decline and decimated by war, accelerated. At the same time the number of new nobles increased dramatically. Opportunities for personal advancement had multiplied because of the general confusion of the times and the need of the crown to reward its faithful followers and to raise additional revenues through the sale of titles. As a result, it is argued, the old nobility was eclipsed and replaced by a class of new nobles drawn from the most affluent and politically astute sections of the Third Estate.[4]

This chapter uses the records of the noble *recherches* discussed in the previous chapter to show how population change and social mobility affected the membership of the Bayeux nobility between 1463 and 1666. The sixteenth century, as we shall see, was a period of unprecedented expansion for the Bayeux nobility, and the dynamism of this expansion was provided by the old nobility itself as much as by a dramatic influx of vast numbers of *anoblis*. The old nobility in the *élection* of Bayeux successfully traversed the sixteenth and seventeenth centuries, in large measure not only preserving, but at times actually managing to increase their numbers. There was a great deal of mobility into the Bayeux nobility during this period, but much mobility was only apparent— that is, it involved simple geographical displacements within the entire Lower Norman nobility rather than wholesale turnovers in the membership of the nobility.

Actual upward social mobility from the Third Estate into the nobility was a much more limited phenomenon than has generally been assumed, and genuinely new nobles never made up more than a small portion of the nobility as a whole. As a result, old families continued to dominate the membership of the nobility of this area from the mid-fifteenth to at least the third quarter of the seventeenth century.

As mentioned in chapter one, records have survived of the noble *recherches* that took place in the *élection* of Bayeux in

1463, 1523, 1540, 1598, 1624, and 1666. Two different kinds of family units are represented in the records of these *recherches*. The first are *lignages*, or noble lines, groups of nuclear families who had a common male ancestor and therefore shared a surname.[5] The second unit was the basic legal and fiscal unit of the old regime—a more restricted nuclear family composed of a married couple and their children or a group of unmarried siblings headed by the eldest son.[6] Changes in the aggregate size of the *élection*'s nobility over time can be traced by comparing the number of nuclear families that appeared in the successive *recherches*.

This information, which is presented in table II.1, shows that there was a tremendous expansion in the size of the Bayeux nobility between 1463 and 1666. The number of nu-

TABLE II.1

Growth of the Nobility, 1463-1666

Date	Number of families	Index
1463	211	100
1523	273	129
1540	309	146
1598	559	264
1624	520	246
1666	592	283

clear noble families living in the *élection* almost tripled, increasing from 211 to 592. The biggest increases came in the late fifteenth and sixteenth centuries: between 1463 and 1523, when the size of the nobility increased by 29 percent, and between 1540 and 1598, when the number of families increased by 81 percent. During the period with the highest rate of growth, 1540-1598, the era of the Wars of Religion, the *élection* absorbed 250 additional families, or better than one per parish. Even in the period with the relatively smallest growth, 1624-1666, some 72 additional families had to be absorbed by the *élection*'s nobility. Overall, between 1463 and 1666, the aggregate size of the *élection*'s nobility increased by 381 families.

The number of individual nobles involved in this expansion is impossible to determine exactly. The 1598 *recherche* seems to have been most complete, identifying all adult males (rather than just family heads) and all minor males.[7] For 559 families a total of 1,296 males were identified, a mean of 2.32 males per nuclear family. Assuming a sex ratio of roughly 1:1, this would mean an average of 4.64 persons per family. By applying this admittedly crude estimate to the number of families in 1463, 1540, 1598, and 1666, it would appear that the individual noble population of the *élection* of Bayeux went from about 1,000 people in 1463 to 1,400 in 1540, 2,600 in 1598, and 2,700 in 1666. This estimate contains a large margin of error, but the magnitude of population growth is obvious.

It is impossible to assess the significance of every aspect of such a tremendous growth in numbers on the *élection* of Bayeux. But some of the more significant quantitative implications are intriguing. Despite its expansion, the nobility never accounted for more than approximately 2.6 to 3.4 percent of the total population in the *élection*.[8] Thus in relative terms the expansion of the nobility did not by itself involve any quantitatively significant shifts in the *élection*'s social structure. But in absolute terms, the noble presence increased considerably between 1463 and 1666. One result of this increase was an accompanying increase in the number of parishes with resident noble families. By 1666 only a few parishes were without resident nobles, and not only did more parishes have nobles living in them, but the mean number of nuclear families per parish inhabited by nobles had also grown from 1.7 to 3.5. By the late sixteenth century, almost all the *élection*'s inhabitants lived within several hundred meters of an indigenous noble family. Such a tangible noble presence had not characterized the Bayeux countryside of the mid-fifteenth century.

It should also be pointed out that the increase in numbers was evenly distributed throughout the *élection*'s nine sergeantries, and since no single sergeantry grew disproportionately to the others, most of the growth took place in predominantly rural parishes. Despite a tripling in numbers, there was no tendency by nobles to abandon the land and establish residences in the city of Bayeux itself. With only 14 percent of its noble families living in the city and outskirts of Bayeux in 1666 (compared to 13 percent in 1463), the Bayeux nobility still remained overwhelmingly a class of *gentilshommes campagnards*.[9]

The significance of this numerical growth for the internal composition of the nobility remains to be determined, but it is important to reiterate that the expansion of the nobility sensed by many commentators at the time of the Wars of Religion did indeed take place in the *élection* of Bayeux.[10] What must now be investigated is whether or not this growth was the result of the wholesale creation of new nobles and took place at the expense of the old nobility. If expansion was the result of massive numbers of *anoblissements*, then for the nobility the sixteenth century must have been, as many historians have argued, an era of great change. Under these circumstances, the sense of crisis, which was expressed by some members of the old nobility at the end of the sixteenth and beginning of the seventeenth centuries, might have been well founded, since they would be fast becoming a much less important part of their own social class.[11]

The *recherches* are particularly valuable because the genealogies they contain allow us to trace the survival of family groups and identify the descent of individual nuclear families from one *recherche* to the next. By tracing the descent of each individual nuclear family and family group and then combining the results, a clear picture emerges of the relative continuity of noble membership and the resiliency of noble blood lines. Table II.2, for example, traces the survival of noble lines

TABLE II.2

Survival of Noble Lines

Starting date for group	Number of lines surviving to:					
	1463	*1523*	*1540*	*1598*	*1624*	*1666*
1463	163	101	89	76	69	60
1523		77	59	46	37	27
1540			41	22	19	16
1598				109	81	78
1624					19	8
1666						63
Family group total	163	178	189	253	225	252

from one *recherche* to the next. All the noble lines who were present in 1463 were treated as a single group, as were the new lines who appeared at each subsequent *recherche*.

As can be seen, despite the fact that the total number of family groups represented in the *élection* increased from 163 in 1463 to 253 in 1598 and 252 in 1666, at all times noble lines were disappearing from the *élection* at a rapid rate.[12] Of the 163 noble lines present in 1463, for example, only 60 (or 37 percent) were still represented in 1666, and other groups showed similar rates of attrition. Of 77 lines appearing for the first time in 1523, for example, only 27 were still living in the *élection* in 1666, while the 41 new lines recorded in 1540 had dwindled to 16 by 1666, a reduction of more than half in a century and a quarter. The number of male-related family groups who continued to be represented in the *élection* from one *recherche* to the next, in other words, was constantly shrinking, and only through the appearance of new groups between *recherches* was it possible for the overall number of different family groups to grow as it did. On the surface, then, there was little continuity in noble membership across time. By 1598, more than half (131) of the noble lines living in the *élection* had appeared since the 1523 *recherche*. By 1666 only

24 percent (60 out of 252) of the family groups represented in the *élection* were the direct descendants of family groups who had been living in the *élection* two centuries previously at the time of Montfaut's *recherche*.[13]

The significance of this continual change in the pool of kinship groups living in the *élection*, however, must be put in perspective, for when the descent of these cohorts of noble lines is considered in terms of nuclear families, a very different picture emerges. Despite the ominous appearance of the turnover of kinship groups, the disappearance of family groups entailed losses by no means as serious as might appear to have been the case. The fact that many noble lines disappeared did not necessarily mean that the nobility was dependent upon constant replenishment to avoid extinction. Noble lines or kinship groups, after all, could contain up to a score or more of related nuclear families. Because the number of families included in these noble lines was so variable, any attempt to trace long-term demographic trends in terms of them contains hidden dangers. The most obvious of these, of course, is that population curves based on changes in the number of noble lines may not reflect population movements at all. The noble line is such an elastic unit that within a given group, even if many lines disappeared, those that remained could have experienced such a large increase in nuclear families that no real decline in total population took place.[14]

For example, if we trace the descent of the nobles maintained by Montfaut in 1463, we find that the number of original noble lines steadily declined between 1463 and 1666 (though the rate of decline leveled off in the seventeenth century). But if we trace the descent in terms of individual nuclear families of this group, we find (table II.3) that as late as 1666 the total number of nuclear families who could trace their origins directly back to 1463 had hardly declined at all. The 163 noble lines alive in 1463 included 211 nuclear families; the 66 lines from this group who survived to 1666 contained 184 nuclear families, a decline in total population of only 13 percent over a 200-year period. Between 1463 and 1598, more-

TABLE II.3

Descent at Subsequent *Recherches* of Nuclear
Families and Family Groups Maintained in 1463

Number in:	Noble lines	Nuclear families
1463	163	211
1523	125	177
1540	104	172
1598	84	229
1624	76	211
1666	60	183

over, these nobles actually increased (from 211 to 229) and
between 1463 and 1624 maintained (at 211) their numbers.

The ability of the nobility as a whole to avoid extinction
over time can be even better illustrated by taking the five
groups of noble nuclear families present at the first five
recherches and counting their direct descendants at the time
of the last *recherche* in 1666 (table II.4). We can then compute
the relative rate of disappearance for each of these five groups
and estimate the number of centuries needed for the complete
disappearance of each group from the *élection* of Bayeux if
there had been no replacements for losses and if these rates

TABLE II.4

Survival Rates for the Nobility, 1463-1666

Period	Families at start of period	Descent in 1666	Percent change	Percent change per 100 years	Centuries required for extinction
1463-1666	211	183	−13.3	− 6.6	15.2
1523-1666	273	259	− 5.9	− 3.6	27.7
1540-1666	314	302	− 3.8	− 3.0	33.3
1598-1666	557	459	−17.6	−25.9	3.9
1624-1666	525	482	− 8.8	−21.0	4.8

had remained constant. As can be seen, the percentage of each group lost over a century's time ranged from 3 to 25.9. In different periods, therefore, the ability of the nobility as a group to avoid extinction differed considerably. In some periods (between 1598 and 1666, for example) the nobility seemed on its way to extinction, as many nuclear families died out or moved out of the *élection*. But across longer periods (notably 1540-1666) the nobility was almost able to maintain its numbers by procreation alone.[15] Indeed, over the shorter periods between individual *recherches*, as we have already noted, the nobility was actually able to increase its numbers without any assistance from social mobility at all.

The ability of nobles to procreate sufficiently to increase their numbers over short periods and practically maintain themselves demographically over long periods played, as we shall see, an important part in the overall expansion of the nobility that took place between the mid-fifteenth and late sixteenth centuries. But the records of the *recherches*, besides allowing us to follow the survival and descent of family groups and nuclear families from one point in time to another, also enable us to identify clearly the new families who had been added to the *élection*'s nobility between *recherches*. Figure II.1 shows how the changes in the numbers of established families from one *recherche* to the next, which were discussed in the previous section, were related to the number of nuclear families who were appearing in the *élection* for the first time.

The magnitude and importance of social mobility in the overall process of expansion and renewal is shown quite clearly by this figure. We have already noted that the number of noble nuclear families living in the *élection* almost tripled between 1463 and 1666 (see table II.1). This tremendous growth was made possible by the simultaneous interaction of actual population increases among resident nobles and constant additions of newcomers to the *élection*'s nobility. As can be seen, only in one period (1598-1624) did social mobility fail to make good whatever population losses occurred among

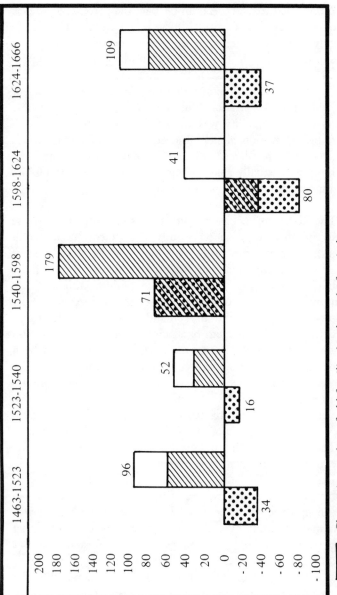

Figure II.1 Changes in the Composition of the Nobility Between *Recherches*

Change in number of old families by the end of period

Number of new families by end of period

Net change (new families + change in number of old families)

established families. And in the sixteenth century such losses were minimal; in fact, actual increases in the number of established families through procreation between 1540 and 1598 more than made up for all losses that had taken place between 1463 and 1540. Since, demographically speaking, the established nobility was more than holding its own in the sixteenth century, additions to the nobility due to social mobility did not just replace extinct families, but resulted in a large net expansion in membership.[16] As a result, in the 1540-to-1598 period, when net population increases among established families took place simultaneously with the greatest amount of social mobility in the whole two-century period, the membership of the nobility almost doubled over a span of less than sixty years.[17] In the early seventeenth century there was a slight shrinkage in numbers, but by 1666 these losses had also been more than made up through continuing additions of newcomers, and the nobility as a whole again experienced a slight increase in numbers.

But while established nobles appeared capable of a degree of demographic resiliency which until now has not been fully appreciated by historians, the fact remains that a great deal of the substantial sixteenth-century, and almost all of the slight seventeenth-century expansion resulted from social mobility. Without the appearance of newcomers among the *élection*'s nobility there would have been a slight reduction, rather than an expansion, in the size of the nobility. The nature of this constant social mobility must now be analyzed before the overall impact and significance of combined population change and social mobility on the internal composition of the Bayeux nobility can be assessed.

A favorite technique of historians who wish to measure the effect of social mobility within a limited group or area is to determine how rapidly the pool of family names changed through the disappearance of established and the addition of new names. It is assumed that the more quickly established names disappear and new names appear, the higher the level of social mobility.[18] This technique, unfortunately, contains a great many pitfalls, one of which has already been elucidated. To all appearances there was a tremendous turnover in the family groups of nobles living in the *élection* of Bayeux, so much so that one could conclude that by the end of the sixteenth, or midway through the seventeenth century, only a minority of the Bayeux nobility could trace its roots back to the mid-fifteenth or early sixteenth centuries. If this were true, of course, it would mean that the membership of practically the entire nobility would have changed during the sixteenth century. But, as we have pointed out, changes in the number of identically surnamed kinship groups of nobles can be extremely inaccurate reflections of the ability of a social group to maintain itself demographically across time. The original Bayeux nobility of 1463, it will be recalled, virtually managed to maintain its numbers across the entire two-century period, despite the disappearance of many kinship groups.

Similarly distorted conclusions about the effect of widespread social mobility on the membership of the nobility may arise if careful distinctions between different types of social mobility are not made. Here again, the information contained in the *recherches* is invaluable, for it identifies the antiquity and origins of those new, socially mobile families who were appearing for the first time in each *recherche*.[19] Table II.5 uses the convention adopted by the *recherche* commissions to divide these newcomers into "old" and "new" nobles: proof of four generations of noble status without ennoblement established a family as old nobility, or *noblesse de race*. The legal and customary dividing line of four generations corresponded to a lapse of about a century, so families who had been noble for more than a century at the time they joined the Bayeux nobility have been labeled "old" and those who had been noble for less than a century, i.e., those who were recent *anoblis*, have been labeled "new." This standard enables us to distinguish between vertically, or upwardly mobile, families and horizontally, or geographically mobile, families.

The sixteenth century was a period of dramatic growth for the nobility of this area, and we have noted the extent to which this expansion was dependent upon a significant amount of social mobility. But, as table II.5 demonstrates, most of the contribution to this growth from social mobility did not involve vast numbers of recent *anoblis*. It is true substantial numbers of fresh faces appeared in each *recherche*.

TABLE II.5

Additions to the Nobility, 1463-1666

	New families				
Date	Noble more than a century	Recent anoblis	Unknown	New family subtotal	Total families
1523	47	41	8	96	273
1540	33	15	4	52	309
1598	89	77	13	179	559
1624	34	5	2	41	520
1666	71	28	10	109	592
Total	274	166	37	477	2,253

Ninety-six recent arrivals appeared in 1523, 179 in 1598, and 109 in 1666. Overall, some 477 newcomers appeared in the five *recherches* that were made between 1523 and 1666. But very few of these apparently mobile families were actually *anoblis* or recently ennobled. A majority (274 families, or 57 percent) of the 477 new arrivals had been noble for more than a century at the time they joined the *élection*'s nobility. They were simply old nobles who had moved into the area from neighboring Norman *élections*. These immigrants were geographically mobile, but their immigration involved no fundamental change in their social status.[20] Only a third (166 families, or 35 percent) of the newcomers were *anoblis* or nobles who were still in their first century of nobility. Most of these were long-time residents of the *élection* who had received letters of nobility from the crown between *recherches*. This group was the product of upward social mobility, and it alone can be considered a genuinely new addition to the Bayeux nobility.[21]

Since *anoblis* or recently ennobled families never made up more than a fairly small portion of all new additions to the nobility of this area, the dramatic increase in the size of the nobility that took place in the sixteenth century was not primarily the result of an increased level of upward social mobility. In fact, most of the dynamism in this expansion was provided by old nobles: the old families who constituted a majority of the new arrivals to the *élection* were being added to an already existing pool of resident old nobles who were themselves in the midst of a modest population increase. For example, the families who had lived longest in the *élection* (since 1463 at least) increased their numbers from 177 in 1523 to 229 in 1598. Therefore the old nobles who immigrated into the *élection* (122 nuclear families between 1523 and 1598) did not simply make up for numerical losses among the oldest members of the *élection*'s nobility. Instead, the addition of large numbers of old noble immigrants, and to a lesser extent *anoblis*, and positive population growth among these new-comers themselves once they had joined the *élection*'s nobility, combined with population growth among the eldest residents of the *élection* to effect a tremendous swelling of the ranks of the nobility.

This combination of population increases and extensive geographical mobility had an effect on the internal makeup and composition of the Bayeux nobility that is at odds with previous descriptions of changes in the membership of the nobility in the sixteenth and early seventeenth centuries. Because immigrating old nobles always outnumbered recent *anoblis* among the fresh faces in the *élection*'s nobility, and long-resident old nobles were expanding their numbers through population growth, *anoblis* or recently ennobled families never made up more than a very small minority of all the nobles in the *élection* (figure II.2). And if we allow for the fact that *anoblis* themselves would have been absorbed into the *noblesse de race* after the passing of a century or more of nobility, we find that the relative number of old families (that is, families that had been noble for at least a century)

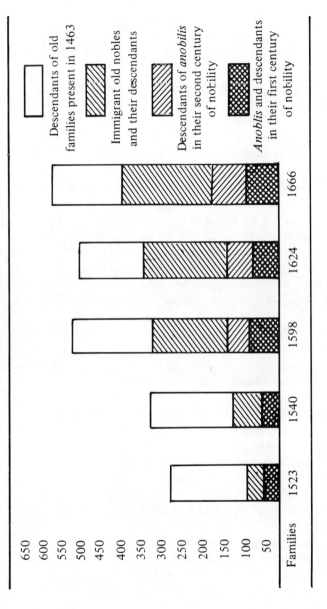

Figure II.2 Origins and Antiquity of the Nobility

Descendants of old families present in 1463

Immigrant old nobles and their descendants

Descendants of *anobilis* in their second century of nobility

Anoblis and descendants in their first century of nobility

650
600
550
500
450
400
350
300
250
200
150
100
50

Families   1523   1540   1598   1624   1666

remained the same from the beginning to the end of the sixteenth century and actually increased during the first half of the seventeenth century. In both 1523 and 1598, 81 percent, and in 1666, 85 percent of all the nobles in the *élection* had been noble for more than a century. Most had been noble much longer: in 1666, for example, 91 percent of the nobles who could be classified as old nobles had been nobles for at least seven generations.

All this suggests that the old nobility was much healthier than has previously been thought, for in this region, at least, old families continued to dominate the membership of the nobility throughout the sixteenth century and even as late as 1666, a date by which they were supposed to have been displaced by waves of *anoblis*.[22] This also suggests that the importance of *anoblissement* in determining the character of the nobility may have been overestimated.[23] To be sure, new families were joining the nobility in increasing numbers in the sixteenth century, but viewed in its totality, the makeup of the Bayeux nobility was determined more by the geographical movements and population increases of its older families than by the addition of recent *anoblis*.

Because extinction and mobility within the nobility appeared to have been taking place simultaneously throughout the old regime, some historians, as we have noted, have suggested that there must have been a direct relationship between the extinction of old and the appearance of new nobles. Both Edouard Perroy and Pierre Goubert, for example, have advanced rather mechanistic explanations of the origins of social mobility into the nobility. The high rate of extinction among the nobility in the county of Forez, Perroy wrote, led to "the necessity to replenish, so to speak, this dying social class by a constant stream of new men."[24] Goubert was even more adamant about the basic cause of mobility into the nobility. Analyzing the reasons for widespread *anoblissement* during the old regime, he wrote that "the speed of extinction of old lines . . . renders inevitable this erection by an authoritarian path [*anoblissement*] if the nobility is to continue to exist."[25] Extensive social mobility into the nobility, in other words, was a necessary response by French society to the harsh facts of demography.

But this simple logic, as we have seen, does not fit the experience of the Bayeux nobility. Not only did the viability of the old nobility obviate the need for massive infusions of new blood, but when real and apparent social mobility are distinguished, we find that the actual numbers of new nobles in the sixteenth and seventeenth centuries, while hardly insignificant, were much more modest than has traditionally been assumed.

The fact that historians have misinterpreted the interplay of population change and social mobility within the nobility raises the question of whether or not, through a similar lack of precision, historians might also have misinterpreted the significance of the actual methods of ennoblement used by commoners to join the nobility. French historians refer to the act of joining the nobility, whatever the method used, as *anoblissement*. They distinguish three methods: ennoblement by royal letter patent, ennoblement by the holding of certain *charges* or offices, and ennoblement by prescription or *aggrégation* (informal assumption of a noble way of life and status that at some point became legally and socially accepted or recognized). Obtaining a letter of ennoblement made a man and his family (and usually their descendants) noble. Some offices, such as that of secretary to the king, carried immediate and hereditary noble status, and some offices endowed their possessor and his family with immediate but not permanent nobility; permanent legal status came after holding the office in the family for two or three generations, or in some cases twenty years. This type of ennoblement was customary in the sixteenth and codified in the seventeenth century.[26] Ennoblement by prescription was a longer and more subtle process. Each historian has had his own romanticized scenario which went something like this: a rich commoner—merchant, officer, notary—purchased a seigneury or noble fief with its manor

59

house. He adopted the leisure life style of a gentleman, wore a sword, styled himself sieur, and signed his legal documents as *écuyer*. His sons served in the *ban* and *arrière-ban*. They and his grandchildren married into local noble families. After several generations the family was reputed to have always been noble. The parish tax collector was persuaded (or coerced) to strike their name from the list of taxable inhabitants. During the next *recherche* for false nobles, the family was not challenged, and its proofs were accepted without question.[27]

What was the relative importance of these different methods of entering the nobility? Historians have put forth many opinions but few facts. One belief is that the number of ennoblements by letter was quite small. Jean-Richard Bloch, in a study of ennoblement during the reign of Francis I, found only 183 letters in a twenty-eight-year period for the whole of France. These were, moreover, usually given or sold only to deserving individuals.[28] Jean Meyer discovered only some 100 letters for the whole of Brittany during the eighteenth century, again granted to deserving individuals.[29] From these facts Pierre Goubert concluded that ennoblement by letter was the least important means of joining the nobility.[30] But since Meyer's conclusions were for the eighteenth century, and Bloch's for the early sixteenth century, it is not clear whether this state of affairs characterized the mid-sixteenth and seventeenth centuries as well.

Historians have differed in their estimations of the importance of prescription as a method of social mobility. Some historians claim that the majority of new nobles used prescription to enter the nobility.[31] In his study of social mobility among the nobility of Forez in the Middle Ages, for example, Edouard Perroy strongly emphasized the fact that the greatest number of new men used informal methods of joining the nobility. Very few nobles received formal recognition from the sovereign power.[32] Writing of the fifteenth and early sixteenth centuries, J.-R. Bloch thought that a large portion of ennoblements stemmed from possession of a noble fief and subsequent acceptance by the nobility and the authorities.[33] As we have mentioned, during the Middle Ages in Normandy the custom was that a commoner who possessed a noble fief for forty years without challenge was entitled to claim noble status. Since letters of ennoblement were quite rare until the sixteenth century and the number of ennobling offices still few, most new nobles must have entered the nobility by this kind of prescription during this period. This would agree with Perroy's conclusions for the nobility of Forez. Louis XI's attempt in 1470 to require payment of the *franc-fief* by all commoners in Normandy who held fiefs, however, led to protests by the Norman Estates. The monarch's response to these remonstrances, the *charte des francs-fiefs*, officially ennobled all commoners who had possessed noble fiefs for forty years. About a score of families in the *élection* of Bayeux could trace their origins as nobles directly to the edict of 1470. As we have argued, however, by purchasing official recognition of past action, the Normans tacitly conceded that such actions had not been completely sanctioned in the past and recognized that the king had the power to demand official certification by letters patent of a previously unquestioned method of becoming a noble. Therefore the edict of *francs-fiefs* marked the end, rather than the beginning, of an era, and in 1579 prescription associated with ownership of a noble fief was made illegal.

It is interesting, however, that in Normandy the era of legal prescription came to an end at just about the same time that the nobility underwent its greatest expansion and was accepting its largest contingents of *anoblis*. Jean Meyer also felt that, in Brittany, entry into the nobility became more tightly controlled in the seventeenth than in the sixteenth century.[34] Informal proofs and noncomprehensive *recherches* in the sixteenth century, he speculated, had made entry into the nobility relatively easy. This was replaced in the seventeenth century by comprehensive *recherches* with rigid, formal proof requirements, presumably reducing the chances of successful prescription. Pierre Goubert also discarded the idea that most new nobles became nobles by prescription because, he claimed, by the eighteenth century old nobles closely supervised group membership, and in any case many potential prescribers eased their way by purchasing a *"solide office anoblissement."*[35]

In general, then, although different historians have been concerned with different periods, prescription has been seen as the most common way by which most men entered the nobility from the Middle Ages until the mid-sixteenth century. But tightened requirements and closer supervision from the end of the sixteenth and beginning of the seventeenth centuries on reduced the importance of prescription until, by the eighteenth century, the chances for successful prescription were small.

If in the second half of the sixteenth century recruitment by prescription decreased in importance while the number of recipients of letters of ennoblement remained unimportant, how did large numbers of new nobles manage to join the nobility? The answer put forth by French historians, of course, is that it was done by men who were ennobled by their offices. The number of *anoblis* by office during the reign of Francis I, according to J.-R. Bloch, greatly exceeded the number of *anoblis* by letters.[36] In the seventeenth and eighteenth centuries, Goubert claimed, ennoblements by office were by far the most numerous of all ennoblements.[37] So, if letters of ennoblement were numerically unimportant and the importance of entry by prescription was declining, methods of entering the nobility must have changed over time: if most new men entered the nobility by prescription in the thirteenth century, most new men in the second half of the sixteenth and throughout the seventeenth centuries became nobles by purchasing an ennobling office. If these assumptions were true, we should find that by the sixteenth century almost all new men were prescriptive nobles or *anoblis* by office while very few were *anoblis* by letter, and that by the mid-seventeenth century almost all new nobles had been ennobled by their offices. But, as we shall see, quite the opposite was true.

The appearance of new families in the ranks of the *élection*'s nobles was the result of two very different kinds of mobility—real upward social mobility and geographic mobility. Real upward social mobility involved the *ennoblement* of an individual through one of the three methods outlined above. Pure geographic mobility involved the immigration of old nobles into the *élection* and did not involve any change in personal legal status. As we saw in table II.5, two-thirds of the apparent mobility into the *élection*'s nobility consisted of immigration by old nobles from other parts of Lower Normandy. Most mobility, in other words, reflected relatively minor geographic displacements within the larger Norman noble community rather than the replacement of slowly disappearing old families by entirely new social elements.

Since noble families who simply moved into the *élection* underwent no ennobling process, they are irrelevant to any analysis of the methods of ennoblement used by upwardly mobile families. In table II.6 the purely geographically mobile families have been removed leaving only new nobles. The information contained in the table is surprising. Although historians have asserted that ennoblement by letter was relatively unimportant, 138, or 83 percent, of the 166 identified families who entered the nobility in the *élection* of Bayeux between 1463 and 1666 owed their noble status to grants of letters patent. Only 28 (or 17 percent) of these *anoblis* families were successful usurpers, or prescriptive nobles, that is, families who were not immigrants, had not received letters of ennoblement, had a record of previous unfavorable *arrêts* from the Cour des Aides, and yet were still accepted as noble. Although, as we shall see, more than half of all *anoblis* were officeholders, there were no clear cases of ennoblement by office. Even if all the new nobles in the "unknown" category were prescriptive *anoblis* or *anoblis* by office, which is unlikely, more than two-thirds of the new nobles would still have entered the nobility using letters of ennoblement. In the *élection* of Bayeux, officials became noble by purchasing a letter of ennoblement; they were not ennobled by their office. Unofficial or gradualistic

TABLE II.6

Methods of Ennoblement

Dates	By letter	By prescription	Unknown	Total
1463-1523	34	7	8	49
1524-1540	7	8	4	19
1541-1598	74	3	13	90
1599-1624	1	4	2	7
1625-1666	22	6	10	38
Total	138	28	37	203
Percentage of total	68	14	18	100

methods of ennoblement were in a definite minority even in the seventeenth century.

Is this striking departure from what modern historians have led us to expect an exception, or part of a wider Norman pattern? It has been previously mentioned that for the reign of Francis I, J.-R. Bloch found only 183 letters of ennoblement, while Meyer counted only 100 for Brittany in the eighteenth century. Yet in an easily accessible work printed in 1862 Abbé P.-F. Lebeurier listed more than 1,300 letters of ennoblement issued to Norman commoners between about 1460 and 1670.[38] These 1,300 letters represent only a partial listing of all the letters of ennoblement granted by the crown in Normandy during that period. Therefore, the conclusion is inescapable that in Normandy a formal grant of a letter of ennoblement was the most common method of becoming a noble. The Norman experience in the sixteenth and seventeenth centuries was quite different from the picture of ennoblement presented as the norm by French historians.

In the two centuries between 1463 and 1666, then, direct royal action in the form of letters of ennoblement was responsible for the greatest part of upward social mobility into the *élection*'s nobility. The entry of newly created nobles in the *élection*'s nobility therefore depended almost exclusively on a type of royal action that was totally unrelated to population factors. For these letters of ennoblement were responses to political and financial exigencies and were prompted by the desire to reward faithful or competent subjects or the need to find sources of revenue for empty royal coffers.[39]

The chronological distribution of letters of ennoblement in Normandy listed by Lebeurier is presented in figure II.3. As can be seen, the most letters of ennoblement were issued during the turbulent years of the Wars of Religion and the Fronde, both periods when the monarchy needed to reward its supporters and increase its revenues. Grants of nobility, in other words, multiplied in times of crisis. Since the only two studies on the operation of ennoblement that we have covered periods before and after this era, it is entirely possible that grants of nobility may have increased during times of crisis elsewhere in France. It may have been a mistake to assume that J.-R. Bloch's and Meyer's conclusions on methods of ennoblement were good for the intervening period and for all of France. Given deterministic assumptions about the steady extinction of established noble families, the misplaced (for Normandy at least) emphasis on entry by prescription and ennoblement by office is understandable. Ennoblement by letter seemed too individualistic and dependent on the whims and political fortunes of the monarchy to be counted on as a dependable method of replacement for a steadily dying nobility. Gradual replacement by prescription or the purchase of offices fits much more logically into a demographically determined system of social mobility. On the basis of the information advanced in this chapter, however, the accepted assumptions about the rate of extinction and explanations of the origins and mechanisms of social mobility into the nobility need, at the very least, serious qualification.

Several sources contain information on the social origins of these *anoblis*. The most important are Lebeurier's listing of letters of ennoblement, which often included information on the offices or occupations of their recipients, and the genealogical information and written comments contained in the

Figure II.3 Letters of *Ennoblement* in Normandy, 1460-1670

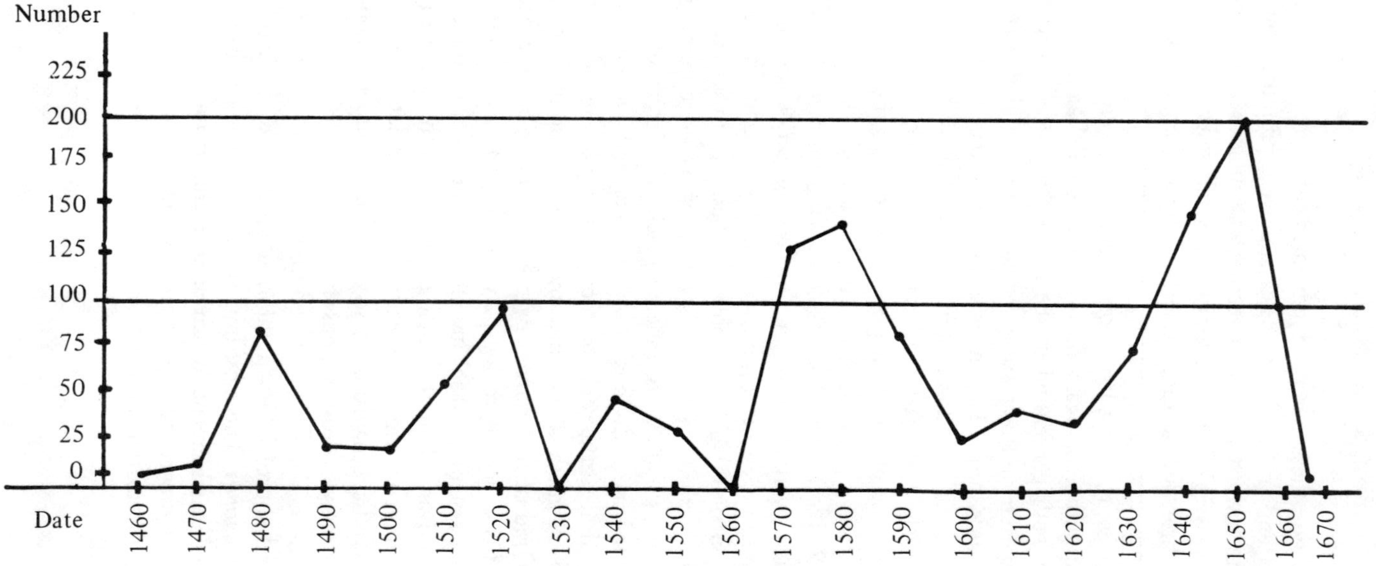

recherches. Out of 174 *anoblis* who are known to have joined the nobility of the *élection* between 1463 and 1666 it was possible to identify the exact social origins of 65, or 37.4 percent. Lebeurier lists the occupations of 538 of the 1,120 *anoblis* who received letters of ennoblement between 1540 and 1670, or 48 percent of that total.

The relative importance of different social origins for *anoblis* in the *élection* of Bayeux over the period 1463 to 1666 and for all of Normandy over the period 1540 to 1670 is presented in table II.7. The smaller sample of *anoblis* from the

TABLE II.7

Social Origins of *Anoblis*

Percentage drawn from:	Election of Bayeux	All Normandy
High robe[a]	4.6	7.4
Justice	26.2	20.3
Finance	30.8	30.2
Military	9.2	14.1
Learned professions[b]	16.9	10.0
Municipal	4.6	13.6

[a] Royal council and courts. [b] Lawyers, doctors, notaries, and clerks.

élection does not seem to differ much from the sample drawn from the entire province. The single exception, the municipal category, is explained by the fact that most of the men identified as bourgeoisie or *échevins* (municipal officials) were from Caen, Rouen, or Dieppe, outside the *élection* of Bayeux.

About 60 percent of the men in these samples were officials of some type. Almost four out of five men (78.5 percent) in the Bayeux sample were officials or professional people (mostly lawyers). It is likely that a minimum of 40 percent of all the *anoblis* entering the nobility of the *élection* of Bayeux belonged to these two categories. However, since some unidentifiable *anoblis* also probably belonged to these groups, and many of the sons of unidentified first-generation *anoblis* are also known to have been officials, it would be safe to say that at least two-thirds, if not more, of the *anoblis* in Bayeux were officials or professionals at the time they were ennobled. It is impossible to be exact about the origins of those *anoblis* who were not officials. Perhaps 10 to 15 percent were ennobled for military services. As for the rest, in his *Vénalité des offices*, which is based mostly on Norman examples, Roland Mousnier asserted that the majority of *anoblis* by letter were former merchants and peasants who had become landed proprietors.[40] Four hundred and twenty-seven of the 829 *anoblis* (52 percent) who appear in Lebeurier's *Etat des anoblis*, but whose origins or occupations are not given, were sieurs of some property when they entered the nobility. They were already established, in other words, as landlords and property owners of some kind. If not the offspring of officials, these men must have been well-to-do peasants or descendants of former merchants, for apart from officials, these were the only groups wealthy enough to buy land.

Very few of the *élection*'s *anoblis* (perhaps 5 percent) were drawn from the ranks of the high robe, that is, the royal council and the sovereign courts. Therefore, the officials who were joining the Bayeux nobility did not own offices that conferred *noblesse graduelle* on their possessors even in the seventeenth century. Although many *anoblis* were officials, they were ennobled by their letters of nobility, not their offices. This is further evidence of the unimportance of ennoblement by office as a means of social mobility into the Norman nobility. Only commoners with positions in the royal household and sovereign courts were gradually ennobled, and recent research has clearly shown that almost all the men who held these offices were already noble when they acquired them.[41] Secretaries of the king and the few commoners actually ennobled by their offices were hardly enough to provide new nobles for a province, much less the whole of France. This is just another example of the slender basis on which previous explanations of mobility by massive ennoblement by office rest, and it raises questions about whether such explanations may also be incorrect for provinces other than Normandy.

CHAPTER III

SOCIAL STRUCTURE:
OFFICIALS AND *NOBLESSE D'ÉPÉE*

WHAT EFFECTS did the kinds of upward social mobility examined in the preceding chapter have on the nobility? Were newcomers quickly assimilated and integrated into the pre-existing social structure and life styles of the majority of nobles as well as into the more personal network of family alliances and relations that characterize every rural aristocracy? Or did their addition to the nobility lead instead to internal social divisions and conflicts between established and new families?

The sixteenth and seventeenth centuries, as every historian of early modern France knows, witnessed a tremendous increase in the number of royal officials, officeholders, and functionaries. The crown indulged in the creation and sale of new bureaucratic offices in order to extend both its political and its tax-gathering power and, less rationally, to provide cash at critical moments for a penurious treasury. The overall rate of growth of officialdom was heavily influenced by the fact that almost all public offices and posts were venal, that is, they were the personal private property (de facto in the sixteenth, de jure in the seventeenth century) of their holders. This meant that old, obsolescent, and superseded posts could be abolished only after they had been repurchased by the crown, a practice that, despite the hopes of successive generations of reform-minded royal counselors, turned out to be prohibitively expensive. As a result, layer upon layer of newly created offices were erected on top of already existing posts.[1]

The significance for French public life and society of the

mass creation of venal offices and officeholders has been thoroughly examined and debated by historians. Among other things, we are now aware that the main institutions of venal officialdom—the sovereign courts in particular—were captured and dominated by the nobility at an early date. And despite the confusion spread by contemporaries and modern historians who insist that newly ennobled officeholders were not "really" noble, the importance of officeholding as an intergenerational method of social advancement for upwardly mobile families has now been rather fully investigated and appreciated.[2]

As we saw in the last chapter, officeholding was an attribute shared by a majority of new nobles. But in the *élection* of Bayeux, as we pointed out, officeholding played a more subtle role in the process of ennoblement than historians have heretofore acknowledged. Although most new nobles came from officeholding backgrounds, contrary to current beliefs almost none were actually ennobled by their office. At the institutional level of an *élection* or *vicomté*, where most of the careers of these new nobles originated, offices did not automatically or even eventually ennoble their holders. Most of the *anoblis* in the *élection* of Bayeux entered the nobility when they were awarded, or purchased, formal letters of ennoblement. A background of officeholding was significant for these men because it indicates that they were sufficiently prominent and affluent either to take advantage of the periodic sale of patents of nobility by the impoverished crown, or to render themselves valuable enough to warrant ennoblement as a reward for their loyalty and services to the crown (or in the case of Henry IV, an aspirant to the crown). Officeholding was not so much the means to nobility (for many officials never became nobles) as an indication that so prominent a social position had been reached that movement into the nobility, for some, became a practical possibility.

But a problem that has rarely, if ever, been explored before, is the effect that officeholding had on the internal social structure of the nobility as a whole. It is obvious that many new nobles were officeholders at the time they were ennobled, but to what extent did their careers as officials carry over into their new status as nobles? For how many nobles was officeholding an important aspect of life, and to what extent, if any, did noble officeholders as a group differ in their social profiles from ordinary nobles? Conventional historical wisdom suggests that this group of officeholding *anoblis* formed a clearly discernible and exclusive subgroup within the nobility, which was despised by the old nobility.[3] Rejected by the old nobility, whose talents, values, and life style differed considerably from their own, these new nobles purportedly preserved their self-identity by intermarrying primarily among themselves and refusing to be assimilated into the larger mass of country gentlemen.[4]

This chapter explores the phenomenon of officeholding among Bayeux nobles and its relation to the integration and assimilation of new nobles into the older nobility. We shall discover that new nobles did not overwhelmingly dominate the group of noble officeholders, and that many individuals from the oldest families in the *élection* also followed official careers. The caste of noble officeholders was never identifiable as a closed preserve for *anoblis*. We shall also discover that new nobles, as a group, tended to abandon their offices as quickly as possible and adopt life styles that were indistinguishable from those of the mass of older families. And since only a tiny minority of new families, once they were ennobled, chose to retain their offices, new nobles, as a separate group, were hardly more tainted by officeholding than old nobles. The operation of social mobility, in other words, did not lead to any essential fragmentation or new internal social divisions among the nobility as a group.

This chapter also analyzes the place of military careers and service in the social structure of the Bayeux nobility. The nobility had originated as a military class, of course, and in the sixteenth and seventeenth centuries continued to base its self-identity and defend its claim to group privileges on the rationale that it was a military service class.[5] Since its own self-identity and, to some extent, the public's perception of it depended on the perpetuation of the idea of the nobility as a military elite, it is important to determine whether the myth of a warrior class really reflected underlying social realities.

Therefore, in addition to its focus on officeholding, this chapter seeks to determine such basic facts as the types, extent, and duration of military service among the Bayeux nobility. As in the case of officeholding, however, a reconstruction of the military aspects of nobility can also be related to the larger question of the assimilation of new nobles into the typical and general social patterns of this local, rural-based class of country gentlemen. Once the typical military profile of the class as a whole was uncovered, for example, it became possible to determine how quickly and completely new nobles took on the military aspects of the older nobility, thereby lessening their social visibility as recent nonnobles and making it easier for them to be assimilated.

As in the case of officeholding among nobles and its role in the social integration of *anoblis*, we shall discover that the place of military service in the life of the nobility was more complex than has commonly been acknowledged. On the one hand, many nobles did at some time serve in a military capacity, and small but substantial numbers of individuals, drawn almost entirely from the oldest families in the *élection*, became important military leaders. As a military service class, then, the Bayeux nobility did contribute its share of talented and energetic individuals. On the other hand, more than half of the Bayeux nobility never performed any military service at all. And even within the militarily active portion of the class, only a very small portion followed what could be called regular or lengthy military careers. Thus the great majority of a class that based much of its self-identity and its claim to privilege on the regular performance of military services, had either not performed any military service at all, or had performed a bare minimum.

This analysis of the military component of noble life will also provide additional evidence of the quick assimilation of new nobles into existing noble social roles. While only a hand-

ful of *anoblis* came from a military background, once ennobled, new nobles tended to pursue regular military careers
and perform military service to the same degree as the older
nobility. It was rare for new nobles to break into the upper
reaches of the military hierarchy as commanders or military
leaders, but on all other counts their record for military service
was indistinguishable from that of other kinds of nobles. The
operation of social mobility, in other words, did not have the
effect of prompting the military nobility to attempt to enhance
its own special identity by excluding new nobles, and new
nobles were therefore able to use military service as a means
to promote their integration into the nobility.

The key to an active career, whether as a soldier or an official, we shall see, was not, as so often has been thought, the
antiquity of a man's nobility, but rather his wealth. An overwhelming majority of officeholders and *nobles d'épée* came
from the richest half of the nobility (see table III.11). It was
wealth, rather than lineage, that the active portion of the
nobility shared, and that enabled newcomers to merge quickly
and easily into traditional noble activities. This basic theme,
that of rapid assimilation of newcomers into a social structure
whose basic attributes were reinforced rather than challenged
by the operation of social mobility, will be taken up again in
chapter four, which analyzes how intermarriage worked to
simultaneously promote the integration of *anoblis* and preserve the self-identity of the nobility as a whole.

Although there are no complete records for the Bayeux nobility, evidence on the extent of officeholding exists in many
forms. Officeholders were highly visible and noteworthy, and
they claimed exemptions of many kinds. They were exempted,
for example, from personal military service in the *ban* and can
therefore be identified in the numerous *ban* musters held in
the *bailliage* of Caen between 1552 and 1639.[6] Furthermore,
both current and past officeholders are noted in the various
recherches.[7] From the information contained in these and
other sources[8] a composite picture emerges of the pattern of

officeholding among the Bayeux nobility and the social profiles of the officeholders themselves which sheds valuable light on how one of the most significant social developments of the sixteenth and seventeenth centuries affected the provincial nobility.[9]

It was possible to identify 182 individual nobles who held offices between 1463 and 1666 or had positions that, if not offices properly speaking, required formal training or had duties similar to those of offices. This last category included such professional people as lawyers, notaries, doctors, and sergeants. This information is presented in table III.1, which breaks the two-century period into two roughly equal periods at 1562 and identifies the antiquity of these officials' nobility.

TABLE III.1

Occupations and Antiquity of Noble Officials and Professionals

Occupation	1463-1562 Old	New	1563-1666 Old	New	Subtotal Old	New	Total
High robe: sovereign courts and royal council	3	—	9	5	12	5	17
Bailliage and vicomté judicial posts	10	8	17	30	27	38	65
Officials in the élection and other financial posts	2	4	5	29	7	33	40
Lawyers	4	5	12	—	16	5	21
Municipal officials	4	—	—	4	4	4	8
Notaries and sergeants	11	4	9	3	20	7	27
Doctors	—	—	2	2	2	2	4
Total	34	21	54	73	88	94	182

This group was almost exclusively local. The largest category was that of judges and counselors in the local courts of the *bailliage* (and *siège présidial* or appellate court) and *vicomté*. A smaller group, comprising less than 10 percent of all officials, held positions in the sovereign courts and royal council. The second largest group was that of financial officials in the *élection*. The next largest group combined several kinds of minor legal personnel: lawyers, notaries, and sergeants employed by or active in the local jurisdictions. Bayeux nobles who held offices, then, tended to come more from the judicial than the financial bureaucracy, and almost exclusively from the world of local offices rather than the high robe.

The number of nobles who can be identified as officeholders increased in absolute terms between the mid-fifteenth and mid-seventeenth centuries, reflecting the overall expansion of French officialdom during the period and a willingness by nobles of all types to obtain newly created offices. But in relative terms, as table III.2, which calculates the percentage of all nobles who were active officials or professional people at various dates shows, the doubling in the number of noble officials that took place between 1563 and 1666 only just kept pace with the overall expansion in the size of the nobility noted in chapter two. As a result, though the size of the officeholding group within the Bayeux nobility expanded, at any single point the number of nobles who were officials or professionals was quite small: for example, in 1552 only fifteen, in 1598 nineteen, and in 1639 some twenty family heads were officials or professionals. Except in 1666, less than 5 percent of the noble family heads living in the *élection* at those times were officials. Despite the expansion of officialdom over the whole period from 1463 to 1666, the size of this group within the

TABLE III.2

Numbers and Antiquity of Noble Officials and Professionals

Type of noble	Number of officials and professionals					
	1552	1562	1568	1598	1639	1666
Old	9	8	8	11	10	24
New	4	5	3	8	10	15
Total	13	13	11	19	20	39
Percentage of all nobles	4.2	3.2	2.7	3.4	3.7	6.6

nobility remained, relatively speaking, about the same—very small.

As we have noted, however, at least two-thirds of the new nobles who joined the Bayeux nobility were officials or professionals. Therefore, even if the officeholders as a group did not become a larger proportion of the nobility over time, it would seem logical that the highly visible *nouveaux arrivés* complexion of this group could easily have led to resentment and exclusion by the older squirearchy (*gentilhommerie*). But, in fact, as a closer examination of tables III.1 and III.2 will show, it would be difficult to make any simple identification of officeholding with the *anoblis* among the nobility.

In the first place, many officials and professionals were old nobles. Of 55 officials and professionals before 1563, 34, or 62 percent, were old nobles. After 1562, 54 of 127, or 43 percent, were old nobles. Over the whole period, therefore, 48 percent, or almost half, of all nobles who were officials or professionals had been noble for at least a century. Some of these old nobles came from families that had been ennobled in the first half of the period and had therefore been noble for much more than a century by the second half. But many more were from *noblesse de race* families that could trace their origins back to at least the time of Montfaut's *recherche* in 1463.

These old nobles tended to be concentrated in judicial offices or to be lawyers, notaries, or sergeants. They were rarely financial officials. The Suhard, for example, were a large old family group that produced several branches of soldiers and captains. But one branch, headed by a Jean Suhard, *avocat postulant* of Bayeux in 1540, turned to the judiciary, and by 1668 two of his descendants, Pierre and Michel Suhard, were lieutenant general and advocate of the king in the *vicomté* of Bayeux.[10] The Hotot family could trace its origins back to at least the 1200s, and in 1587 a Jean Hotot was captain of a cavalry company of fifty men. But in 1609 we find Noel Hotot as a counselor to the king, civil and criminal lieutenant for the *bailli* of Caen at the *siège* of Thorigny; in 1639 his son Charles held the same post.[11] The de la Rivière were another ancient family that did not disdain holding office. François de la Rivière was lieutenant general in the *vicomté* in 1540, and Jean de la Rivière in 1562, at the same time that Guillaume de la Rivière was *guidon* for the Admiral de Châtillon.[12] A member of a younger branch of the very old Verigny family held the office of king's attorney at Caen in 1562 while another Verigny became a counselor in the Grand Council.[13] Many nobles from old families, in other words, belonged to the official and professional part of the *élection*'s nobility.

Because almost half of all the noble officials in the *élection* were drawn from the *noblesse de race*, it is impossible to identify the official and professional class of the nobility exclusively with the *anoblis*. It is true that nobles who held financial offices were almost always (33 cases to 7) new nobles, and even a slight majority of the men who held judicial offices (43 cases to 39) were new nobles. Over the whole period 51 percent of the men identified as officials were new nobles, although new nobles never constituted more than 15 to 20 percent of all the nobles in the *élection*. And table III.2 which indicates the antiquity of nobles who were active as officials at various dates, shows that between 1568 and 1639 new nobles became a larger part of all active noble officials. But the importance of old nobles among the *noblesse de fonctions* was never permanently changed. Because of the aging of some families and the tenacity with which some old nobles held on to their offices, by 1666 old nobles again formed the great majority of noble officials as they had in the first half of the sixteenth century.

The key to the continuing importance of older families among officeholders, despite the fact that at least two-thirds of the new nobility came from officeholding backgrounds, lay in the fact that most new nobles quickly abandoned their offices once they became noble. A few new nobles, however, perpetuated family dynasties of officials. The d'Escrametot family, for example, were prescriptive *anoblis* and officials at Bayeux from the 1530s, holding first the office of *vicomte*, then, for

77

four generations, the office of *élu* in the *élection* of Bayeux.[14] The Hamel family, ennobled in 1579, were lawyers and then lieutenants in the *vicomté* for four successive generations.[15] The l'Escally, ennobled in 1543, were advocates of the king and then lieutenants and counselors of the king for at least four generations.[16] But such dynasties were rare and often their members turned eventually to careers unconnected with offices: for example, Germain l'Escally, a *maître d'hôtel extraordinaire du roy*, served as captain of an infantry company in 1597; another member of this official family commanded a company of the bourgeoisie of Bayeux under Matignon in 1649; and a third, Lambert l'Escally, a lieutenant in the *vicomté* of Bayeux in the seventeenth century, lost two sons in battle.[17]

A much more common pattern was for officials who were ennobled to leave their offices very quickly.[18] For example, Christophe Cyresme, a notary and secretary of the king, became *vicomte* of Bayeux in the 1540s and married the daughter and sole heir of Herve Daneau, *écuyer*, the former *vicomte*. His son, Anthoine Cyresme, also became *vicomte*, but succeeding generations of this family were simple country gentlemen, one of whom, Jean-Baptiste, was serving in the Vendôme in 1666.[19] Lucas Acher was administrator of the barony of Neuilly for the bishop of Bayeux in 1503. His son Guillaume was an *élu* at Coutance when he was awarded letters of nobility in 1523. Succeeding generations never again held offices: in 1552 Guillaume's eldest son, Guillaume, sieur of Mesnil-Vité, was a man at arms in the service of the king while in 1562 Jean, his younger brother, held the post of captain of chateau Neuilly. Henry Acher, sieur of Mesnil-Vité, a fourth-generation noble, was a gentleman of the order of the king and captain general of the seacoast in the *bailliage* of Cotentin in 1587.[20] Pierre Paysant was *vicomte* of Bayeux when in 1543 or 1544 he was ennobled and changed his name to Manvieux, the name of his principal fief and parish of residence. His sons served in the *ban*, and his grandson was a member of the duke of Montpensier's company of gendarmes.[21]

Officials, in other words, tended to move on quickly to careers unconnected with offices. Furthermore, when an official family expanded, its new branches rarely continued as officeholders. For example, while a younger branch of the Bunel family, descended from a receiver of the *taille*, ennobled in 1596, filled the office of *lieutenant général et criminel* for three successive generations, the eldest branch became country gentlemen, and by 1639 were being styled *gens d'épée*.[22] The Bourran, sieurs of Castilly, had been condemned as usurpers in 1463. Geoffroy Bourran, a forester, did not attempt to prove his nobility during the *recherche* of 1523, but his descendants were accepted as noble in 1540, a fairly clear case of perseverance and prescription. The Bourran pursued several different careers: we find a Guillaume Bourran as a trooper in the duke of Beuvron's company in 1587, while in the 1660s two brothers, Philippe and François, became advocates and counselors at the Parlement of Rouen. But Philippe then left the law to become captain, later general, of the coast guard at Grandchamp.[23] A final example might be Gilles Blais, a soldier ennobled for military service to the king in 1492. Around 1568 a fourth-generation descendant of this family's second branch became a treasurer general of France and moved to Caen, where a descendant of his later became a counselor at the Parlement. But the eldest and third branches remained behind in the *élection* to live their lives as simple gentlemen.[24]

Thus, though many new nobles may have been officials when they joined the nobility, very few seem to have remained officials past their first generation of nobility. This general trend is illustrated by table III.3, which indicates the generation of nobility of all the new nobles who were identified as officials or professional people in table III.1. Seventy-one percent of new nobles who were also officials and professionals were first- or second-generation nobles. Very few were third- or fourth-generation nobles. Therefore for the most part only the newest of these new nobles were officials. Their entry into the nobility did not have the cumulative effect of forming an ever growing *noblesse de fonctions* because in most cases

TABLE III.3

Generation of Nobility of
Officeholding and Professional *Anoblis*

Generation of nobility	Number of nobles	Percentage of total
First	51	53.7
Second	16	16.8
Third	15	15.8
Fourth	13	13.7
Total	95	100.0

newly ennobled officials were not permanently added to the pool of existing noble officeholders, but instead, left their offices to merge with the mass of older nobles who were not officials.

One result of this trend was that very few new nobles remained officials through their first century of nobility, and the percentage of all new nobles in the *élection* who were officials or professionals at various times was very small. In 1552, for example, only 4 out of 60, in 1598 only 8 out of 138, and in 1666 only 14 out of 171 new noble family heads were active as officeholders or professionals. Despite the fact that probably two-thirds of the new nobles were officials or professionals when they joined the nobility, it would be incorrect simply to equate the new nobility with the world of offices in the *élection* of Bayeux.

The goal of most new nobles, officials or not, was entrance into the rural squirearchy. Most new families settled in the countryside: in 1598, for example, of 113 new noble family heads living in the *élection*, 89, or 79 percent, were living in the countryside outside Bayeux or its outskirts. In 1666, of 106 new noble family heads, 86, or 81 percent, lived in the countryside. A majority of these new nobles, moreover, seem to have been landowners of some kind. Of the 1,367 *anoblis* listed by Lebeurier for all of Normandy between the mid-fifteenth and the mid-seventeenth centuries, 721 were styled seigneur or sieur of some property, indicating that they owned some land or an estate.[25] Of the 106 new noble family heads living in the *élection* of Bayeux in 1666, for example, 69, or 65 percent, were sieur or seigneur of some parish. As landowners and inhabitants of the country new nobles, especially newly ennobled officials, rather than forming a caste inside the nobility, were adopting the rural way of life characteristic of older gentlemen families.

An accurate assessment of the importance of the military aspects of noble life rests on answers to two separate but related problems. The first, of course, is to determine what portion of the nobility actually were *noblesse d'épée*, or military nobles, that is, nobles who performed occasional military service when it was required, or pursued regular and extended military careers. The second problem is to compare the social profiles of the active military element of the nobility to the social profile of the class as a whole. In this way we can determine the degree to which the military aspects of noble life were a preserve of the *noblesse de race* and the degree to which they were a readily available avenue for the assimilation of new nobles into the way of life of the established nobility.

No unified register of the military service of the Bayeux nobility exists, but the records that have survived, primarily *ban* and *arrière-ban* musters for the second half of the sixteenth century and surveys of military fitness and service by royal officials in the seventeenth century, give an interesting and detailed enough overall view of the extent and nature of military service among Bayeux nobles. Records of the *ban* musters of 1552, 1562, 1568, 1587, and 1597, a *ban*-inspired survey of military suitability in 1639, and a survey of military service records made in 1666 provide the starting point.[26] The *ban* muster, whether called out in expectation of a coming campaign as in 1552, or during emergencies such as the relief of the siege of Amiens in 1597, was the chief official means by which the crown tried to harness the military potential of the provincial nobility in the sixteenth century. Theoretically, almost every noble fiefholder in the *élection* owed military service, but by the mid-sixteenth century fiefholders could often avoid their obligation of personal service by making a payment worth one-fifth of the annual revenue of their fief. These payments were collected in a *ban* treasury which was then used to support a *ban* company drawn from the ranks of those who were willing or preferred to serve in person. All fiefholders, therefore, either served in the *ban* company itself or contributed to its upkeep.[27]

At the end of the sixteenth and the beginning of the seventeenth centuries, the crown, disenchanted with the effectiveness of *ban*-raised companies, which were as unreliable as their term of service was short, began to try to enforce an effective service obligation on all nobles, rather than just fiefholders, but chose to retain the *ban* organization in forcing service, on pain of financial penalty, onto all eligible family heads. Thus even though the principle upon which the *ban* was based, that of military service by fiefholders, was being abandoned in favor of a broader interpretation, the records of the *ban* continued to identify all the male nobles who were eligible for service, contributed to the treasury, attended the muster, or were chosen to serve in the *ban* company. In addition to identifying all those affected by *ban* service in a particular year, the *ban* records also identify those who, though fiefholders, were already on active service as *homme d'armes* or commanders, and were, therefore, exempt from serving in or contributing to the *ban* in that particular year. By adding the number chosen to serve in the *ban* to those already serving in some military capacity we can obtain an idea of the number of militarily active family heads in peak years of military activity.

Table III.4 shows the levels of military activity among Bayeux nobles at six different dates between 1552 and 1639. At those dates between 13 (1568) and 38 percent (1597) of all the eligible family heads in the *élection* performed active military

TABLE III.4

Active Military Service, 1552-1639

	1552	1562	1568	1587	1597	1639
Eligible for *ban* service	208	198	189	211	265	466
Already serving	16	15	10	28	18	15
Served in *ban* company	25	23	14	9	84	94[a]
Total active service	41	38	24	37	102	109
Percent already serving	8	8	6	13	7	3
Percent serving in *ban*	12	12	8	4	32	20
Total percent active service[b]	20	19	13	18	38	23

[a] The 1639 *ban* was never actually held. This figure represents those found capable of serving.

[b] Totals may not add up because of rounding.

service of some kind. In general, however, less than one-tenth of the family heads in the *élection* served in non-*ban*-related military positions. Most of these men were regular military personnel, that is, military commanders or soldiers in quasi-regular military formations. In addition to these regular military types, the *ban* was able to muster for service anywhere from another 4 (1587) to 32 percent (1597) of all the eligible family heads in the *élection*.

These figures reflect two concurrent military developments. The first was the deterioration during the Wars of Religion of the effectiveness of the *ban* as a means of mobilization. In 1552, before the wars, and in 1562, a time of confusion but before the major lines of religious and political opposition had become crystallized, the crown was able, in effect, to draft 12 percent of the eligible nobility for active service in any year. If we combine those who served in the *ban* with those already on active service at those dates, the number of militarily active family heads rises to one-fifth of the total. But by 1568 and 1587, the *ban* only yielded, respectively, 8 and 4 percent of all eligible nobles. General war weariness may have played a role, but most of the ineffectiveness of the *ban* can probably more accurately be traced to the distrust of various religious and political groups of an institution they did not control and which they feared might be used against them. In the 1560s, for example, Protestants often absented themselves from the *ban* muster by pleading illness,[28] and by 1587 the *ban* had almost completely broken down, producing only 4 percent of those eligible for service. Nevertheless, the overall percentage of militarily active nobles remained almost as high in 1587 (18) as at mid-century, but primarily because the percentage of family heads already on active service (13) was already twice as high as at most other dates. The level of military activity in 1587 was high, but the *ban* was ineffective because most of those who were militarily active were serving with the various partisan units of the Huguenots and Catholic League, rather than directly for the monarchy.

At the end of the sixteenth and beginning of the seventeenth centuries the second military development alluded to, the extension of a military obligation to all nobles rather than just fiefholders, was well underway, and the *élection* began producing roughly two and one-half times the number of noble soldiers produced earlier in the sixteenth century. In 1597, for example, with the Wars of Religion over, the *ban* mustered one out of every three eligible family heads for the relief of Amiens, and total participation (38 percent) was at the highest mark of the entire period between 1552 and 1639. This high level of participation, however, was a result of levying stiff financial penalties on those who were not already serving or refused to serve, and the extension of a military obligation to men who were not fiefholders. More than one-quarter of those threatened with penalties for not serving were not listed as fiefholders on the *ban* muster.

By 1639, dissatisfaction with the results of the *ban* led Louis XIII to attempt to extend the obligation to serve or make contributions to all nobles, and to use the *ban* contributions to support regular infantry units rather than the traditional noble cavalry units.[29] A preliminary survey of the military (and financial) capabilities of 466 nobles was made which showed a very low percentage (3) of regular military men, while an additional 20 percent of all noble family heads were said to be capable of military service.[30] So in the mid-seventeenth, as in the mid-sixteenth century, between one-fifth and one-quarter of the nobility was capable of active military service in a single year. In absolute terms the seventeenth century was producing more soldiers, primarily because the definition of eligibility and the size of the nobility had simultaneously expanded. Depending upon the circumstances, then, the proportion of militarily active nobles differed considerably. In times of civil disturbance and civil war (1568, for example) less than one out of seven nobles may have been militarily active, while in times of relative domestic accord (1597, for example), by applying maximum coercion, as many as four out of ten nobles may have served in some military capacity.

The number of nobles on military service in a single year, however, does not accurately represent the overall importance of military nobles in the nobility as a whole. It does not include nobles who, while militarily inactive in a specific year, may have been active in other years, or those who, though willing, were not chosen to serve in the *ban* company. Furthermore, as the 1597 and 1639 documents show, fiefholders were not the only nobles capable or even willing to serve. In fact, there is a great deal of evidence to suggest that much more than one-fifth of the nobility should be classified as genuine *noblesse d'épée*. In 1552, for example, some 52 nobles who held no fief appeared voluntarily at the *ban* muster and offered their services or made nominal contributions to the *ban* treasury.[31] Most of these were men like Cléophus Hue, who declared he owned no property, yet nevertheless offered to perform military service for the king.[32] In 1562, 103 of the nobles who attended the *ban* muster were presumably ready to serve but simply were not chosen to serve in the *ban* company, while 66 nobles in addition to those already serving or judged fit for service are referred to as *homme d'épée* or *gens d'épée* in 1639.[33] A 1666 document which recorded the service record of almost every noble in the *élection* identifies over 200 nobles who had served at one time or another in a military capacity.[34]

If we add those men who were willing but not chosen to serve in the *ban* in 1552 and 1562 and those referred to as *gens d'épée* to those actually serving or considered capable of service in 1639, we will arrive at a more accurate appraisal of the total size of the *élection*'s military nobility. Table III.5 shows the proportion of *noblesse d'épée* among the nobility of the *élection* by comparing these 1552-62 and 1639 figures,

TABLE III.5

Size of the *Noblesse d'épée*

	1562	1639	1666
Total population (family heads)[a]	404	547	592
On active military service	41	109[b]	17
Other military nobles	154	66	204
Total *noblesse d'épée*	195	175	221
Percent *noblesse d'épée*	49	32	37

[a] Estimated in 1562 and 1639.
[b] Includes those capable of service.

as well as those representing the 1666 nobles who had military experience, to the total number of noble family heads living in the *élection* in 1562, 1639, and 1666.[35] As can be seen, by this count the total percentage of *noblesse d'épée* rises appreciably over the total of those actually on active service in a single year. In 1552-62, about 40 percent, in 1639 about 32 percent, and in 1666 about 37 percent of all nobles can be considered military nobles. If we also count the 7 percent of the nobility in 1666 who, though they had never performed any military service, nevertheless had close relatives—unmarried brothers or sons—who had served as soldiers, then the percentage of the nobility in 1666 who could be considered military nobles rises to 44. This is comparable to the 49 percent in 1552-62 and indicates that, despite the low 1639 figure, no serious secular decline in the relative importance of the military nobility had taken place between the mid-sixteenth and mid-seventeenth centuries.

These figures suggest that a military way of life affected many nobles; indeed, it may have affected proportionately more nobles than any other group in French society. Bayeux nobles fought in Italy, Hungary, Holland, Flanders, Denmark, Sweden, and the Vendôme.[36] They contributed members to all factions during the Wars of Religion and were represented at the siege of Amiens in 1597, at Bordeaux in 1593 and 1616, and at La Rochelle in 1622.[37] Several score became chateau, company, and regimental commanders, masters or *aides de camp*, artillery officers, royal lieutenants general for Lower Normandy, and marshals of France. Hundreds more served as *homme d'armes* in the cavalry, as infantrymen, or more rarely, as sailors. Military experience, then, was widely shared and military performance and reputations public knowledge. Many examples of individual exploits, honors, and occasional dishonors are noted in the military surveys of 1639 and 1666.

Families that had many members actively serving or killed in action were considered noteworthy: Jean l'Archier, for example, a *noble de race* who by 1666 had taken part in fifteen campaigns, had one son serving in the army, another who had been killed in action, and a brother who had lost his life at the battle of Arras.[38] Veterans of many years of active service were often highly esteemed: Robert d'Aigneaux, an old noble with thirty years of service, was described, along with his younger brother, who had taken part in ten campaigns, as "very brave."[39] Hervieu Hebert, an old noble by 1666 (from a family ennobled in 1543), was "highly esteemed" for his twenty-five years of experience.[40] Jacques du Pont, a Huguenot old noble aged twenty-two in 1666, was notable for having served in the army since the age of thirteen.[41] Men who had been wounded in action or had in some way done something out of the ordinary were also considered noteworthy. Tanne-guy Saint-Ouen, for example, though only twenty-one in 1666, had lost an arm, and François de Mesnil, after suffering several sword wounds, had been made prisoner for a year.[42] Charles Chartier, ennobled in 1636, had fought in eight campaigns, been wounded, and, it was noted, recognized by the king himself for his actions.[43] Henry Saon, an old noble, had, less fortunately, "been accused of flight [i.e., cowardice]," while the possessions of the father of Pierre Boisdelles, a *noble de race*, "were dissipated in the service."[44] Many more examples could be cited, but suffice it to say that military activities and careers were an integral part of life for large numbers of Bayeux nobles, and a way of life that was always before them in the living examples of experienced relatives and neighbors and in the oral recountings of their deeds.

Despite distinguished individual and collective military records, however, the fact remains that by even the most liberal estimate, using a very inclusive definition of military service, less than half of the Bayeux nobility could be said to have been genuine military nobles or *nobles d'épée*. Less than half of the official military class of French society, in other words, had ever performed military service of any kind. And table III.6, which is based on the 480 individual service records recorded in 1666, shows quite graphically that even most of those who could be considered *noblesse d'épée* had performed only the minimum of military duties.[45] Fully 57 percent of these nobles had never performed any military service at all, and another 28 percent had served in four or less campaigns (most only one or two). Only 10 percent had served in ten or more campaigns, and only 1 percent had twenty years or more of experience.

Less than 1 out of 100 nobles surveyed in 1666, in other words, had completed the equivalent of a modern regular army officer's average term of service. This minimal activity, moreover, is just as striking when we take into account the

TABLE III.6

Length of Military Service in 1666

Years of service or number of campaigns	Number	Percent
No service	275	57
One to four	136	28
Five to nine	20	4
Ten to nineteen	43	9
Twenty or more	6	1
Total	480	99

age structure of noble family heads. In 1666 the ages of some 335 nobles (not counting minors) were recorded along with their service records, and when, as in table III.7, we divide these nobles into age cohorts, and then analyze the length of their military service, the nonmilitary character of the majority of all nobles, whatever their age, is strikingly reconfirmed.[46] We would expect as nobles grew older and had more opportunities for service that the percentage of militarily active nobles would increase, and to a certain degree it did: a higher percentage of nobles between the ages of 40 and 59 served at least once than those aged 20 to 39. And, as might be

TABLE III.7

Length of Military Service by Age Cohort

Years of service or number of campaigns	Percentage of age group					
	20-29	30-39	40-49	50-59	60-69	70+
No service	62	67	55	45	55	70
One to four	32	26	24	33	28	15
Five to nine	6	1	5	5	6	5
Ten to nineteen	—	6	11	17	9	5
Twenty or more	—	—	5	—	2	5
Total	100	100	100	100	100	100

expected, as nobles aged, the proportion of those who had served in ten campaigns or more, increased. But the fact remains that in every age bracket but one, a majority of nobles had never served at all, and even in the 50-59 age bracket, 78 percent had either not served or had served in four or less campaigns.

By even the most generous of standards, only one-fifth of the nobles in the 40-to-69-year-old cohorts can be said to have had extensive military service. There was also a surprising lack of experience among the younger groups (20-39 years) who were, presumably, at the height of their physical powers and would have been fit for service even if they were still too young to have had extensive experience. What this table clearly indicates is that in every generation of nobles a majority would never perform any military service at all, another third would take part in only one or two campaigns, and only about 15 to 20 percent would see appreciable military action and follow regular and extended military careers.

At the top of the *élection*'s military hierarchy were those individuals who attained military posts of responsibility and note—lieutenants general for the king in Lower Normandy, troop or chateau commanders, masters and *aides de camp*, and lieutenants and captains of the coast guard. Between 1463 and 1666 some seventy-five members of the Bayeux nobility attained such elite positions. The antiquity of these elite members of the *noblesse d'épée* is analyzed in table III.8.

Old families totally dominated this small regular military establishment, providing 91 percent of its members. All eight royal lieutenants general came from ancient families while among military commanders old nobles outnumbered new by a ratio of nine to one. The increases in the numbers of new nobles in the *élection* after 1500 had little effect on the composition of this group, for new nobles, and in fact most old nobles, almost never made their way directly to the top of the military establishment.

The post of lieutenant general for the king was dominated

TABLE III.8

Antiquity of Elite Members of the *Noblesse d'épée*

Position	1463-1562 Old	New	1563-1599 Old	New	1600-1666 Old	New	Subtotal Old	New	Total
Lieutenant general for Lower Normandy	2	—	2	—	4	—	8	—	8
Troop, coastal, and chateaux commanders	27	2	7	3	26	2	60	7	67
Total	29	2	9	3	30	2	68	7	75

by the Matignon family from the early sixteenth century: five of the eight Bayeux nobles who held that post were Matignons. The Matignons also produced several notable military commanders: a Jacques Matignon was colonel general of the Swiss in Italy in 1525, Odet Matignon was marshal of the camp for Henry IV in 1595, and Jacques Matignon was a marshal of France and lieutenant general of Lower Normandy in 1578.[47] The Bricqueville, sieurs of Bricqueville, Luzerne, and Colombières were another old family that produced a remarkable series of soldiers in the sixteenth century, including François de Bricqueville, one of the greatest Protestant captains of his day. This series of commanders culminated, after the abjuration of his branch of the family, in Gabriel de Bricqueville, lieutenant general for the king in Lower Normandy in the 1660s.[48] The Longaulnay family was another old military dynasty, producing many notable commanders, including Herve Longaulnay, lieutenant general for the king in Lower Normandy from 1553 to 1590, and Anthoine Longaulnay, marshal of camps and arms for Henry IV.[49]

Few families could match the brilliance of the Matignon, Bricqueville, or Longaulnay families, but many produced one or two prominent military men. The ancient Foullogne fam-

ily, for example, boasted an *aide de camp* to the duke of
Longueville in 1634; Jean d'Escageul was an *aide de camp*
to the duke of Beuvron, and captain and governor for the
League at Bayeux in 1589; and Joachim Montfriart was a
grand master of the camp in the 1620s.[50] Some families de-
voted themselves to a particular post, like the Pierreponts, who
were captains of the coast from the mid-sixteenth to the mid-
seventeenth century.[51] Some families served under the
amirauté or were officers in the *ban*. In 1562, for example,
Charles Villiers was *cornette* of the *ban* while in 1587 his son
Guillaume was exempt from *ban* service as captain of the *plat
pays* at the same time that two other Villiers served as men at
arms in the company of a sieur of Pierrecourt.[52] Old families
like the Taillebois or Suhard also built military careers around
their leadership of the *ban* contingent. Old nobles did not
hesitate to serve as treasurers of the *ban* either: Thomas
Suhard held this post in 1562.[53]

When we analyze the antiquity of the entire *noblesse d'épée*,
however, rather than just the relatively tiny group at the top
of the military hierarchy, we find that *anoblis* were well represented. In 1552-62, for example, 26 percent (table III.9) of
the *noblesse d'épée* were new nobles, while, in 1597, 19 percent
of the nobles who went to the relief of Amiens were recent
anoblis. In 1639, 22 percent and in 1666, 20 percent of the military nobles in the *élection* came from the most recently ennobled section of the nobility. Taken as a whole, new nobles

TABLE III.9

Antiquity of the *Noblesse d'épée*

Antiquity of family	Percentage in:			
	1552-62	*1597*	*1639*	*1666*
Old noble	74	81	78	80
New noble	26	19	22	20
Total	100	100	100	100
Number of nobles	178	109	153	221

were penetrating into the *noblesse d'épée* and taking part in the military aspects of noble life in numbers that equaled and even exceeded their numerical importance among all nobles.

Although there were some exceptions, new nobles may not have been able to penetrate into the highest levels of the military hierarchy, but then, neither had most *nobles de race*, for the higher functions were basically a monopoly of a very small group of very ancient and esteemed families—the traditional *noblesse d'épée* often cited by historians. But in all other respects *anoblis* seem to have participated and been absorbed into the existing, or developing, military establishment in the same proportions as the *nobles de race*. Antiquity, in other words, was not, unless the very highest ranks were involved, a good predictor of potential military activity.

Nor is there any evidence to suggest that those *anoblis* who did belong to the *élection*'s military nobility served any less extensively than their fellow military *nobles de race*. On the contrary, where we are able, as in 1666, to compare the relative lengths of service of old and new nobles, we find that, if anything, new nobles were more active on the average than old nobles. As table III.10 demonstrates, not only was the percentage of new nobles performing some kind of military service higher than among old nobles, but a slightly higher per-

TABLE III.10

Lenth of Military Service by New and Old *Noblesse d'épée*

Years of service or number of campaigns	Number		Percentage	
	Old	New	Old	New
No service	234	41	59	48
One to four	105	31	27	37
Five to nine	16	4	4	5
Ten to nineteen	36	7	9	8
Twenty or more	4	2	1	2
Total	395	85	100	100

centage of new nobles also belonged to the group of nobles with extensive (five campaigns or more) military experience.

It was not unusual, then, for new nobles quickly to step into military roles, or, a fact that has often been overlooked, to combine a military career with officeholding. Henry Baucquet, for example, from a family ennobled in 1581, served in two campaigns despite the fact that he held the office of *vicomte* of Thorigny.[54] François d'Escrametot, a prescriptive *anoblis*, was the third successive member of his family to hold the post of *élu* at Bayeux; he also served as an *homme d'armes* under Matignon at Bordeaux in 1593, and his eldest son Michel, an assessor at Bayeux, also served under a Matignon in 1622 (at La Rochelle) and 1646.[55] Nor was it unusual for the sons and grandsons of newly ennobled officeholders to serve exclusively as soldiers, reflecting the habit of abandoning the world of offices mentioned earlier. The father of François and Jean Marconetz, for example, was a lieutenant in the *élection* of Bayeux when he was ennobled in 1595. But by 1666 one of these second-generation *anoblis*, François, had become captain of a regiment while the other brother, Jean, had seen service as an *homme d'armes* for twenty years.[56] The Godefroy family, condemned as prescriptive nobles in 1666 but later maintained in their nobility (as 1585 *anoblis*) produced a captain of the coast who was held "in very good regard in the province . . . and acquits himself diligently of his charge."[57] Jean Petit-Coeur, a fourth-generation prescriptive noble also challenged in 1666, was able to produce a testament to his service at the siege of Bordeaux in 1616, after which he had served as grand master of waters and forests until 1630, when he began service as a cavalry lieutenant. In 1666 he produced a folio of twenty documents to prove that all his sons were on active duty with the royal army.[58] In 1666 Lambert l'Escally, a retired lieutenant in the *vicomté* of Bayeux, whose family had been ennobled in 1543, had lost two sons in action with the royal army.[59]

Thus, in the same way that most new nobles gave up their offices in order to merge with the majority of country gentlemen, they were also quick to adopt the military habits of the class they had joined. Apparently, there were no insurmountable barriers to their participation in the type of activity that was considered quintessentially noble. In the military field as in the world of noble officeholders, there was little that distinguished the new nobility from the old. The antiquity of a man's family had little correlation with the type of posts he held or careers he followed. The internal social structure of the nobility did not exhibit the serious social, functional, and caste divisions between old nobles and new that have often been thought to have existed among the sixteenth- and seventeenth-century French nobility. On the contrary, new nobles were accepted into the existing social roles without apparent disruption or isolation, while old nobles shared fully in those new roles, such as officeholding, that have often been viewed as a threat to the *noblesse de race*.

The most crucial internal division in noble society was simply one of wealth: between those who, whatever their social background, were affluent enough to undertake active military and civil roles, and those who were not. Table III.11, for example, shows the comparative income rankings of noble officials and professional men, and nobles who held military commands or had served in some military capacity, in 1552-62, 1639, and 1666.[60] Officials and professionals almost always (58 of 70 cases) came from the richest half of the nobility, a majority (36 of 70, or 51 percent), in fact, from the richest quarter of the nobility. Almost three-quarters of the *élection*'s military nobility belonged to the richest half of the nobility, 43 percent (169 of 391) to the richest quarter alone. Following a military or civil career, in other words, was basically a privilege of the well-to-do.

The determining effect of wealth on the pursuit of an active career can also be demonstrated by estimating the total proportion of all poor and relatively well-to-do nobles who were capable of following an active career. In 1639, for example (figure III.1), a large majority of the richest half of the no-

CHAPTER III

TABLE III.11

Income Ranking of Officials, Professionals, Military Commanders, and Other *Noblesse d'épée*

Occupation	Poorest half	Income ranking Third-richest quarter	Richest quarter	Total
No. of officials and professionals in:				
1552-62	1	7	7	15
1639	2	6	12	20
1666	9	9	17	35
Subtotal	12	22	36	70
No. of *nobles d'épée* in:				
1552-62	13	9	46	68
1639	12	38	66	116
1666	81	69	57	207
Subtotal	106	116	169	391
Total	118	138	205	461
Percentage of total	26	30	44	100

bility were officials or military nobles. But only a small minority of the poorest half of the nobility had served in these capacities. And in 1666, members of the richest half of the nobility were almost twice as likely to have served in such positions as nobles from the poorest half of the nobility.

Therefore, from a structural standpoint, the crucial division within the nobility was between rich and poor nobles. This structure effectively prevented large numbers of nobles from undertaking politically effective social roles. There were, for example, very few poor nobles who served as soldiers. Most poor nobles were old nobles, but their lineage did not fit them in any way for a military career or office they could not afford. Poor nobles, in fact, whether old or new, were excluded from full participation in most traditional noble activities except the

Figure III.1 The Influence of Wealth on the Occupational Structure
of the Nobility in 1639

Poorest Half

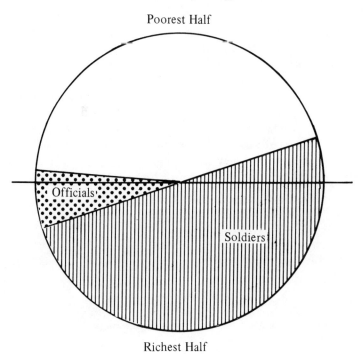

Richest Half

enjoyment of noble status itself. Many owned no fief nor
could they style themselves sieur: the names of 59 percent of
the nobles appearing in the 1597 *recherche*, for example, and
40 percent of those in the 1666 *recherche*, were recorded with
no seigneurial title. Although most of these poor nobles possessed a nonnoble tenure of some kind, and enjoyed a standard
of living better than that of most commoners, they had an
insignificant part to play in the seigneurial regime and in the
administration of local justice, and their revenues were too
small to support even a modest military or official career.

If a lack of income prevented sizable numbers of nobles
from fully following traditional noble ways of life and en-

97

gaging in significant social action, the intermingling of old and new men into the *noblesse d'épée* and squirearchy reveals the opposite side of the coin. For wealth was the means both to an effective integration of new elements and the continued dominance by older families. New men who could afford to do so, could without liability, for example, undertake military careers or merge in an economic sense into the seigneurial regime. Substantial old families were, of course, able to accept these newcomers easily since, in terms of wealth and social position, they had more in common with each other than with their more disadvantaged fellow nobles. And, as we shall see in the next chapter, new nobles merged easily into the established nobility in a personal sense, through intermarriage.

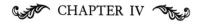 CHAPTER IV

MARRIAGE PATTERNS AND
SOCIAL INTEGRATION

IN THE PREVIOUS CHAPTER we observed that the nobility's internal social situation was considerably more complex than many historians have thought. In the first place, the nobility had not become subdivided into two mutually opposed camps of *anoblis* officeholders and old *noblesse d'épée*. The number of officeholders was actually quite small, exhibited rapid turnover, and was at least as much a preserve of old nobles as new. The military nobility, which included less than half the nobility, was well penetrated by *anoblis*, who served in the same proportions as members of older families. Therefore at least half of the nobility, whether *nobles de race* or *anoblis*, does not fit into the stereotyped social divisions whose supposed mutual antagonisms have been a major focus and concern of historians since the sixteenth century. We concluded that the sixteenth and seventeenth centuries simply did not witness the erection of significant structural social barriers between old and new families. Occupationally and functionally, old and new nobles seem to have been mixed and thrown together in the most significant social categories without regard to their social origins. New nobles, in other words, were integrated into a preexisting social structure which remained basically unchanged over the entire period.

But the question of the degree of social integration of newcomers cannot be conclusively settled by a single analysis of occupational, age, and status groups alone. The more subtle problem of whether or not the old nobility was willing to accept new nobles on a deeper level—that of friendship and family association through marriage alliances—remains to be explored. It is often difficult to determine what has happened in this area of social history, since we are dealing with the virtually unrecorded and private realm of individual and collective personal experience. Yet an accurate appraisal of the internal social dynamics of the Bayeux nobility would be incomplete without such information, since our estimation of its coherency and unity as a class must, in the end, depend in part on our reading of relations within the nobility itself and between it as a group and the rest of society.

This chapter approaches the problem by analyzing the marriage patterns of the Bayeux nobility over the whole period between 1463 and 1666. It will identify the types of marriage ties that existed between the most important subgroups within the Bayeux nobility, and between the nobility as a whole and nonnobles. It will show that many of the assumptions that historians now hold about noble marriage patterns do not fit the actual historical experience of the Bayeux nobility and will propose a significant revision of current ideas about the internal dynamics of the nobility as a class during the sixteenth and early seventeenth centuries.

The marriage patterns of venal officeholders, magistrates, and the upper nobility have been analyzed elsewhere,[1] but the marriage patterns of the mass of ordinary provincial nobles who made up the overwhelming majority of the Second Estate have not previously been analyzed in any systematic and quantitative manner. Nevertheless, two theories about the marriage behavior of the nobility are now in vogue. One is that the nobility as a whole had strong tendencies toward endogamy, or marriage within its own ranks, and that this endogamy was an important part of the self-definition of the nobility as a social group. This tendency toward estate-directed endogamy is seen by some historians as one of the most original characteristics of a unique society of orders which they feel existed in France in the sixteenth and early seventeenth centuries.[2]

A second theory holds that, just as the nobility as a whole set itself apart from other social groups by refusing to intermarry with them, certain noble subgroups also refused to intermarry with one another. This theory finds special favor with those historians who like to characterize the Renaissance nobility as an essentially fragmented or internally divided social group. The sixteenth and seventeenth centuries, they believe, witnessed the ennoblement of large numbers of venal officeholders, merchants, and financiers. The ranks of the nobility had to stretch to accommodate these new nobles whose talents, values, and life styles differed considerably from those of the old established families. Social tensions flared between the two groups. Old nobles despised the new families and refused to accept them as true nobles. In return, the new nobility, conscious of the power they possessed as officials of a burgeoning absolute monarchy, demanded public recognition as a Fourth Estate on an equal footing with the older nobility. Both groups strengthened this tendency to reject one another by refusing to intermarry, with the result that the nobility became internally divided along quasi-class lines. The tensions that arose from these internal social divisions, it is argued, provide the best key to understanding noble behavior during the political conflicts and crises of the sixteenth and early seventeenth centuries.[3]

We have already had occasion to question the factual accuracy of part of the second of these theories, but the best way to determine definitively the accuracy of both is simply to analyze the marriage patterns of a large and representative group of provincial nobles like the nobility of the *élection* of Bayeux. The records of the *recherches*, once again, provide the main source of information. Families made extensive use of the marriage contracts of their individual members to prove their nobility to the *recherche* commissions, and although the marriage contracts themselves have not survived, the records of the *recherches* contain the date of marriage and wife's name for 1,979 Bayeux noblemen. Since approximately 4,300 noble nuclear families lived in the *élection* for at least some time between 1463 and 1666, the 1,979 marriages represent about half of all the marriages entered into by Bayeux noblemen between the mid-fifteenth and mid-seventeenth centuries.

In order to determine to what extent and at what periods the Bayeux nobility was marrying only within the nobility itself and if different groups inside the nobility refused to intermarry, the surnames of these 1,979 wives were checked against a directory of all the noble families who lived in Lower Normandy between 1463 and 1666. This directory was created by combining the results of the 1463, 1598, and 1666 *recherches*, which covered the eight *élections* and more than 1,500 parishes of the *généralité* of Caen, an area of approximately fourteen thousand square kilometers.[4] Names were matched by computer. The general directory of nobles was searched at the appropriate date for the surname of each nobleman's wife. If no match was found, it was concluded that the wife came from the Third Estate. If a corresponding name or names was found, the program then determined what kind of nobles they were, that is, whether they were *nobles de race* or *anoblis*, or some combination of the two in cases where several different noble families shared a surname.[5]

This was not, however, a completely error-free process. To produce genuine and accurate results, two important conditions had to be met. The first, of course, was that most Bayeux noblemen had to have married within Lower Normandy so that their wives' families, if noble, could be found in the directory of all Lower Norman nobles. The *élection* of Bayeux, fortunately, was located in the center of Lower Normandy, bordered on the north by the English Channel, and surrounded by the other *élections* of the *généralité* of Caen. To have married outside Lower Normandy, most Bayeux nobles would have had to travel at least seventy kilometers to the east, and much further in other directions. The information in the *recherche* suggests that this almost never happened and that most nobles sought wives much closer to home. The focus of marriage was first the *élection*, and then the region: more than 70 percent of the marriages made by Bayeux noblemen, for example, were with women who bore the names of noble families living in the *élection* of Bayeux itself, a percentage that rises to over 90 if the surrounding *élections* of Carentan, Coutances, Virc, and Caen are included. Such regionality is further demonstrated by the fact that three-quarters of all immigrant noble families, whether recent *anoblis* or old nobles, came from the adjacent *élections* of Lower Normandy.

The second condition that had to be met was that the name-matching process itself did not mistakenly identify wives who came from nonnoble families as noblewomen just because they shared a surname with some noble family. Although this situation sometimes arose, it did not turn into a serious problem. In most of these cases, the bride of the Bayeux nobleman was also referred to in the records of the *recherches* as a *damoiselle*, the honorific title used by women of quality, which indicates that even if the woman's surname was shared with commoners, it was probably the noble family that was meant. Though there is a chance that some erroneous identifications were made, they were probably too few to distort the overall results.

Some examples will make clear the manner in which this process worked. In 1644, for example, Michel Estoc, from an old, but undistinguished family that had lived in the *élection* since at least the middle of the fifteenth century, married Marie Dieu, or Le Dieu. Now between the *recherche* of 1598 and the date of this marriage, there were no noble families named Dieu or Le Dieu living anywhere in Lower Normandy, though a Le Dieu family was ennobled in the *élection* of Carentan in 1656. In this case, our nobleman would be counted as having married a commoner, though she was probably from a bourgeois family that achieved noble status twelve years after her marriage.[6]

The case of Jean de Cuves, sieur of Longueville, a *noble de race* who married a Margueritte du Brebeuf in 1504, provides an example of a more positive identification. In 1463 there were two noble families named Brebeuf living in Lower

Normandy, both from the old nobility, one in the *élection* of Bayeux, another in the *élection* of Coutances. In 1598 there were also two Brebeuf families, both from the old nobility, living in the *élection* of Bayeux. In this case, our nobleman was counted as having married a woman from an old noble family like his own, because the only nobles named Brebeuf living in Lower Normandy between the *recherches* of 1463 and 1598 were old nobles.[7] The marriage of Mathurin Hue, a third-generation *anoblis* from a family ennobled in 1595, to a Damoiselle Anne Le Boucher in 1632, provides an example of a third type of identification. Between 1598 and 1666 there were several different noble families named Le Boucher living in Lower Normandy, mostly in the *élections* of Caen and Falaise, so Mathurin Hue's wife was counted as a noblewoman. But since some of the Le Boucher were *nobles de race* while others were *anoblis*, it was impossible to tell if he married a woman from an *anoblis* family like his own, or from one of the *noblesse de race* families of Lower Normandy.[8]

Figure IV.1 shows the percentages of marriages that Bayeux noblemen made with other nobles and with commoners in each decade between 1430 and 1669. This figure shows clearly that the marriage patterns of the Bayeux nobility across this lengthy period were characterized by a very high degree of endogamy. Decade after decade, Bayeux noblemen consistently chose their wives almost exclusively from within the nobility itself.[9] In the twenty-three decades between 1430 and 1669, the percentage of marriages made outside the nobility exceeded 20 only twice. This happened once in the 1460s, the period immediately following the close of the Hundred Years' War, and once in the 1550s, the period immediately preceding the outbreak of the Wars of Religion. But the era of the Wars of Religion does not show an excessive number of marriages with commoners, nor does that other period of great social unrest, the Fronde. The overall picture is that over the more than two centuries between 1430 and 1669, the Bayeux nobility consistently intermarried almost exclusively with itself and the

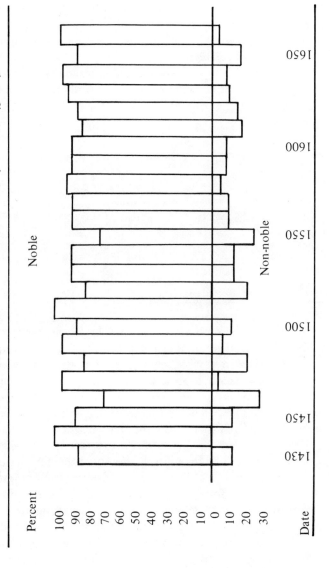

Figure IV.1 Noble Marriages with Nobles and Commoners, by Decade, 1430-1669

rest of the Lower Normandy nobility. Enough marriages with commoners were consummated to avoid a castelike marrying pattern, but as some historians have suspected, the nobility seems to have been successful in guarding its distinctiveness as a social group through a highly discretionary and exclusive system of marriage alliances.

Table IV.1, which shows the overall figures on wives' social origins for the entire 1430-1669 period, vividly demonstrates the strength of the nobility's social cohesiveness. Over this

TABLE IV.1

Social Origins of Noblemen's Wives, 1430-1669

		Wife's origin		
		Third		Third
	Nobility	Estate	Nobility	Estate
Bayeux Nobles	N	N	%	%
Old nobles	1,481	191	89	11
New nobles	272	35	89	11
Total	1,753	226	89	11

period 1,753 of the 1,979 marriages made by Bayeux noblemen were with women from other noble families. Only 226 of the 1,979 marriages were with commoners. The nonnoble wives appear to have come, in general, from two different groups. The first group was composed mostly of the daughters of local commoner families, well-to-do farmers or seigneurial officials, perhaps, who lived in or near the same parish as the noble family with whom the match was made. Good examples of such marriages can be found in the history of the d'Aigneaux, a noble family who had lived in the parish of Deux-Jumeaux since at least the fourteenth century. In 1634 Charles d'Aigneaux, sieur of Douville, married Renée Davy, daughter of a man of modest condition from the parish at Cerisy, in order to legitimize their children, the first of whom had been born in 1606. In 1659 Robert d'Aigneaux, sieur of Douville and an *homme d'armes* in the company of the duke of Longueville, married, in his second marriage, a Jacqueline Magne, who was from a nonnoble family living at Deux-Jumeaux which owned enough property for its members to style themselves sieurs of Val.[10]

Daughters of bourgeois families, mostly from Bayeux, but often from Caen and sometimes from Coutances or St. Lô provided a second group of commoner wives whose relatives were often minor officials and officeholders. In 1657, for example, Jean d'Aigneaux, sieur of Grand-Mare, married a Marie Gouye, daughter of a *huissier audiencier* at the *présidial* of Caen.[11] Another example of this type of marriage, probably a very rich one, was made by François de la Rivière, *écuyer*, sieur of Romilly and Gonnets, lieutenant general in the *vicomté* of Bayeux, founder of the Hérils branch of the de la Rivière family, which could trace its roots back to the twelfth century, who in 1532 married Jacqueline de Cossey, only daughter and heiress of Guillaume de Cossey, sieur of Herils, a *receveur des tailles* at Bayeux.[12] As that group of nobles with the most recent ties to the Third Estate, the new nobility would have been in a better position than older nobles to sustain relationships across class boundaries. But the pressure toward self-association within the nobility itself was apparently so strong that new nobles, as a group, found it desirable to reverse previous patterns and limit themselves almost entirely to marrying within their new status group. Over the whole period, nobles made almost nine out of every ten marriages with other nobles. The fact that new nobles showed exactly the same degree of group loyalty as did old nobles further underscores the pervasiveness and strength of this pattern of estate-directed endogamy.

Knowing that the marriage patterns of Bayeux nobles as a group were strongly endogamous does not, however, shed much light on the nature of the marriage alliance system within the nobility itself. As previously mentioned, some historians argue that in the sixteenth and early seventeenth centuries the old and new nobility formed mutually exclusive groups which refused to intermarry. Table IV.2, which compares the marriage patterns of these two groups within the Bayeux nobility over the 1430-1669 period, shows that, as many have suspected, old nobles had a significantly stronger tendency to marry women from old noble families, and not marry women from new noble families, than new nobles did.[13] But these figures also show that new nobles were certainly not being denied the opportunity of concluding marriage alliances with older noble families. In fact, at least 58 percent of all the new nobility's wives came from old noble families. New nobles, in other words, were intermarrying more rapidly with the older nobility than with their fellow *anoblis*.

TABLE IV.2

Old and New Noble Marriage Patterns, 1430-1669

		Wife from:			
Bayeux nobles	Old nobility	New nobility	Nobility[a]	Third Estate	Total
Old nobles	1,108	200	173	191	1,672
New nobles	179	55	38	35	307
Old nobles	66%	12%	10%	11%	99%
New nobles	58%	18%	12%	11%	99%

[a] Could be either old or new noble.

This point is reinforced by table IV.3, which illustrates the relative degree of endogamy characteristic of both new and old nobles by calculating the range of minimum and maximum possible intragroup marriages for both groups. Marriages with commoners have been excluded from this table, and marriages with women from families whose antiquity was unknown were counted once each way as matches with either old or new nobles. Old Bayeux families, for example, made 11 percent of their marriages with women from families that could have been either old or new nobles. If all these mar-

TABLE IV.3

Possible Ranges of Intermarriage by
Old and New Nobles[a]

Bayeux nobles	Percentage of marriages with:	
	Similar nobles	Dissimilar nobles
Old nobles	75–86	14–25
New nobles	20–34	66–80

[a] Based on 1,753 marriages with other nobles.

riages had been with other old nobles, then fully 86 percent
of the marriages by old nobles would have been with other
old families. If all had been with *anoblis*, then only 75 percent
of their marriages could have been endogamous matches. The
actual percentage of endogamy, then, lies somewhere between
75 and 86 percent.

In terms of group loyalty, old and new nobles could hardly
have been more dissimilar. Old nobles married other old
nobles between 75 and 86 percent of the time, a high degree
of inbreeding. New nobles, on the other hand, married other
new nobles only 20 to 34 percent of the time. At least two-
thirds of their marriages were outside their own group. We
may conclude, then, that though the old nobility as a whole
did marry fairly exclusively with other old nobles, the argument that new nobles were excluded from the rest of the nobility and were forced, in effect, to intermarry only among
themselves, does not seem to be valid. *Anoblis* were two to
three times as apt to marry a woman from a *noblesse de race*
family as they were to marry a woman whose father, like
themselves, was an *anobli*.

But the fact that old nobles mostly married women from
other old noble families is not surprising if the proportion of
old to new families among the Lower Norman nobility as a
whole is considered. Throughout the entire period the proportion of *anoblis* families to all noble families sometimes sank
as low as 10 percent, never exceeded 20 percent, and generally

fluctuated around 15 percent.[14] This means that old nobles could not have made more than a small minority of all their marriages with *anoblis* in any case, because there just were not enough new nobles around to support a higher level of intermarriage. The fact that old nobles did make between 14 and 25 percent of all their noble marriages with women from *anoblis* families indicates that despite the high degree of inbreeding that characterized their marriages, the number of matches old families made with *anoblis* was very close to the limit of all such possible matches, given the relatively small numbers of *anoblis* available. Despite surface appearances, then, the old nobility may have been assimilating the new nobility as rapidly as it could. Similarly, though it would have been theoretically possible for *anoblis* to restrict their marriages entirely to their own group, they were making between two-thirds and three-fourths of all their noble marriages outside their own group. Therefore, both old and new nobles appear to have been marrying each other at near the maximum possible rate. This suggests that while hostility may in fact have existed between these two groups, it did not affect the social realm in which marriage alliances were concluded.

Despite the figures presented above, it is still possible that most old and new nobles were avoiding each other. In the first place it is possible that older nobles made finer distinctions between new nobles than those adopted here. Almost all historians who have written on the matter have agreed that after a certain amount of time, usually three or four generations, new families would be able to shed their *anoblis* status and be accepted in their turn as relatively old families.[15] But if a pattern existed in which first- and second-generation *anoblis* were shunned by the old nobility, but third- and to an even greater degree fourth-generation nobles were found to be more acceptable, we could have arrived at the aggregate statistics examined above, and yet still had an almost complete exclusion of the very newest nobles by old nobles. Furthermore, before concluding that all old nobles were readily marrying new nobles, we must determine what portion of all old noble lines were actually involved in marriages with *anoblis* and commoners. A small number of old noble lines, for example, might have been responsible for all the marriages with *anoblis* or commoners. If this was the case, it would have been possible for there to have been many old noble-new noble matches, while four-fifths of the old nobility still pursued a rigidly exclusionary pattern of intermarriage. And, since these aggregate figures do not reveal whether intermarriage between old and new nobles was continuous or intermittent, it also is possible that such intermarriages might have been made at very high rates in some periods but not at all in others. Therefore, the periodicity of intermarriage between the two groups must also be determined.

The question of whether or not different generations of new nobles had varying degrees of success in their attempts to intermarry with old nobles is explored in table IV.4, which shows the marriages of Bayeux *anoblis* by generation of nobility. These figures show that there were significant differences between the behavior of fourth-generation *anoblis* and *anoblis* in their first three generations of nobility.[16] Fourth-generation *anoblis* married a significantly higher percentage of *nobles de race* than did other *anoblis*. The oldest of the new families, in other words, tended to make better marriages than

TABLE IV.4

Marriages of New Nobles by Generation

| | | Percentage of marriages with: | | | | |
Generation	Number of marriages	Old nobility	New nobility	Noble[a]	Third Estate	Total
First	38	63	13	8	16	100
Second	83	58	24	11	7	100
Third	110	51	16	15	17	99
Fourth	107	70	13	11	6	100

[a] Could be either old or new noble.

the newest of the new families. Apparently once an *anoblis* family had completed its third and entered its fourth generation of nobility, it became somewhat easier or more desirable for it to arrange more matches with *noblesse de race* families.

What these figures demonstrate in an even more impressive way, however, is that new nobles, no matter what their generation, were never excluded from the rest of the nobility. In fact, it is almost impossible to find an *anoblis* line that was not able to make some matches with the *noblesse de race* sometime during its first three generations of nobility.

A typical example was the Cabazac family, which immigrated from Cahors and attempted to claim noble status during the 1540 *recherche*. Their claim was rejected on the grounds of insufficient proof. They obtained letters of ennoblement in 1545, though they remained in litigation over their nobility with the Cour des Aides until 1605. We might expect this kind of family to have had difficulty finding matches with *nobles de race*, but in fact Thomas Cabazac, one of the recipients of the letter of ennoblement, married a Damoiselle Marie de Baudre, from the old nobility, while Pierre de Cabazac, Thomas's eldest son, married a Damoiselle Anne d'Amours, also from a very ancient line, in 1583. In 1594, Thomas's second son, Jean Cabazac, who lived in Bayeux, married a Camille Andre, from a family ennobled in 1544, but the third generation of Cabazacs made matches with a Le Breton and a de la Mare, both old noble families.[17]

This pattern of marrying into the old nobility early and often was shared by most *anoblis* lines. Some new families, in fact, married only *noblesse de race* women. The Acher family, sieurs of Mesnil-Vité, are excellent examples. According to their own claims they had been ennobled by *franc-fief* in 1471, but according to the version accepted by the crown, they were recipients of letters of ennoblement in 1523. The recipient of this *anoblissement*, Guillaume Acher, sieur of Mesnil-Vité, was an *élu* at Bayeux and, by 1548, a *gentilhomme ordinaire de la chambre du roy*. His father, Lucas Acher, had been an administrator of the barony of Neuilly for the bishop of Bayeux, while his mother, Fleurie de Gascoing, was a relative of a bourgeois cleric, Jean de Gascoing, prior of Hauteville-la Guichard. He married, in 1518, Damoiselle Margueritte Pellévé, from a wealthy and important *noblesse de race* family in the *vicomté* of Vire. His son Jean, sieur and patron of Mesnil-Vité, Cartigny, Montreuil-sur-Vire, Villiers, Auney, La Chapelle, and Estables, married outside Lower Normandy with a Damoiselle Claude du Croq, daughter of Henry du Croq, seigneur of Mesnil-Terribus and other lands in the *vicomté* of Arques, which Jean inherited. Jean's eldest son, Henry, seigneur and patron of Mesnil-Vité and other lands, and a third-generation *anobli*, had so far shed the family's original financial background as to become captain general of the seacoast in the *bailliage* of Cotentin, *gentilhomme ordinaire de la chambre du roy*, and a chevalier of the order of St. Michel. In 1595 he married Damoiselle Lucrece de Marguerie, from one of the oldest and most distinguished houses in Lower Normandy, seigneurs of Motte-Airel. Finally, his son, Jean, also seigneur of Mesnil-Vité, and with whom the male line of the Acher family ended, married Hélène de la Ménardiere, the only daughter of Marc de la Ménardiere, sieur of Cuverville, a *noble de race*.[18]

Overall, each of the first three generations of *anoblis* made at least a majority, or, if we exclude marriages with commoners, two-thirds of all their marriages with old nobles. Thus when an *anobli*, whatever his generation, married a noblewoman, she was twice as likely as not to have come from a *noblesse de race* family. So to speak of the isolation of new nobles from the rest of the nobility is, from the point of view of the new nobles themselves, nonsensical.

As noted above, a small number of old noble lines could have made all their marriages with *anoblis* and commoners while most of the rest of the old nobility pursued a rigidly exclusionary pattern of intermarriage. If this were true, it would be incorrect to suggest, as we have been doing, that relations between the old and new nobility were characterized by reciprocity rather than exclusion and isolation. Table IV.5

attempts to settle this question by showing the degree to which individual old noble lines were actively involved in alliances with commoners and *anoblis* alike. Only the marriages of the 107 oldest family groups in the *élection*, those who were already old nobles in 1463 or similarly ancient lines who moved into the *élection* between 1463 and 1666, and for whom we have at least five examples of marriages each, are included in this table. The members of these 107 noble lines represent the purest *noblesse de race* or *noblesse d'épée* families living in the *élection* of Bayeux during this period. If any strict or exclusionary intermarriage pattern based on a concept of *noblesse de race* status existed in Lower Normandy, this group of nobles would be the one we would most suspect of having practiced it. Therefore in this table all marriages with unidentifiable noblewomen have been assumed to be marriages with other old nobles, in order to give these old families every benefit of the doubt in their uncertain marriages, and arrive at a conservative estimate of the extent to which they had remained untouched by *mésalliance* (marrying beneath themselves).

The results given in this table undermine the idea that any significant or large group of old nobles successfully managed

TABLE IV.5

Mésalliance by the Oldest *Noblesse de Race* Lines[a]

Lines that:	Number	Percentage
Married commoners	21	20
Married commoners and *anoblis*	48	45
Married *anoblis* but not commoners	29	27
Married neither *anoblis* nor commoners	9	8
Total	107	100

[a] Based on 1,311 marriages.

to exclude the new nobility from their alliance systems. Only 9 out of 107 of these *noblesse de race* lines, or 8 percent, could legitimately claim to have married only other *noblesse de race* families between 1463 and 1669. Only 8 percent, in other words, had never concluded marriages with *anoblis* or commoners. Fully two-thirds of these noble lines had at sometime married commoners and 72 percent, or almost three out of four, had concluded marriages with *anoblis*. Almost half (48 percent) of these noble lines had married *both* commoners and *anoblis* sometime during the two centuries.

A branch of the ancient Clinchamps family, sieurs of Moudan, in the parish of Livry, which concluded all twelve of its marriages with other *nobles de race*, and the Garsalles, sieurs of La Vacquerie and other lands, who also married all twelve times into the most ancient *gentilhommerie*, were, contrary to most that has been written on the subject, exceptions to the rule.[19] More common were such families as the Pierreponts, one branch of which, captains of the seacoast and military captains who had immigrated from the *élection* of Caen, made most of their alliances with other old families (ten out of eleven) but also made at least one marriage with an *anobli* family, the Marcadey, ennobled in 1543 and 1577.[20] More common still were such families as the Fayel, a huge line which, out of 43 marriages, contracted three with commoners and four with *anoblis*, or the d'Escageul, another old *gens d'épée* family of note which produced many soldiers including a captain of the Holy League, and who made two of their sixteen marriages with commoners and one with an *anobli*. Also common were old families like the Guyenro, sieurs of Fontenailles and other lands, who between 1440 and 1616 made six marriages with such ancient families as the Hotot, the Grimouville, and the St. Gilles, and then in four marriages between 1617 and 1646 married a Manvieux and an André, *anoblis*, and a Fumée and a Tremblay, commoners.[21]

If 92 percent of the oldest lines in the *élection*, the group that supposedly most jealously guarded its identity as old nobles, had been touched by *mésalliance* at least once in its history, it makes little sense to talk about the old nobility as a status group that defined itself through a rigorous endogamy that excluded other nobles. On the contrary, though matches with new nobles formed only a minority of all their marriages, such marriages were being concluded at a near maximum rate, and by almost every old noble family group in the *élection*.

The periodicity of this extensive intermarriage is examined in table IV.6, which shows the distribution of marriage choices made by all old Bayeux noblemen in several large periods between 1460 and 1669. As suspected, over time there were sig-

TABLE IV.6

Marriage Patterns of Old Nobles, 1460-1669

| | | Percentage of marriages with: | | | | |
| | | Old | New | | Third | |
Period	Marriages	nobility	nobility	Noble[a]	Estate	Total
1460-1499	154	77	3	10	10	100
1500-1559	328	62	16	9	13	100
1560-1599	396	74	10	7	9	100
1600-1669	728	60	14	13	13	100

[a] Could be either old or new noble.

nificant variations in the rates at which intermarriage took place, and the marriage patterns of old nobles were relatively more open in some periods than in others.[22] But the chronology of relative openness and closeness revealed by these figures departs somewhat from conventional ideas about the periods at which the old nobility is supposed to have withdrawn into itself. For these old nobles, the period following the close of the Hundred Years' War and that during the era of the Wars of Religion were relatively more ingrown than the first half of either the sixteenth or the seventeenth century. This is interesting because the first half of the sixteenth century is often viewed as the golden age of the landed nobility, a time of peace and prosperity before the twin tidal waves of price revolution and religious war.[23] Yet insofar as these marriage patterns reflect the effect of social mobility and assimilation on the old nobility, the first half of the sixteenth century seems to have been significantly more open than the era of the Wars of Religion. The figures for the era of the Wars of Religion do suggest a certain turning inward of old nobles, for the fraction of endogamous marriages rose to a minimum of three-quarters, compared to a minimum of two-thirds of all marriages in the previous period. This increased inbreeding, however, was never as strong as it had been in the period following the Hundred Years' War, though it may be evidence of an attempt to return to earlier patterns of stronger exclusiveness after the relatively more open era in the first half of the sixteenth century. Whatever the cause of the drawing inward between 1560 and 1599, however, it was followed, surprisingly, by the least exclusionary patterns of the whole two-century period. The first two-thirds of the seventeenth century, the era of the Fronde and of arguments over precedence between *anoblis* and *nobles de race*, the period when enmity between new noble and old was supposedly at its height, turns out, to have had the lowest barriers to intermarriage between the two groups of any period since the mid-fifteenth century. The factors that operated to reduce the relative frequency of marriages between *anoblis* and *gentilhomme* during the second half of the sixteenth century had disappeared by the beginning of the seventeenth century. And the political hostility between old noble and new which may have existed at the center of the realm in the first half of the seventeenth century appears to have had little or no counterpart at the local level of French society during that same period.

In conclusion, it does appear that the Bayeux nobility defined itself socially by practicing a strict endogamy. Marriages with commoners never made up more than a small fraction of all marriages by Bayeux noblemen—over the whole two

centuries only 11 percent of the total. It does not appear, however, that the hostility between *nobles de race* and *anoblis* expressed in some polemics and memoirs and at meetings of the
Estates General took concrete form in the development of
separate and irreconcilable subgroups within the nobility, at
least not at the level of the *élection* of Bayeux and Lower Normandy. On the contrary, there was a high level of intermarriage between the two groups in which almost every noble
line in the *élection*, whether old or new, participated. Whatever barriers may have existed between old families, no matter
how old, and new families, no matter how new, they did not
prevent intermarriage between the groups.

Indeed, it can be argued that extended intermarriage
strengthened, rather than weakened, the social cohesiveness of
the estate or order of nobles. For by opening their ranks to
the new nobility the old nobility removed, in effect, any necessity for newly ennobled families to continue their ties to the
Third Estate. Extensive intermarriage between the two groups
preserved and reinforced the tendency toward estate-directed
endogamy upon which so much of the nobility's identity as a
group rested. In terms of the viability of the concept of a society of orders or estates in sixteenth- and early seventeenth-
century France the experience of the Bayeux nobility shows
rather clearly that an order or estate based principally on
shared legal status could also serve as a meaningful primary
social group, despite great internal differences in wealth and
social status.

If investigations into the nobility of other parts of France
were to turn up evidence similar to that for the Bayeux nobility, characterizations of the sixteenth- and early seventeenth-
century French nobility as an essentially fragmented or internally subdivided social group would have to be discarded.
Explanations of the role that French nobles played in the conflicts and crises of the sixteenth and seventeenth centuries that
depend on the assumption that the nobility was divided along
quasi-class lines based on antiquity of family and that those

divisions are the key to a full explanation of the nobility's social behavior will have to be modified.

Historians would reap a number of dividends if they ceased to concentrate on the notion of a seriously subdivided nobility. This analysis, for example, shows a society whose mechanisms of social mobility and assimilation, at least among its highest social elite, functioned smoothly and effectively throughout a period of fairly constant religious and political conflict and change. What the example of the nobility of the *élection* of Bayeux demonstrates, in other words, is not the clash of artificially defined social groups, but a combination of stability and flexibility that enabled French society as a whole, and the French nobility in particular, to continue functioning effectively long after the conditions that had originally produced them had ceased to exist.

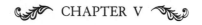

CHAPTER V

INCOME AND INDEBTEDNESS

No INVESTIGATION of the sixteenth- and seventeenth-century nobility would be complete, of course, without an evaluation of its economic health. If the class as a whole was badly off economically, or if internal divisions of wealth and income coincided with other aspects of social structure in such a manner as to lead to the historians' traditional description of internal social divisions along quasi-class lines, the picture drawn here of a relatively thriving social class, with minimum internal structural barriers and maximum, conflict-free, integration of new social elements, would lose most of its significance. Therefore this chapter and the next explore noble finances, indebtedness, and landholdings. We will show that the nobility as a whole, and within the nobility, the *noblesse de race*, successfully navigated the troubled economic waters between the mid-sixteenth and mid-seventeenth centuries, and even showed a slight improvement in economic position, both relatively and absolutely.

It is, unfortunately, impossible to determine exactly the total absolute income of the Bayeux nobility in the sixteenth century. But information on noble fief incomes contained in the *ban* of 1552 can be used to illustrate the general nature of income distribution among nobles at a time predating the era of the Wars of Religion.[1] The *ban* muster of 1552 listed 259 local nobles liable for military service. According to their statements the 259 nobles shared a total income from fiefs of 20,752 livres. This revenue was very unevenly distributed: the mean revenue from fiefs was 80 livres per year, but three-quarters of the nobility had revenues smaller than the mean. Fifty-two poor nobles had no revenues at all from fiefs. Most wealth was concentrated in the hands of a few very rich nobles. For example, the richest nobleman in the *élection*, Jean de Péllé-vey, had a larger income from fiefs than the 140 poorest nobles combined.[2] Although the distribution of fief revenues in 1552 does not provide us with the exact incomes of Bayeux nobles at that date, it most probably represents a fair approximation of income distribution as a whole among the nobility at that time, and therefore can be compared to the actual income distribution among nobles at later dates.

For the seventeenth century there is a great deal more information on noble incomes. In the 1639 *Estat des gentils-hommes*, royal officials recorded the estimated annual income of every noble family in the *élection*.[3] According to these estimates, 456 noble families shared a total annual income of approximately 637,250 livres.[4] This corresponded to a mean family income of about 1,404 livres a year, but most incomes were far under the average. Two hundred thirty-six families were considered "poor" (*"homme de peu"* or *"homme de petitte consideration"*), which in this case clearly meant they enjoyed annual revenues of less than 400 livres. The largest incomes were concentrated among a relatively small number of families. Only 33 families were worth 5,000 or more livres a year, and the 2 richest nobles in the *élection*, Gabriel de Bricqueville (25,000 livres) and Philippe d'Espiney (20,000 livres), together had a larger income than the total income of the 236 poorest nobles combined.[5]

In conjunction with Chamillart's *recherche*, royal officials also recorded the estimated annual income of every noble family in the *élection* in 1666.[6] According to these estimates, 553 noble families shared a total annual income of approximately 1,039,450 livres.[7] The mean income for individual families was therefore 1,880 livres a year, an increase of 476 livres over the corresponding 1639 figure. But, as in 1552 and 1639, there were large numbers of relatively poor nobles: 204 family heads were "poor" or had annual incomes of less than 500 livres. Once again, only relatively few nobles (43) had incomes of more than 5,000 livres, and the richest nobleman in the *élection*, Louis d'Epinay, had a larger income (50,000 livres) than the total combined incomes of the 204 poorest nobles.[8]

Such disparities in wealth are striking, and many historians have used the existence of significant numbers of relatively poor nobles in the seventeenth century to argue that a decline of the nobility had taken place in the previous century. But since no attempt has been made to compare the actual incidence of poverty in the seventeenth century with the incidence of poverty at earlier dates, it remains to be determined if these large numbers of poor nobles were in fact the product of the second half of the sixteenth century, the era of the Wars of Religion.

If we assume that the distribution of fief revenues represents a fair approximation of income distribution among the nobility as a whole in 1552, we can then compare it to the actual distribution of income in 1639 and 1666.[9] If the nobility was becoming impoverished between the mid-sixteenth and mid-seventeenth centuries, we should find substantially larger numbers of relatively poor nobles in 1639 and 1666 than in 1552. And if large numbers of old nobles were becoming poorer at the same time that wealthy *anoblis* were joining the nobility, we should find evidence of an increasing concentration of wealth among nobles, and an increase in the new nobles' share of total income.

Figure V.1 compares the distribution of income among the *élection*'s nobility in 1639 and 1666 with the distribution of income from fiefs in 1552. This comparison indicates that no significant change in the structure of noble income distribution took place between the mid-sixteenth and mid-seventeenth centuries. At both times, for example, the poorest half of the nobility received less than a tenth of the total income while the richest tenth received more than half the total. This suggests that the presence of large numbers of relatively poor nobles was a permanent feature of noble social structure, not

Figure V.1 Noble Income Distribution in 1552, 1639, and 1666

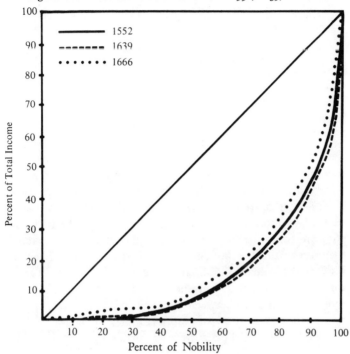

a development of the Wars of Religion, for large numbers of poor nobles existed even before the Wars of Religion, and their proportional strength among the nobles of the *élection* remained the same between 1552 and 1666.[10] Nor is there any indication of an increasing concentration of wealth among nobles. The degree of inequality in the distribution of wealth is indicated by the distance of the plotted curves from the diagonal line in figure V.1. As can be seen, the degree of inequality hardly changed between 1552 and 1666. Incomes had not become more concentrated in fewer hands: if anything, incomes had become slightly more evenly distributed by 1666.

Nor did the relative economic positions of old and new nobles change dramatically between the mid-sixteenth and mid-seventeenth centuries (table V.1). In both 1552 and 1639,

TABLE V.1

Income of Old and New Nobles, 1552, 1639, and 1666

| | (in %) | | |
	1552	*1639*	*1666*
Old nobles' share	79.9	78.5	84.4
New nobles' share	20.1	21.5	15.6
Total	100.0	100.0	100.0

for example, old nobles controlled four-fifths, and in 1666, 84 percent, of the total income, proportions that accurately reflected their numerical importance among all nobles. New nobles—that is, from families that had been noble less than a century—controlled about one-fifth of the wealth in 1552 and 1639 and one-sixth in 1666, figures that also closely parallel their proportional representation among all nobles. There is little evidence here of substantial new noble inroads. Therefore, old nobles successfully negotiated the period of slightly more than a century between 1552 and 1666 with no deterioration in their position in relation to the new nobles.

A closer look at the structure of fortunes among the *élection*'s nobility explains the relative stability of old noble fortunes. Figure V.2 uses the mean income figures for all nobles in 1552, 1639, and 1666 to divide the nobility into its richest and poorest segments. These richer and poorer segments are then divided into groups of old and new nobles. It is true that many of the old nobles in the *élection* were relatively poor. In fact, poor nobles from old families made up a majority of all nobles at all three dates. But old nobles were not much more disadvantaged than new nobles, for a sizable majority of the new nobility was also relatively poor at each date.

Not only was poverty not restricted to old families, but old nobles were not always poor. On the contrary, throughout this period most of the very richest nobles in the *élection* were members of the *noblesse de race*. Between 1552 and 1639, and again between 1639 and 1666, old families actually improved

Figure V.2 The Antiquity of Rich and Poor Nobles
in 1552, 1639, and 1666

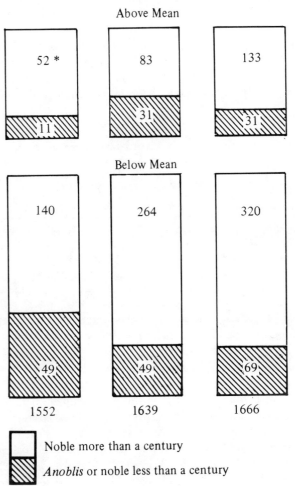

Above Mean

| 52 * | 83 | 133 |
| 11 | 31 | 31 |

Below Mean

| 140 | 264 | 320 |
| 49 | 49 | 69 |

1552   1639   1666

☐ Noble more than a century

▨ *Anoblis* or noble less than a century

* Number of nuclear families

their positions among the thirty richest nobles in the *élection* (table V.2). Furthermore, these were genuinely old families: only one out of the twenty-five old families in 1639, and one out of twenty-six in 1666, had been noble for less than a century and a half; most had been noble much longer. The ability of this small group of very rich nobles to maintain its wealth across time was an important factor in the continuing relatively strong position of the old nobility as a whole.

TABLE V.2

Antiquity of the Thirty Richest Nobles, 1552, 1639, and 1666

| | Antiquity in: | | | | | |
| | 1552 | | 1639 | | 1666 | |
Ranking	Old	New	Old	New	Old	New
Richest ten	8	2	9	1	10	0
Second ten	7	3	9	1	8	2
Third ten	8	2	7	3	8	2
Total	23	7	25	5	26	4

Although large numbers of poor families certainly existed among the nobility of the *élection* of Bayeux (as in most areas of France) by the middle of the seventeenth century, and most of these poor nobles were from old families, it would be wrong to infer that an eclipse in the position of old nobles had taken place. Between the mid-sixteenth and mid-seventeenth centuries the relative overall economic position of the old nobility appears to have remained stable or even slightly improved. Old families had not become poorer relative to new nobles. On the contrary, their share of total income actually increased, and old families were able to improve their dominant position among the richest segment of the *élection*'s nobility.

A more difficult question to answer, of course, is whether or not the economic position of the nobility as a whole im-

proved in absolute terms or relative to the rest of society between 1552 and 1666. Here, unfortunately, our internal comparisons of relative income distribution are not helpful: since
the 1552 *ban* does not contain estimates of total noble incomes,
it is impossible to make any meaningful comparison, in absolute terms, between 1552 and later years. (Strong circum-
stantial evidence of the continuing economic health of the
nobility as a whole during the 1552-1639 period will, however,
be presented in the next chapter.) Absolute comparisons can
only be made between 1639 and 1666, but since this period
encompasses the time of the Fronde, during which economic
complaints are supposed to have been a major factor in noble
unrest, such a comparison should still be of major importance.

Almost all the evidence we have developed to this point indicates that substantial increases in noble income took place
between 1639 and 1666. Mean family income, we noted, rose
from 1,404 livres in 1639 to 1,880 livres in 1666, a 34 percent
increase. The median family income increased during the same
period from slightly less than 400 livres a year in 1639 to 1,000
lives a year in 1666. Although increases in real income may
have been somewhat less than these nominal increases, they
must nevertheless have been substantial, since this was not a
period of high inflation.

A closer comparison of income levels (table V.3) shows that
the most dramatic gains between 1639 and 1666 accrued to the
poor and middle-income nobility. Between 1639 and 1666 the
percentage of families with less than 500 livres a year decreased from 53.1 to 36.9. A substantial number of families, in
other words, rose above the level of about 500 livres annual
revenue, which the officials compiling these income surveys
considered the dividing line between poverty-stricken families
and the rest of the nobility. At the same time, the percentage
of families who enjoyed revenues of between 2,000 and 4,999
livres and were therefore included in the substantial "middle
class" (or *bons ménagers*)[11] of the nobility, almost doubled
(from 11.5 to 21.5). Evidence of increased incomes can also
be found at the top of the income pyramid—the number and

TABLE V.3

Distribution of Annual Revenues, 1639 and 1666

Revenue in Livres	Number of family heads		Percent family heads	
	1639	*1666*	*1639*	*1666*
Less than 500	242	204	53.1	36.9
500–999	65	70	14.3	12.7
1,000–1,999	63	118	13.8	21.3
2,000–2,999	23	64	5.0	11.6
3,000–3,999	23	41	5.0	7.4
4,000–4,999	7	14	1.5	2.5
5,000–9,999	17	28	3.7	5.1
10,000–14,999	9	4	2.0	.7
15,000–19,999	5	3	1.1	.5
20,000–50,000	2	7	.4	1.3
Total	456	553	99.9	100.0

percentage of individual family heads with annual incomes of 20,000 livres or more, for example, more than tripled (going from two to seven individuals).

All this evidence points to a substantial improvement in noble fortunes at a time when, according to many historians, the impoverishment of the nobility as a whole was deepening. Whether the improvement represented a reversal of earlier stagnation or was simply the continuation of sixteenth-century economic vitality will be discussed in the next chapter when information on landholding and bankruptcy settlements is presented.

Incomes, of course, represent only one side of the financial ledger. The deficit side—the extent of indebtedness, the nature of the creditors, and the frequency of bankruptcies—is equally important in any evaluation of the nobility's economic health and its balance of payments with other groups in society. We have already noted the relative poverty, in monetary terms, of a large portion of the nobility (though noble poverty was decreasing rapidly in the seventeenth century). There are also descriptions scattered throughout the various documentary sources that hint at the great indebtedness of individual well-to-do families. For example, Gabriel de Bricqueville, marquis of Colombières, a member of one of the oldest and most illustrious *noblesse d'épée* houses in Lower Normandy, was described in 1639 as "very burdened by his debts," despite an annual income of 18,000 livres.[12] In 1666 Joachim Fayel, another old noble of great military experience and 4,000 livres revenue, was described as "ruined."[13] Therefore moderate to great wealth was no guarantee of solvency, but, as we will demonstrate below, neither was noble poverty necessarily synonymous with economic ruin.

Systematic records of noble indebtedness do not exist, but for the middle decades of the seventeenth century (ca. 1640-1675) a reasonably accurate picture of the incidence and consequences of noble indebtedness can be developed from the records of involuntary bankruptcies and seizures of immovable property (*décrets des héritages*) in the *bailliage* of Bayeux, which at that time covered the northern three-quarters of the *élection* of Bayeux.[14]

Although *décrets* of the property of commoners vastly outnumber those of the nobility, between 1622 (when the first noble record is found) and 1675 (when the period we are interested in ends) there were 142 cases of Bayeux nobles who were so hopelessly in debt that their creditors had their property seized and sold at public auction in order to recover overdue loans and obligations.[15] During this period one hundred manors (*lieu et entrétenant*) and 7,130 acres of land (including a few urban and industrial properties), with a capital worth approximately 1,020,575 livres, were seized from Bayeux nobles (see chapter six). At least 266,795 livres worth of property was sold at auction and the proceeds distributed to creditors.

An evaluation of the relative frequency of these *décrets des héritages* is important in assessing their significance. The 142 seizures took place over fifty-four years, but there were few in the 1620s and 1630s, and an average of 5 to 6 a year in the 1650s, 1660s, and 1670s. It is not clear, however, if this increasing frequency actually reflected an increasing rate of bankruptcy. It is more likely that the incidence of *décrets* was just as high in earlier years but that the records have not survived as well.[16] A few cases also represent successive seizures of different properties belonging to the same individual. Taking everything into account, and leaving room for a fairly wide margin of error, the best estimate that can be made is that between 1622 and 1675 approximately one out of every ten noble families in the *élection* had its property seized for nonpayment of debts and obligations.

The general identity of these families and their creditors, and the overall financial result of their bankruptcies, we shall see, fits the traditional stereotype of an economically ruined nobility hardly at all. In the historians' usual picture the victims of indebtedness and bankruptcy are always the ancient and impoverished rural *noblesse d'épée*. The beneficiaries of their decline are always grasping bourgeois merchants and officials or hard-eyed *anoblis*, "*mal noble*," fresh from the rational and calculating "real world" of the Third Estate. But of 142 noble bankruptcies that took place in the *élection* of Bayeux between 1622 and 1675, 54 or 38 percent were bankruptcies of *anoblis*. New nobles, in other words, though they made up only about 15 percent of the entire nobility at that time, accounted for more than a third of all noble bankruptcies.

The stereotype of economically ruined nobles is further undermined by table V.4, which shows the annual incomes of ninety-three of these bankrupt nobles.[17] Not only, relatively speaking, did old nobles have fewer bankruptcies than *anoblis*, but poor nobles were no more likely to have had their property seized than their more well-to-do fellows. Quite as many nobles in the 1,000-4,999 livres income range, for example, had their property seized for debts as did nobles with incomes of less than 500 livres. Bankruptcies, in fact, seem to have struck, in terms of income levels, at a fairly representative cross sec-

TABLE V.4
Income Ranking of Bankrupt Nobles

Income in Livres	Antiquity		
	Old	New	Total
0–499	22	19	41
500–999	7	1	8
1,000–4,999	28	13	41
5,000 or more	2	1	3
Total	59	34	93

tion of the nobility. This would seem to suggest that factors such as personality, individual incompetence, economic mismanagement, or even luck, may have had more to do with the financial ruin of an individual house than simple and indiscriminate economic and social determinism.

If any groups can be considered the most systematically unstable financially, they were in fact the *anoblis* and officeholders. Only 35 percent of the 142 bankrupt nobles (some of whom were *anoblis*) came from the *noblesse d'épée*. But some 28 of the 54 new nobles whose property was seized were either the direct descendants, or close relatives (almost always the sons) of officials, or held offices themselves. Furthermore, 5 of the old nobles who went bankrupt were also officeholders, which means that at least a quarter of all the cases of bankruptcy took place among the group that has traditionally been regarded as the most sophisticated and rational of all nobles in its financial management.

It is also illuminating to make a systematic comparison of the social identity of *décrétants*, that is, the individual creditors who actually initiated a *décret* (and therefore stood in the most favored position to collect legal damages resulting from nonpayment) with the identity of the nobles whose land they had caused to be seized. Table V.5 subdivides the ninety-three bankrupt Bayeux nobles whose income is known into groups

TABLE V.5

Social Identity of *Décrétants*

Bayeux nobles	Old nobles	New nobles	Noble[a]	Décrétants' backgrounds		Noble[a] officials	Bourgeois officials	Other commoners	Total
				Old noble officials	New noble officials				
Old nobles									
Poor (0-999 livres)	16	—	1	3	—	1	1	8	30
Rich (1,000+ livres)	15	2	1	1	—	1	3	6	29
Subtotal	31	2	2	4	—	2	4	14	59
New nobles									
Poor (0-999 livres)	8	—	—	3	3	—	3	3	20
Rich (1,000+ livres)	2	4	—	2	3	—	—	3	14
Subtotal	10	4	—	5	6	—	3	6	34
Total	41	6	2	9	6	2	7	20	93

[a] Could be either old or new noble.

of poor and rich, as well as old and new, nobles, and identifies the social background of their *décrétants*. What this table shows very clearly is that the majority of suits pursued against old nobles, whether poor or rich, were initiated by other *nobles de race*. Fifty-three percent of the bankruptcies of poor old nobles (sixteen out of thirty), for example, were initiated by nonofficeholding *nobles de race*, and another 10 percent (three out of thirty) were initiated by officeholding old nobles. Fifty-five percent of the suits against rich old nobles (sixteen out of twenty-nine) were also initiated by other *nobles de race* (one of whom was an official). New nobles, especially *anoblis* officials, played a larger role in *décrets* of bankrupt Bayeux *anoblis*, but even here, old *nobles de race* played the major role (fifteen out of thirty-four, or 44 percent).

Overall initiative for foreclosures on bankrupt nobles is shown by table V.6, which collapses the *décrétants* into four general categories of ordinary nobles, officeholding nobles, bourgeois officeholders, and other members of the Third Estate. As can be seen, the main initiative for proceedings against indebted Bayeux nobles came from their fellow nobles. Seventy percent of the foreclosures on poor, and 72 percent of the foreclosures on rich nobles, were initiated by other nobles. Overall less than one-third of all *décrets* were initiated by commoners, whether officials or not. When a poor noble was forced into bankruptcy in the *élection* of Bayeux, therefore, it was usually at the request of some other country gen-

TABLE V.6

Social Identity of *Décrétants*, Summary

| Bayeux nobles | Décrétants' backgrounds in % | | | | Total |
	Ordinary nobles	Noble officials	Bourgeois officials	Other commoners	
Poor (0-999)	50	20	8	22	100
Rich (1,000+)	56	16	7	21	100

133

tleman, or, less often, a noble official who was also usually a *noble de race*, rather than a predatory bourgeois.

It is, of course, easy to find examples of the stereotyped noble bankruptcy in the *élection* of Bayeux in the seventeenth century. In 1669, for example, Jacques le Maire, a poor old noble (from a family ennobled in 1453), who had served in three campaigns, had his estate seized at the request of Pierre Agnetz, a merchant bourgeois of Bayeux, for payment of five years' arrears of 5 livres hypothetical rent.[18] And in 1671 Jean and François Nollant, brothers and *nobles de race*, had their manor seized by Pierre Bertrand, master tailor and bourgeois of Caen, for payment of 84 livres for merchandise purchased in 1667.[19] In 1671 Anthoine de Reviers, a *noble de race* with annual revenues of 4,000 livres, had his manor and ninety-eight acres of land seized at the request of a Charles Gueroult, a commoner and advocate in the *siège présidial* at Caen,[20] while in 1674 the estate (manor and seventy acres) of Jean Suhard, an old *noble d'épée* who had an income of 4,000 livres and had fought in fifteen campaigns, was seized on the behalf of Marin Gaubot, a bourgeois of Bayeux.[21]

But such selected examples turn out to be very misleading. Far more typical of the relations involved in the initiation of noble bankruptcies in the *élection* of Bayeux were those in the case of Jacques Canivet, a fourth-generation *anoblis*, with 800 livres revenue and experience in ten military campaigns (and whose brother was the king's advocate in the salt warehouse at Bayeux), whose flour mill and 8 acres of land were seized in 1662 on the behalf of Magloire Bailleul, a lieutenant general in the *vicomté* of Bayeux.[22] Or Gilles Cauvet, a third-generation noble whose father had been a receiver of the *taille* (with an income of 10,000 livres in 1639), precipitated into bankruptcy by Jean de Foullognes, an ancient *noble de race*, for arrears of a rent in kind.[23] A final example of the inapplicability of the traditional stereotypes could be the 1656 bankruptcy of Charles du Hamel, a poor new noble (family ennobled in 1578), whose estate, a manor and 150 acres of land worth 26,600 livres, was seized and sold at auction at the request of Jacques Lambert, a *noble de race* (with an annual income of 2,000 livres), who also happened to hold a post in the salt warehouse at Bayeux.[24]

The identity of those individuals who initiated *décrets des héritages* alone, however, does not give a complete picture of the nobility's creditors. Once a nobleman's property had been seized, inventoried, and assigned to a temporary receivership on the basis of competitive bids, public notice of the suit was broadcast in the affected parishes and all creditors, including the *décrétant* who initiated the action, were given the opportunity to enter claims against the estate. These claims form an important part of the dossiers of those twenty-six cases for which fairly complete records have survived; they identify all claimants and reveal the monetary value of their claims (figure V.3).[25]

The information contained in figure V.3 should go a long way toward dispelling the myth of the ruthless bourgeoisie preying on ancient and impoverished noble families. Bourgeois officials and merchants and other members of the Third Estate were important creditors of bankrupt nobles, but the majority of creditors came from within the nobility itself. In fact, since 53 percent of all the creditors of *nobles de race* came from the old nobility alone, it would be more accurate to say that the typical creditor of a bankrupt old noble was more likely than not another old noble. Nonnobles figure more prominently among the creditors of the new nobility (43 percent, in all), which means, contrary to much that has been written, that if any group of Bayeux nobles were to be singled out as the principal target of predatory commoners, it would be the *anoblis*, that part of the nobility most recently removed from the Third Estate. Even among creditors who were officials, moreover, nobles outnumbered commoners, so that when bankrupt nobles had officials as their creditors, they tended to be other nobles, and *nobles de race* more often than the most recently ennobled officials.

The importance of nobles among all creditors, however, is

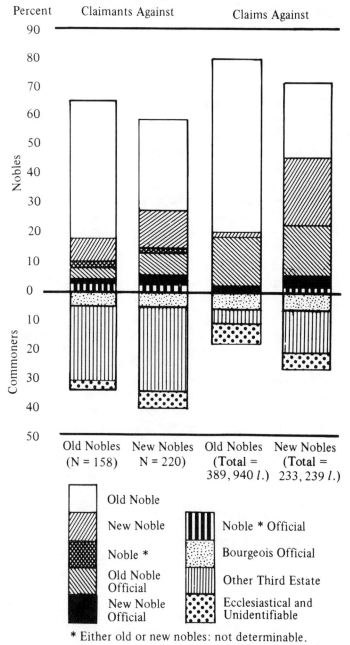

Figure V.3 Identity of Claimants and Amount of the Claims against Bankrupt Bayeux Nobles

demonstrated even more dramatically when we take into account the value of the claims that were filed against the proceeds of the sale of the properties of bankrupt nobles. By value, more than 70 percent of the claims against bankrupt *anoblis* and more than 80 percent against *nobles de race* were filed by their fellow nobles. An astonishing 78 percent of claims against *noblesse de race* families came from other *nobles de race*.[26] Only a negligible 3 percent of the total claims against old nobles belonged to *anoblis* and only 4 percent to bourgeois officials. Furthermore, 37 percent of the claims filed against *anoblis* also belonged to old nobles. This suggests that, contrary to almost everything that has been written on the subject, the most active creditor of the nobility was the nobility itself. And among all noble creditors, it was principally the rural *gentilhomme* segment of the old nobility, rather than recently ennobled officials, who were most active, and who stood to gain the most from the financial wreckage of their less fortunate fellow nobles.

Not all claims in a bankruptcy, however, were fully paid. Disbursements to claimants from the proceeds of the auctions of the property of bankrupt nobles were made on the basis of strict chronological preference: the oldest debts were paid first (with special provision made for the initiator of the *décret*). Many creditors received no payment at all because the proceeds from the sale of a bankrupt's property were exhausted before their claims were considered. So before any conclusion about the ultimate beneficiaries of the financial collapse of individual noble families can be reached, the actual distribution of the proceeds from the sale of bankrupt estates (rather than just the claims on estates) must be analyzed.

Twenty-two complete records of the payments that were actually made to claimants have survived: twelve records of bankrupt *nobles de race* and ten of bankrupt *anoblis*. The sale of their property produced 182,949 livres to be distributed to creditors. But about one-sixth of this total (31,671 livres) did not go directly to creditors as settlements for outstanding debts.

Legal fees came to 11,200 livres, seigneurial charges (*traisièmes*) on the sale price of the properties came to 11,773 livres, and 8,698 livres were deducted in order to continue permanent ground and hypothetical rents (*défalcations*). This left 151,278 livres for the settlement of creditors' claims, distributed as shown in table V.7, which confirms that the vast majority of all payments to creditors went to nobles. Sixty-nine percent of the 64,350 livres paid out from the sale of property belonging to bankrupt *nobles de race* went to other nobles, 53 percent, in fact, to other old nobles. Seventy-seven percent of the 86,298 livres paid from the sale of property of bankrupt *anoblis* also went to other nobles, 38 percent to their fellow *anoblis*. Officials received a fairly small portion (16 percent) of settlements from the estates of old nobles, but a more substantial portion (36 percent) of payments from the estates of new nobles, reflecting perhaps the recent officeholding backgrounds of most *anoblis*.

The true significance of these figures, of course, lies in the

TABLE V.7

Payments to Creditors

Type of creditor	Percentage from the sale of property of:	
	Old nobles	New nobles
Old nobles	50.7	19.4
New nobles	10.8	29.9
Nobles[a]	—	.3
Old noble officials	2.4	18.4
New noble officials	4.0	2.9
Noble[a] officials	.7	6.6
Bourgeois officials	8.8	8.4
Other Third Estate	22.4	6.4
Clergy	.3	6.9
Unidentifiable	—	.8
Total	100.1	100.0
Total in livres	64,350	86,928

[a] Could be either old or new noble.

preponderance of nobles as ultimate beneficiaries of noble bankruptcies and all that this implies about the balance of payments between the nobility as a whole and the rest of society. For every livre paid out to the creditors of bankrupt old nobles, 10 sous went to other old nobles and 3 sous to new nobles. For every livre paid to the creditors of bankrupt new nobles, 7 sous 6 deniers went to the *noblesse de race* and 6 sous 6 deniers to other *anoblis*. If we assume that two-thirds of all the payments made to creditors of bankrupt nobles came from the sale of estates of bankrupt old nobles and one-third from the sale of the lands of bankrupt *anoblis* (which would accurately reflect their proportional representation among bankrupt nobles as a group), then two-thirds of the total settlement from all noble bankruptcies would have been awarded to other nobles, and three-quarters of the settlements from the estates of bankrupt *nobles de race* would have been returned to the old nobility.

The actual portion of settlements that remained in noble hands was, in all probability, even higher. For example, nobles also collected 51 percent (old nobles 40 percent) of the 20,471 livres in seigneurial dues and payments (*traisièmes* and *défalcations*) which were a byproduct of the forced sale of noble estates (ecclesiastical institutions, principally the bishopric of Bayeux, received 40 percent of these payments). Furthermore, even before the actual settlement of a bankruptcy, nobles had often received some part of the settlements which were eventually paid to commoners. Many of the obligations of bankrupt nobles had originally been held by other nobles who, rather than attempt to collect in full on bad debts, transported the obligation, in return for payment of less than its face value, to officials or merchants who specialized in the collection of bad debts. A substantial portion of the awards made to members of the Third Estate, in other words, had already made its way into the hands of members of the nobility.

This analysis, therefore, strongly supports the earlier conclusion that the nobility as a whole, and within the nobility the oldest families, navigated the troubled economic waters of the second half of the sixteenth and first two-thirds of the seventeenth centuries with no deterioration, and indeed some improvement in their overall economic position. When nobles encountered serious financial difficulties, the web of obligations in which they found themselves enmeshed turns out to have been spun chiefly by other nobles. When overdue dowry payments, neglected hypothetical rents, and overdue obligations proved too much for the finances of an individual nobleman and he was forced into bankruptcy, the settlement of his estate went most of all to the profit—not of the rapacious bourgeoisie—but of his fellow nobles, neighbors, and relatives. The structure of credit transactions and financial obligations, while certainly not excluding financially astute members of the Third Estate, was dominated primarily by the nobility itself.

Therefore the ultimate effect of financial catastrophe was merely to enrich one segment of the nobility (the lenders) at the expense of another (the borrowers). That this should have been the case is further evidence of the basic economic stability and financial resiliency of the nobility as a whole in the sixteenth and seventeenth centuries.

CHAPTER VI

LANDHOLDINGS AND
BANKRUPTCY SETTLEMENTS

WITH THE EXCEPTION of an occasional property within the city of Bayeux itself, almost all noble landholdings in the *élection* of Bayeux were organized into rural estates, or manors, consisting of a dwelling, specialized agricultural buildings, and associated fields and pastures. Many of these manors were also fiefs, which were distinguished from nonnoble tenures in Normandy by the fact that they were held by virtue of an act of homage and enjoyed certain seigneurial rights dating back to the founding of the feudal system.[1]

The property and rights associated with individual fiefs varied greatly, but, in general, the land associated with a fief was divided into two parts: the *domaine fieffe* and *domaine non fieffe*. The *domaine fieffe* was that portion of land held by tenants in return for varying seigneurial dues and services. Although the fiefholder technically owned the land held by tenants, tenants in fact exploited their tenures as their private property, and the customary dues and services they owed, unchanged since the Middle Ages, frequently amounted to little more than token payments.[2]

The *domaine non fieffe*, organized as a manor, represented the core and most valuable part of most fiefs. Over this *domaine non fieffe*, or *manoir seigneurial*, the lord had complete control: he could farm it himself or rent it out under any terms he could command. The principal difference between the manor portion of a fief, and a manor that was not a fief, was that the nonfief property did not include a *domaine fieffe* with its tenants and associated feudal rights.

In addition to the seigneurial rights and profits, however, possession of a fief also entitled its owner to use an honorific title, a valuable asset in a society that cherished external marks of prestige. Fief owners also partook of the warrior mystique which still clung to the feudal structure. More important, until the late fifteenth century mere possession of a fief had automatically ennobled a commoner. Although that path to nobility was closed in the sixteenth century, fief owner-ship and the prestige of lordship remained the goal of every noble and all aspirants to noble status.

The first part of this chapter explores the patterns of fief ownership that characterized the *élection* of Bayeux during the early sixteenth and mid-seventeenth centuries. The second part analyzes the disposal of the property of bankrupt nobles and provides an insight into the ability of the nobility and its different subgroups to function successfully in that part of the land market which fell outside the fief system. By combining the results of this chapter with the information on noble incomes and indebtedness presented in the previous chapter, we will be able to arrive at a final conclusion about the economic vitality of the Bayeux nobility in the sixteenth and seventeenth centuries.

There were between 450 and 500 fiefs in secular hands in the *élection-vicomté* of Bayeux.[3] Some three-quarters were held by local nobles. Approximately two-thirds of the resident noble family heads held fiefs. Most nobles possessed only a single fief, and it was quite unusual for a family to possess more than three. The size and value of fiefs varied considerably, but most fiefs seemed to have contained between 100 and 1,200 acres of land, with at least 100 acres, usually more, remaining in the hands of the seigneur as his dwelling and seigneurial manor.[4] In 1611, for example, the fief d'Aigneaux, held by Etienne de Grimouville, sieur of Sully, contained a manor and domain of 30 acres of land, with 180 acres held by tenants.[5] In 1604 the fief of Damigny, possessed by Jean de Longaulnay, chevalier, sieur of Damigny, consisted of a manor and domain of 400 acres, and 200 acres *domaine fieffe*.[6] The castellany of d'Aubigny, property of Adrien de Novince, in 1667 contained 1,200 acres *non fieffe* alone.[7]

Whatever their extent, almost all fiefs had for their core a traditionally Norman group of manor buildings which served as a noble residence. The degree of grandness and state of repair may have varied, but the buildings on even the smallest fief must have served to distinguish all but the very poorest of nobles from the rest of their rural neighbors. The fief d'Aigneaux mentioned above, although a smaller fief, had, in addition to thirty acres of land in the hands of its owner, a manor house, grange, cider press, stables, cellars, smithy, and pigeon coop (a traditional part of a noble tenure) on a single acre totally enclosed by walls and the buildings themselves.[8] The fief of Damigny also consisted of an enclosed manor house (*chasteau*) with a two-acre open courtyard, and in addition to the standard buildings, was further dignified by an oven, a chapel, and several gristmills on the Seulles river.[9] The manor of the castellany of d'Aubigny included a château with four pavillions, enclosed by walls and water-filled ditches, the whole surrounded by a large pond.[10]

The value of fiefs, of course, also varied widely. Some fiefs were worth 10,000 or more livres a year.[11] De Longaulnay's fief of Damigny, described above, was by its owner's declaration worth "ordinary years, in its totality, all charges deducted, 450 livres."[12] But by 1680, its lands augmented, the now castellany of Damigny was estimated by a royal official to be worth 5,000 livres annually.[13] The fief of Brebeuf, with a manor of 160 acres (including 30 acres of woods) and a *domaine fieffe* of 516 acres divided into twelve *vavassoreries*, was worth "ordinarily, all included, 200 livres," in 1627.[14]

Cash income from the *domaine fieffe*, or tenants, was, as in many other parts of France, often very small, since the nominal value of many payments, fixed by custom, had changed little since the Middle Ages. But many fiefs that may have produced little in the way of cash income from tenants often possessed valuable rents in kind. The fief of Banville, owned by Jacques

143

de Cyresme, consisting of a seigneurial manor of 644 acres, including two windmills and two water mills, the right of presentation to the parish church of Banville, a market, and a jail, is a good example. The 576 acres of *domaine fieffe* produced only fifteen and one-half livres in seigneurial rent a year.[15] But cash rents from its tenants, while quite small, were not an accurate guide to the total value of the seigneurie. The lord of Banville also collected each year from his tenants 420 bushels of wheat, 31 bushels of barley, over 100 assorted poultry, 1,220 eggs, and 3 different, and substantial, types of labor obligations.[16] The estimated annual value of Banville, in 1680, was between 4,000 and 5,000 livres.[17]

Like Banville, most fiefs seemed to have included a mill or two, an oven which tenants were required to use for a fee, and the right to collect other substantial, if irregular dues, for example, *traisièmes*. Even the smallest of fiefs provided its owner with a manor house, windmill, arable land, orchards, and sometimes woods. Even if income (in cash or kind) from seigneurial dues was small, the *domaine non fieffe* and the buildings of many fiefs must have provided their owners with a comfortable if not luxurious living.

The fiefs owned by the Bayeux nobility therefore comprised several hundred manor houses and châteaux and their associated buildings, orchards, woods, and grounds—most of the important nonurban noble residences in the area. They represented the most important part of noble landholdings in the *vicomté*. Any drastic or permanent change in the economic fortunes of the Bayeux nobility almost certainly would have been reflected in the pattern of ownership of these fiefs. Any significant losses of fiefs by the nobility to commoners would, of course, be evidence in favor of a decline of noble fortunes relative to the Third Estate. Any significant shift in the balance of ownership to the advantage of the newer families within the nobility would be evidence in favor of a relative decline in the position of older families. Any shift in favor of the nobility as a whole, or within the nobility in favor of the oldest families, on the other hand, would provide very strong reinforcement of the argument developed in the preceding chapter for the economic vitality of the nobility in the *élection* of Bayeux in the sixteenth and seventeenth centuries.

Many historians have argued that large-scale land transfers from the nobility to the bourgeoisie took place in the sixteenth century, and examples of the sale of fiefs and seigneuries to nonnobles are often cited as proof of noble decline.[18] But the question of whether or not such isolated examples accurately reflect significant long-range shifts in noble land holdings has never really been investigated. *Ban* rolls and censuses provide a ready source of information on the ownership of fiefs in the *élection* of Bayeux. The *ban* of 1552, for example, lists 431 fiefs and their owners, and a census of 1640 recorded the owners of 487 fiefs.[19] From such documents, and with the help of family dossiers derived from the *recherches*, we can reconstruct the ownership of the vast majority of fiefs in the *élection* and trace changes in the proportion of fiefs held by different groups of nobles and nonnobles at different times.

Table VI.1 shows the proportion of fiefs owned by different groups between 1503 and 1640. Two groups of fiefs are rep-

TABLE VI.1

Group Holdings of Fiefs, 1503-1640

| Type of owner | Percentage of fiefs held in: | | | | |
	1503	*1552*	*1552*	*1597*	*1640*
Old nobles	74	73	57	63	62
New nobles	12	17	21	18	19
Nonresident nobles	6	2	10	7	12
Commoners and unidentifiable	9	8	12	12	7
Total	101	100	100	100	100
Total number of fiefs	262	215	431	417	487

resented in this table: the first includes 262 fiefs listed in a census of 1503, 215 of which also appeared in the 1552 *ban*.[20] Although the census of 1503 only includes about half of the *élection*'s fiefs, a comparison of the ownership of fiefs that were listed in *both* 1503 and 1552 gives some idea of the extent of change in the first half of the sixteenth century. The second group includes the more than 400 fiefs listed in the *bans* of 1552 and 1597, and the census of 1640.[21] The most obvious conclusion to be drawn from this table is that, as far as fiefs were concerned, no dispossession of the nobility by nonnobles took place during the century and a half between 1503 and 1640. Nobles always held at least 88 percent of all the fiefs in the *élection*, and between 1597 and 1640 increased their share to 93 percent. Within the nobility, the old nobles who were supposed to be in particularly bad straits increased their share of fiefs from 57 percent in 1552 to 63 percent in 1597, and still controlled 62 percent of all fiefs in 1640. During the same period, the number of fiefs owned by new nobles declined slightly.

Furthermore, the changes that took place in the relative value of each group's share of fiefs were exactly the opposite of what we would expect if the nobility had in fact been in financial difficulty. Table VI.2 uses the income values of fiefs as given in the *ban* rolls to compute the total income from fief-holdings of different groups of nobles, and nonnobles, between 1552 and 1640. The figures given in the *ban* grossly under-valued real fief incomes, but accurately reflect the relative value of fiefs compared to one another. They may therefore be used to estimate the approximate relative value of each group's holdings. As can be seen, fiefs held by nonnobles never accounted for more than 13 percent of the total stated income from fiefs. Among nobles, old families steadily increased their share of fief income, from 52 percent of the stated total in 1552, to 65 percent in 1597 and 72 percent in 1640. If the properties of nonresident nobles are subtracted from the total, old nobles always accounted for more than 90 percent of the total fief income enjoyed by local nobles.

TABLE VI.2
Distribution of Fief Income, 1552-1640

| Type of owner | Percentage of total value[a] owned in: | | | | |
	1552	*1562*	*1587*	*1597*	*1640*
Old nobles	52	60	62	65	72
New nobles	17	14	11	12	12
Nonresident nobles	23	19	15	13	15
Commoners and unidentifiable	8	8	13	11	2
Total	100	101	101	101	101
Total number of fiefs	431	415	445	417	312

[a] Based on the stated values in the *ban* rolls of the indicated year. The 1640 column uses 1597 valuations.

An analysis of fief holdings, therefore, produces no evidence of a dispossession of the nobility as a whole, nor of old nobles, between the first half of the sixteenth and the middle of the seventeenth centuries. Whatever changes in fiefholding were taking place, they operated to reinforce, rather than disrupt, existing patterns of ownership. The key to this stability is to be found in the reciprocal nature of losses and gains of fiefs by the different groups. Between 1503 and 1640, for example, at least 335 fiefs changed owners. Table VI.3 shows the net results of these changes. Of the 335 fiefs that changed owners, 285 were given up by nobles. Of these 285 fiefs 251 simply went to other nobles. Nobles lost 34 fiefs to nonnobles in these transactions, but 41 other fiefs were reacquired from nonnobles. The net result of all these changes was a small increase in the number of fiefs held by nobles. A similar pattern is evident in exchanges between nobles. Old nobles, for example, lost a total of 189 fiefs over the period, but 121 of these simply passed to other old nobles. Since old nobles also acquired 69 fiefs from other nobles and nonnobles, they gained one more fief than they lost. Even in exchanges with new nobles, old nobles had an advantage: they lost 25 fiefs to new nobles, but new nobles lost 31 fiefs to old nobles.

TABLE VI.3

Changes in the Ownership of Fiefs, 1503-1640

	To old nobles	To new nobles	To nonresident nobles	To nonnobles	Total
From old nobles	121	25	23	20	189
From new nobles	31	19	8	4	62
From nonresident nobles	11	7	6	10	34
From nonnobles	27	11	3	9	50
Total	190	62	40	43	335

Many historians assume a constant transfer of property from nobles to commoners and from old nobles to new nobles and commoners in the sixteenth and seventeenth centuries. Such changes are often considered an inevitable result of the price revolution and the rise of the bourgeoisie. No such changes, however, occurred in the *élection* of Bayeux. On the contrary, nobles, rather than commoners, and within the nobility, old nobles, were the groups that profited from the many changes in ownership taking place in the sixteenth and seventeenth centuries. It was possible for the nobility or the old nobles to maintain their position because they more than held their own in the massive changes in ownership that were taking place. But in addition, the ordinary processes of social mobility into and within the nobility itself contributed to this remarkable continuity in collective fief ownership and buttressed the position of the class as a whole. In the first place, even those fiefs acquired by commoners had a way of eventually returning to noble ownership when their new owners, in their turn, were ennobled. The high percentage of *anoblis* who were already fiefholders at the time of ennoblement has already been mentioned.[22] In the second place, the simple passage of time contributed to the stability of the holdings of the *noblesse de race*. If old nobles simply held their own in changes of ownership (as they did) they were bound, over time, to increase their total holdings as new nobles gradually became old nobles. For example, by 1640, all the new nobles who had joined the Bayeux nobility before 1540 could be considered old nobles (most had been noble for more than six generations), and their property counted as part of the old-noble total. The whole complicated process of net exchanges, ennoblement, and the passage of time operated to buttress the status quo rather than disrupt it.

Not all noble property was held in the form of fiefs. Nobles could also own nonnoble tenures, so before any final judgment about the ability of the Bayeux nobility as a whole to compete successfully with other groups can be made, it is essential to develop some measure of the degree of noble activity that existed in the land market outside the noble fief system. Information about the properties seized under the *décrets des héritages* mentioned in the preceding chapter provides such an opportunity.[23]

Almost all the real estate seized from nobles by means of *décrets* between 1622 and 1675 was inventoried in some detail. The *décrets* provide the rental value (from which the capital values can be derived), or, in the case of most property that was actually sold, the sale value. Table VI.4 summarizes the extent and value of these properties, estimating the values of properties for which no price (sale or rental) was given by multiplying their acreage by the mean price per acre for all other seized property of that type.

In the aggregate, the lands seized from bankrupt nobles form an impressive total, though it must be remembered that the seizure and sale of these properties was spread over a fifty-four-year period. One hundred and thirty-five separate properties with a total extent of at least 7,130 acres and an estimated capital value of approximately 1,020,575 livres were involved.[24] The 7,130 acres corresponded to approximately 4 percent of the total area of the northern two-thirds of the *élection* of Bayeux. In value this capital sum of 1,020,575 livres equaled

TABLE VI.4

Extent and Value of Properties Seized by *Décret* from Bayeux Nobles, 1622-1675

Source of valuation	Manors			Land only			Total		
	Number of properties	Total acres	Value[a]	Number of properties	Total acres	Value[a]	Number of properties	Total acres	Value[a]
Sale price	25	1,833	241,810	8	361	17,033	33	2,194	258,843
Rental price	39	2,924	451,740	12	166	30,780	51	3,090	482,520
Estimated	31	1,605	234,330	13	241	21,931	44	1,846	256,261
Subtotal	95	6,362	927,880	33	768	69,744	128	7,130	997,624
Sale price only[b]	5	—	20,951	2	—	2,000	7	—	22,951
Total	100	6,362	948,831	35	768	71,744	135	7,130	1,020,575

[a] In livres.
[b] Sale price given but no description of property. Eight other properties, including two manors, are known to have been seized, but their composition and value were not specified.

the income for an entire year of the entire Bayeux nobility, and as a capital sum could generate an annual income of approximately 34,000 livres.[25]

One hundred of the 135 seizures involved manors organized in the same way as the manor portion, or *domaine non fieffe*, of noble fiefs. Each manor (*lieu et entrétenant*) consisted of a dwelling with specialized agricultural buildings, usually enclosing a courtyard, and varying amounts of land. On the average this type of property tended to be somewhat smaller than the manor portion of noble fiefs: the 95 manors that are fully described had a total extent of 6,362 acres or, on the average, 67 acres, with an average capital value of approximately 9,767 livres per manor, which corresponded roughly to an annual value of around 320 livres. Although smaller, such nonnoble tenures were composed of almost exactly the same elements as the *domaine non fieffe* of fiefs. The estate of Lambert le Vaillant, sieur of Ferty, seized in 1669, for example, consisted of a manor house with stable, a combination grange and stable, vegetable garden, and fruit trees, all enclosed by hedges and ditches, two mills, and 126 acres of land, put into temporary receivership at a price of 755 livres a year.[26]

In the preceding chapter we analyzed the kinds of nobles who went bankrupt, the identities of the initiators of suits that led to bankruptcies, the principal creditors, and the value of settlements paid from the sale of seized estates. We did not, however, analyze the actual disposal of properties that were sold at auction. Most of these properties, though organized as manors, were nonnoble tenures, so an analysis of the purchasers of these properties should provide an accurate insight into the ability of the nobility to compete with other groups in the open market for such nonfief properties.

Of the property seized from nobles between 1622 and 1675, records have survived of the sale by auction of thirty-nine properties, including thirty manors, totaling 2,184 acres, for a total price of 266,795 livres. The identities of the purchasers of these properties are shown in table VI.5. Old nobles, again,

TABLE VI.5

Purchasers of Bankrupt Nobles' Properties, 1622-1675

Identity of Purchasers	Property of bankrupt old nobles				Property of bankrupt new nobles			
	Number manors	Other property	Total acres	Sale price[a]	Number manors	Other property	Total acres	Sale price[a]
Old nobles	10	1	419	63,232	2	—	105	15,485
Old noble officials	1	1	181	16,846	2	—	187	30,700
New nobles	1	—	72	8,000	1	1	254	10,495
New noble officials	1	1	41	4,731	—	—	—	—
Bourgeois officials	—	—	—	—	4	1	377	47,546
Other bourgeoisie	6	1	406	50,563	1	2	94	11,695
Unidentifiable	—	—	—	—	1	1	48	7,502
Total	19	4	1,119	143,372	11	5	1,065	123,423

[a] In livres.

were most active as purchasers of the property of bankrupt old nobles. Ordinary *nobles de race* purchased ten of the nineteen manors that were seized from bankrupt old nobles and auctioned off. When one other nonmanor property purchased by old nobles and two properties purchased by old noble officials are added, the old nobility purchased 54 percent of the total acreage and 56 percent of the total value of property sold from the estates of bankrupt old nobles. Bourgeois merchants from Bayeux and Caen were the second most active group, purchasing seven properties containing 36 percent of the acreage and 35 percent of the value of the old noble estates that were sold. The almost nonexistent role played by *anoblis* and bourgeois officials is also noteworthy, since traditionally these groups are thought to have greatly benefited from the sale of property belonging to bankrupt *nobles de race*.

Indeed the disposal of the property of bankrupt *anoblis* further confirms the reversal of the traditionally held views about the victims and beneficiaries of noble bankruptcies, for members of the Third Estate, primarily advocates from Bayeux and Caen, were the principal purchasers of the properties of bankrupt *anoblis*. Bourgeois purchasers accounted for 44 percent of the total acreage and 48 percent of the value of the auctioned *anoblis* properties. Even in this case, however, old nobles were the second largest group of purchasers, buying four of the eleven manors representing 27 percent of the acreage and 37 percent of the value of bankrupt *anoblis* estates.

We can collapse these categories, as in table VI.6, in order to evaluate the overall participation of the nobility in purchasing, at very competitive public auctions, the lands of their bankrupt fellow nobles. As can be seen, nobles, as a group, dominate the purchasers of bankrupt nobles' properties just as they dominated among creditors, claimants, and settlements of bankrupt estates. In the sale of these mostly nonnoble tenures, undertaken at public auctions, often with spirited bidding, *nobles de race*, those nobles most often maligned for their economic incompetence, were the principal purchasers. If both new and old nobles are counted, then the nobility as a whole

TABLE VI.6
Purchasers of Bankrupt Nobles' Properties, 1622-1675, Summary

Identity of purchaser	Number manors	Other property	Total acres	Percent acreage	Sale price[a]	Percent value
Old nobles	15	2	892	41	126,263	47
New nobles	3	2	367	17	23,226	9
Commoners	11	4	877	40	109,804	41
Unidentifiable	1	1	48	2	7,502	3
Total	30	9	2,184	100	266,795	100

[a] In livres.

purchased a sizable majority of all auctioned property: eighteen of thirty manors and four other properties containing 58 percent of the total acreage and 56 percent of the value of all property sold. Members of the Third Estate were certainly not unimportant participants in the purchasing of bankrupt estates, but what is most striking is the successful level of activity of the nobility itself. Furthermore, in some cases the bourgeoisie who were listed as purchasers were the concealed agents of nobles.[27] Therefore table VI.6 probably understates the extent to which nobles were successfully involved in the seventeenth-century land market in nonnoble tenures.

This chapter has presented further evidence of the economic vitality of the Bayeux nobility between the mid-sixteenth and mid-seventeenth centuries. The nobility as a whole, and within the nobility, old nobles, seem to have actually increased their landholdings. This is not to say that the land market or the economic life of the nobility was uneventful and that no nobles suffered economically or were ruined because of financial difficulties during this period. On the contrary, all the evidence points to an extremely fluid and competitive economic situation. For example, more than half of the fiefs in the *élection* changed owners, some several times, between 1552 and 1640. And, in the seventeenth century more than one hundred families were forced into bankruptcy by creditors and had their lands seized and sold at auction. Many examples of the ruin of *noblesse de race* and *noblesse d'épée* families could be found, and *anoblis*, or bourgeois merchants, lawyers, and officials often were able to gain possession of their fiefs and manors. More striking, however, is the fact that the nobility itself was able to take advantage of this extremely fluid situation to improve its overall economic position.[28] The nobility achieved net gains from the buying and selling of fiefs and were the principal initiators and beneficiaries, in all respects, of the bankruptcies that did take place among their fellow nobles.

Furthermore, the identities of active and affected nobles, both victim and victors, when viewed in their totality, turn out to be quite different from what would have been expected given the formulas of much conventional historiography. The group that profited most from the conditions of the time was the *noblesse de race*. *Anoblis*, on the other hand, though often assumed to be better economic managers than the old nobles (presumably because of their recent emergence from the bourgeoisie), seemed, in fact, to have been much more poorly adapted to the fluid economic situation of the sixteenth and seventeenth centuries than the old nobility. They went bankrupt more frequently and were completely overshadowed by the activity of an aggressive *noblesse de race* in the land and estate market.

As a group, then, the Bayeux nobility emerged as a winner in the historical sweepstakes between bourgeoisie and Second Estate which some historians insist on seeing as the principal development of the early modern period. When the economic fortunes of all, rather than a select and unrepresentative portion of the nobility are considered, it becomes clear that the nobility was master, rather than victim, of economic and social developments that have often and, it is here suggested, so erroneously, been seen as its nemesis.

CHAPTER VII

CONCLUSION: THE SOCIOECONOMIC BASIS OF ARISTOCRATIC RELIGIOUS ACTIVISM

THE BAYEUX NOBILITY, as a class, emerged virtually unscathed from the social and economic changes that took place between the mid-fifteenth and mid-seventeenth centuries. That it did so challenges some widely held views of the early modern French nobility, and of the history of early modern France itself. Many current interpretations of early modern French history rest on the double assumption that on the one hand, the old nobility was in economic difficulty during this period and on the other, that resentment of their economic difficulties lay behind the internal struggles between old and new nobles as well as the seemingly endless noble rebellions and protests which form the backdrop to the emergence of modern France.

Yet the Bayeux nobility as a whole, and within it the oldest families, actually improved its economic condition during the sixteenth and seventeenth centuries. Furthermore, during this period it established a stable and cohesive internal social balance between the oldest elements and the *anoblis*, who were integrated in such a way as to defuse potential conflicts while strengthening the class as a whole. Obviously, if conditions in the *élection* of Bayeux were not exceptional, and are found to be representative of conditions among the early modern French nobility as a whole, those explanations of noble participation in the conflicts and struggles of the sixteenth and early seventeenth centuries that rely on the assumption that the nobility was in serious economic difficulty or split internally along class lines, will no longer be valid. This chapter tries to anticipate this possibility and sets forth an alternative explanation of the social origins of early modern noble behavior based on the assumption that the nobility was strong and healthy instead of weak and in decline. We will test the validity of this new explanation against the concrete example of the Protestant movement among the nobility of the *élection* of Bayeux and suggest the implications this new interpretation could have for the more general history of the period.

It is not surprising, really, that many explanations of noble participation in the various historical developments of six-teenth- and seventeenth-century France should depend on the assumption that the principal force behind their actions was weakness, rather than strength. There has always been abun-dant, though superficial, evidence to support various theories of a declining nobility or to indicate that the class was split into warring factions of old and new. But since there has been practically no in-depth socioeconomic research that attempted to reconstruct accurately the history of all the members of the Second Estate in a single area over a significantly long period, there has been no way to test empirically the validity of such explanations. Besides showing that the Bayeux nobility was not in decline and that, in fact, exactly the opposite was true, the evidence presented in previous chapters of this work also suggests that historians have been laboring under a funda-mental misunderstanding about the manner in which the internal structure of the provincial nobility shaped the possi-bilities of individual and collective noble behavior. In par-ticular, historians have misjudged the role that wealth and lineage played in the social structure of the nobility. Attempts to explain their motivation in terms of such stereotyped group categories as that of the old, poverty-stricken, *noblesse d'épée,* or rich *anoblis* officeholders, have simply overlooked or ig-nored several of the most basic realities of noble social struc-ture. This in turn, we suggest, has led to a major misinterpretation of the historical role of the nobility, as a group, in the various conflicts and struggles of the sixteenth and seventeenth centuries.

We have previously noted that there was little correlation between the lineage of a noble family, that is, the antiquity of its nobility, and the occupation, wealth, or choice of marriage alliances of its members. The traditional division of the early modern nobility into groups of poor old soldiers and new rich officials simply does not apply to the *élection* of Bayeux. For one thing, many old nobles were rich, and many new nobles were poor. More than half of them, whether old or new, performed no military service whatsoever, while *anoblis* performed military service at practically the same rate as the older nobles. Many officeholders came from the oldest families in the *élection*, and few *anoblis* remained officeholders once they had entered the Second Estate. Furthermore, there seem to have been no barriers to intermarriage between old and new families. Only about half of the Bayeux nobility, in fact, can be fitted into the two traditional general categories of soldiers and officeholders, and the single most important determinant of whether a noble was active as a soldier or official was not the antiquity of his family, but simply his wealth, for as we noted earlier, almost three-quarters of the nobles who were active in these roles came from the richest half of the nobility. Participation in these activities, in other words, was basically a privilege of the wealthy and well-to-do.

From the point of view of explaining the potential for effective political activity by nobles, the only *crucial* social distinction may have been the division between rich and poor nobles, a social distinction that would closely correspond to the division between those nobles who pursued active social roles and were capable of significant political activity, and those who were not. An accurate multidimensional model of noble social structure, by demonstrating the way in which the various socioeconomic attributes of individuals coincided, shows quite clearly how the categories of nobles that historians have traditionally used simply do not provide an adequate framework for an explanation of the social structural origins of political activity by nobles. The structure of noble society effectively prevented large numbers of nobles from taking politically effective social roles. Thus, any political or military initiative undertaken by nobles, if it was to be significant or successful, had by definition to include large numbers of the most substantial members of the Second Estate. Yet historians have habitually regarded almost every manifestation of noble activism in this period as an essentially negative protest by the oldest and impoverished part of the nobility. It is hard to believe, however, that any movement of nobles could have presented a threat if it had been composed solely of resource-less, impoverished, and inexperienced nobles, for they would have possessed none of the attributes necessary for effective political action.

Would it not be at least as logical to conclude that the French nobility was so politically active in the sixteenth and seventeenth centuries precisely because it was strong enough to resist developments that it saw as contrary to its own interests? From our knowledge of the internal structure of the nobility, we should suspect that the oldest poor nobles were actually the least active and committed of all nobles. To the extent that any movement of nobles was successful, it must have included the most prosperous nobility, who constituted the core of those with political and military experience. And since the most active part of the nobility was in fact its most prosperous part, it would follow that splits and conflicts among groups of nobles who were capable of substantial political or religious action and opposition would be more easily explained in terms of ideological commitment and personal loyalties than in terms of conflicting economic inter-ests. The nobility's willingness and ability to engage in signifi-cant political and religious opposition to the crown should be viewed as evidence that its most substantial members felt powerful and secure enough to engage the developing central government in a not always unequal contest for political control.

An investigation of the social and economic background of the Calvinist nobility of the *élection* of Bayeux provides us with an opportunity to test these propositions. Since, as in the rest of France, only a part of the nobility joined the Protestant movement, by comparing this group to the Bayeux nobility as a whole, we can determine whether the Calvinist nobility formed a socially distinct group within the nobility. And since the Calvinist movement in the sixteenth century was synonymous with political opposition to the crown, an analysis of the socioeconomic backgrounds of its members should also shed some light on the general social origins of political and religious activism among nobles.

The area of the *élection* of Bayeux was a beehive of Protestantism in the second half of the sixteenth century: the diocese of Bayeux alone contained several dozen Calvinist meeting places.[1] In 1562, the city of Bayeux was briefly seized by armed Calvinists under the leadership of a local noble, François de Bricqueville, sieur of Colombières. In 1568 it was successfully besieged by a Calvinist force under Admiral Coligny. The 1560s witnessed many outrages against people and property by the partisans of both religious camps, including a sacking of the Bayeux cathedral by Protestants.[2]

An August 11, 1569 *arrêt* by the Parlement of Rouen condemned persons of the "new pretended religion" in the *vicomté* of Bayeux who had taken up arms, committed excesses, or given aid to the "enemies of his majesty."[3] Many members of the Bayeux nobility were condemned to be stripped of their nobility, have their property confiscated, and hung. The late 1560s saw a trickle of abjurations by Protestants, which swelled to a torrent after the Saint Bartholomew's Day massacre.[4] Many Protestant nobles abjured, including 35 who had previously been condemned by the *arrêt* of 1568. Some Protestants who refused to participate in the *ban* of 1568 because they did not trust its leadership also had their lands seized.[5] From these sources, we can identify more than 200 Bayeux nobles as Protestants in the period from 1568 to 1573. For the period after the Wars of Religion, the 1597 *ban*, called out by

Henry IV for the relief of the siege of Amiens, provides the best source for Protestant identities.[6] Initially, most Protestants refused to serve in this *ban*, and they can be identified by comparing those listed as having been fined in 1597 with earlier and later lists of Protestants.[7] The identity of Protestant noble family heads at the end of the period with which we are concerned is provided by Chamillart's *recherche* of 1666.[8]

The oldest and poorest rural nobility has often been thought to have been the best recruiting ground for Calvinism, and a large portion of the old rural nobility in the *élection* of Bayeux were, in fact, relatively poor. So it would theoretically have been possible for the nobility as a class to have improved its overall economic position in the sixteenth century while the Protestant movement drew its noble membership from that part of the old nobility which did not take part in this general prosperity. But table VII.1, which indicates the number and antiquity of nobles who can be identified as Protestants between 1568 and 1666, shows that this was hardly the case.

Calvinism reached its peak among the nobility of this area at the end of the 1560s, when more than 200 nobles belonged to the Protestant camp, or approximately 40 percent of all nobles in the area. Large-scale abjurations after Saint Bartholomew's Day, casualties from the remaining thirty-five years of civil strife, and the effect of Henry IV's personal abjuration combined to greatly reduce the number of Protestant nobles by 1597. At that date only 70 family heads can be identified as Calvinists, or approximately 13 percent of all nobles, a reduction of almost two-thirds since the 1560s. By 1666 the Calvinist noble community, restricted almost entirely to the area of the Vez estuary, counted only 61 family heads, or barely 10 percent of the entire Bayeux nobility.

As can be seen, the Protestant movement among Bayeux nobles was never the exclusive preserve of the old nobility, for a surprising number of *anoblis* were also Protestants. *Nobles de race* did predominate among the Calvinist nobility: nobles who had been noble for at least a century made up 81 percent of the membership in 1568-73, 73 percent in 1597, and 75 per-

TABLE VII.1

Number and Antiquity of Protestant Nobles

Antiquity	Number of nobles in:			Total	Percentage of nobles in:		
	1568-73	1597	1666		1568-73	1597	1666
Found noble by							
Monfaut in 1463	157	45	33	235	81	64	55
Ennobled 1464-1499	16	6	6	28	8	9	10
Ennobled 1500-1559	21	7	6	34	11	10	10
Ennobled 1560-1666	—	12	15	27	—	17	25
Total	194	70	60	324[a]	100	100	100

The diagonal line separates old nobles from new nobles. Those below the line had been noble for less than a century, those above it for more than a century.

[a] There were in addition nine families in 1568-73 and one in 1666 whose antiquity could not be determined.

cent in 1666. But new nobles took part in the Calvinist movement in proportions at least equal to their numbers within the nobility as a whole. As far as their antiquity was concerned, Protestant nobles therefore seem to have been drawn from a representative cross section of the nobility. In fact, the proportion of recent *anoblis* who were Protestants appears to have increased over time, and if any single trend stands out, it is the increasing dependence of a steadily shrinking noble Protestant community on new nobles for its continued survival. By 1597, for example, 17 percent, and in 1666, 25 percent of the Protestant nobility came from families who had entered the nobility after the beginning of the Wars of Religion. In 1666 almost half of the Protestant nobility (45 percent) belonged to families who had entered the nobility since the mid-fifteenth century, a higher proportion of relatively new families than among the nobility as a whole. Thus, contrary to much that has been written concerning the antiquity of Protestant noble houses, in its earliest stages the Protestant movement in the *élection* of Bayeux drew its members from a cross section of the nobility, and by the end of the sixteenth and middle of the seventeenth century had come to depend very heavily on the newest nobility for its continued survival.

A great deal of nonquantifiable evidence can also be used to show that Protestant nobles as a group were clearly representative of the nobility as a whole and were not recruited exclusively from a small and socially distinct section of it. The bulk of the movement, as might be expected, was made up of country gentlemen who, of course, formed the vast majority of all nobles. But all types of nobles took part in the early Protestant movement. The professions were represented by advocates and converted clerics. Officeholders and their close relatives also took part.[9] Professional soldiers like François de Bricqueville, who had acquired a military reputation in the Italian Wars and died defending St. Lô against royalist forces under Matignon in 1574, were also represented.[10] By 1666, attrition and legal sanctions left military careers as the only honorable profession open to Protestant nobles. But in

its earliest and most successful stages the Protestant nobility
drew its membership from a socially representative cross section of the nobility as a whole.

Table VII.2, which classifies Protestant nobles according to
their wealth as well as their antiquity, shows that Protestant
nobles, tended on the whole to come from the richest half of
the nobility.[11] Seventy-two percent of the Protestant nobility
in 1568-73, and 77 percent in 1666 belonged to the richest half
of the nobility. At the height of the movement in the 1560s,

TABLE VII.2

Income Ranking of Protestant Nobles, 1568-73, 1597, and 1666

Date	Type of noble	Poorest half	Came from: Second-richest quarter	Richest quarter	Total
1568-73	Old	17	22	30	69
	New	6	4	4	14
Subtotal		23	26	34	83
1597	Old	16	8	9	33
	New	5	1	3	9
Subtotal		21	9	12	42
1666	Old	10	17	14	41
	New	3	4	8	15
Subtotal		13	21	22	56
All Dates	Old	43	47	53	143
	New	14	9	15	38
Total		57	56	68	181
Percentage of total		31	31	38	100

41 percent of the Protestant nobility had fief incomes that placed them in the richest quarter of the nobility as a whole. Even in 1597, at the end of a long period of ruinous civil strife and persecution, Protestants represented an exact cross-section of the nobility with 50 percent belonging to the poorest half, and 50 percent to the richest half.

When we turn our attention to the antiquity of these families, it becomes clear that a majority (100 of 181, or 55 percent) of all Protestant nobles during the period were *nobles de race* who belonged to the richest, rather than the poorest, half of the nobility. Of all the old nobility who were Protestants, those who came from the richest quarter (53 of 140, or 37 percent) actually outnumbered those who came from the poorest half (43 of 140, or 31 percent).

The relatively substantial nature of the Protestant squirearchy can also be strikingly illustrated by comparing the relative incomes of Protestant family heads in 1666 (table VII.3). In 1666 Protestant family heads had a mean income of 2,451 livres a year compared to a mean income of 1,880 livres for the nobility as a whole, and a median income of 1,500 livres, which was also substantially higher than the 1,000 livres per year median figure for all nobles.[12] As Table VII.3 shows rather graphically, Protestant family heads were less than half as likely as other nobles to have incomes under 500 livres

TABLE VII.3

Comparative Incomes of Protestant Nobles, 1666

Annual income in livres	Protestant nobles %	Other nobles %
0–499	17.5	39.1
500–999	7.0	13.3
1,000–2,000	36.9	28.2
More than 2,000	38.8	19.4
Total	100.2	100.0

a year, and more than twice as likely to enjoy incomes of more than 2,000 a year.

In this case conventional explanations of the origins of Protestantism among nobles as basically a response to underlying economic ruin and deprivation appear to be fundamentally incorrect. In the *élection* of Bayeux Calvinism did not draw its impetus from poverty-stricken and discontented old *noblesse d'épée* families. Protestant nobles, on the contrary, were drawn from a fairly representative cross section of the nobility, tending if anything to be substantial, rather than ruined, nobles. The advent of Protestantism therefore produced a schism that ran from the top to the bottom of noble society.

How, then, can we best explain the inroads into the Bayeux nobility made by Calvinism in the 1560s? Given our inability to confirm the more traditional materialistic explanations, it would be tempting to emphasize the nonmaterialistic causes of conversion to Protestantism. For if Protestantism was not simply part of a reaction to underlying economic and social developments, then the only plausible interpretation that remains to the historian must rely on the power of ideas, or in this case religious conviction, to influence both individual and collective human behavior. Unfortunately, it is easier to disprove incorrect theories of economic causation than to prove to the satisfaction of all the potency of religious conviction.

Our study of the socioeconomic history of the Bayeux nobility, however, does provide two clues to an understanding of the role of the nobility in Calvinism. The first, which can now be restated in a more positive way, is that among the Bayeux nobility Protestantism was embraced by relatively affluent nobles. The very fact that it was a movement of prosperous and substantial nobles made it a serious and potentially dangerous movement, for if it had been composed predominantly of the dregs of the nobility it could never have been the threat to public order it did become, or enjoy the very real, though short-term successes that its substantial human, material, and spiritual resources made possible. Protestantism was formidable, in other words, because it was based on the desperate actions of a substantial section of a prosperous and powerful nobility rather than the desperate actions of a ruined and poverty-stricken section of the nobility.

The fact that Protestant nobles were relatively affluent members of the nobility, however, does not entirely rule out status anxiety, or insecurity, as a prime cause of individual and collective discontent. Religious belief obviously played a central and unifying role in the Protestant movement, but it is also clear that for a high proportion of the Bayeux nobles who became Protestants in the 1560s doubts had been raised about the legal validity of their noble status some time in the century preceding the Wars of Religion. In fact, of 203 individuals who can be identified as Protestants in the period 1568 to 1573, 108, or 53 percent, belong to families whose claim to nobility had been openly and officially challenged during the previous century or was of such recent vintage as to be extremely precarious.[13] These 108 affected individuals belonged to 62 family groups. Thirty-six of these families were challenged by their own parish or by local royal officials and were able to obtain favorable *arrêts* from the Cour des Aides only after long legal struggles. Some of these cases were pursued for decades and entailed extremely humiliating experiences, from being struck from the list of tax-exempt persons and having to participate in a public hearing on their family's origins, to having a coat of arms broken by an unruly crowd.[14] Families who had been ennobled by the edict of *francs-fiefs* in 1471-1473, and therefore had tacitly admitted an earlier usurpation of noble status seem to have been especially open to challenge, as were recent old noble immigrants. Ten family groups, though eventually confirmed in their status, were also sharply challenged by the 1540 *recherche*. Eleven more, ennobled in the 1540s and 1550s, cannot have felt secure, given the propensity of local officials to engage in the persecution of families who had indubitably longer and better established claims to nobility than their own.

Therefore a sizable number of Protestant nobles, both old

and new, had good reason to feel insecure about the permanence of their nobility. The hostility this insecurity must have engendered may have disposed many toward active opposition to the monarchy. The crown, after all, had made increasingly stringent attempts to regulate noble status since Montfaut's *recherche* of 1463-64. These efforts threatened customary personal status and privileges which had been virtually unregulated before the 1460s. By the 1560s the Bayeux nobility had undergone at least three major reformations at the hands of the financial agents of the crown. Families had their lineage and credentials repeatedly checked, and in some cases, repeatedly challenged. The fact that such a large portion of Protestant nobles fit into a specially threatened category of insecure families is persuasive evidence that the hostility that past and anticipated threats to their nobility must have aroused may have disposed an important part of the nobility to use the Protestant movement as a logical outlet for its opposition to the legalistic assault on its social position by the crown.

Status insecurity, of course, has often been used to explain the adherence of so many French nobles to Calvinism. But the insecurity and hostility that supposedly drove nobles into religious opposition to authority has almost always been seen as a reflection of economic decline and deprivation. The central point of the arguments developed in the past several pages, however, is that while there is strong evidence that status insecurity may have played an important role in predisposing many Bayeux nobles toward Calvinism, this insecurity was not the result of economic decline, nor was it confined to a single group of ancient families. All the evidence we have presented in this work indicates that the sixteenth century was a time of prosperity for the Bayeux nobility as a group. Since Protestant nobles seem to have been more healthy, economically speaking, than other nobles, any status insecurity they felt must have originated in other aspects of their experience than the economic sphere. Here, we are arguing, the repeated efforts of the crown to regulate the legal status of nobles struck, for a variety of reasons, at a cross section of individual nobles, old and new, *nobles d'épée* and officeholders alike. The fiscal and legal initiatives of royal government themselves, because they threatened the nobility of many families, rather than economic decline or interclass conflicts between old and new families, provided the principal source of status insecurity for nobles.

Under such pressure an important and substantial cross section of the nobility chose to rebel against royal authority, combining their political grievances with the very real religious grievances which had become more apparent to Frenchmen in the sixteenth century. The substantial nature of those nobles who rebelled helps to explain the tenacity with which the Protestant nobility fought for its cause. For without the participation of some of the wealthiest and most powerful elements of the nobility, Protestantism would never have become the important and dangerous movement it proved to be. Noble participation in the Calvinist movement of the sixteenth century, and in other movements that involved active military and political participation by nobles, should be viewed as evidence of the ability of some of the most substantial members of a powerful and prosperous class to respond to purely political and religious grievances with effective collective action, rather than as the death throes of an obsolescent class.

It would be rash, of course, to insist on such a dramatic reversal of traditional interpretations on the basis of the single example of the nobility of the *élection* of Bayeux. But because similar basic research into communities of the nobility in other regions of early modern France has not yet been done, it is impossible to tell just how representative the Bayeux nobility may have been. The fact that the traditional interpretation of the nobility was found to be groundless when put to its first comprehensive test, strongly suggests that similar research into the nobility of other parts of France may show that the experience of this class in Bayeux was not unrepresentative.

If the French nobility as a whole passed through the sixteenth and early seventeenth centuries as successfully as the nobility of the *élection* of Bayeux, the implications for the interpretation of early modern French history would be profound. If the nobility was not declining, the personal and ideological struggles that plagued France during this period could no longer be interpreted as simple manifestations of a more fundamental struggle between a declining nobility and a rising bourgeoisie. The relation between the emerging state and the nobility would also have to be reexamined. If the nobility was strong and healthy, its rebellions, remonstrances, and demands might be taken as evidence of its ability to resist developments that were contrary to its interests rather than as evidence of its weakness.

This is not to deny the growth of a centralized and powerful monarchical government, but merely to suggest that the developing governmental institutions may have been forced to accommodate themselves to the prevailing aristocratic social regime as much as the nobility was forced to conform to the new political regime. How else can the continuous dominance of old regime society and government by nobles be understood? Aristocratic control of such key institutions as the church, provincial estates, Parlement, and royal council were never challenged, nor was the social and seigneurial regime on which noble preeminence rested significantly modified before it was destroyed by the Revolution.

The final social and political form of the old regime, in other words, may have been conditioned less by victory over a declining nobility in the sixteenth and seventeenth centuries than by compromises with the nobility. For this class was strong and prosperous enough to ensure that the emerging political regime served its social interests as well as it served the political interests of *raison d'état*.

Of course this study has focused only on the nobility of a

small area of early modern France. Is this area unique? The question of the extent to which conclusions about it apply to the rest of France cannot at this point be answered. What we have found does not fit with many of the large generalizations made about the nobility in the past. Is it therefore time for a major reevaluation of the nobility? Only similar studies of other provincial nobilities can provide an answer.

ABBREVIATIONS

ADC   Archives Départementales de Calvados
ADSM   Archives Départementales de la Seine-Maritime
AN   Archives Nationales
BMR   Bibliothèque Municipale de Rouen
BN   Bibliothèque Nationale
Chamillart Buisson de Courson, A. du. *Généralité de Caen. Recherche de la Noblesse faite par ordre de Roi en 1666 et années suivantes, par Guy Chamillart.*

 NOTES

INTRODUCTION

1. See particularly Davis Bitton, *The French Nobility in Crisis, 1560-1640*; and Jean-Richard Bloch, *L'anoblissement en France au temps de François Ier*.

2. Jean-Pierre Labatut, *Les ducs et pairs de France au XVIIᵉ siècle*.

3. See, for example, Pierre Goubert, *Beauvais et le Beauvaisis de 1600 à 1730*, I, 206-221; Pierre Deyon, *Amiens: capitale provinciale*, 266-276, 552; and Robert Forster, *The House of Saulx-Tavanes*.

4. Robert Forster, *The Nobility of Toulouse in the Eighteenth Century*; Jean Meyer, *La noblesse bretonne au XVIIIᵉ siècle*; Katherine Fedden, *Manor Life in Old France*.

5. Lucien Romier, *Le royaume de Catherine de Médici*, I, 160-216, esp. 170-182. An earlier but similarly pessimistic view of the nobility's predicament was G. d'Avenel, *La noblesse française sous Richelieu*.

6. Gaston Roupnel, *La ville et la campagne au XVIIᵉ siècle*, 234-235, 313; Henri Drouot, *Mayenne et la Bourgogne*, I, 30-46, II, 311-316; Paul Raveau, *L'agriculture et les classes paysannes*, 37-136, esp. 119-120, 244-245.

7. Pierre de Vaissière, *Gentilshommes campagnards de l'ancienne France*, 2-3, 35-58, 218-231.

8. See, for example, Roland Mousnier, *Les XVIᵉ et XVIIᵉ siècles*, IV, 106-107.

9. Bitton, *The French Nobility*, 1-3, 7-18, 27-63, 77, 92-99, 115-117, and the "Bibliographical Essay on the Economic Fortunes of the Nobility," 168-177. Bitton concludes the bibliographical essay by asserting that "there is enough evidence . . . to show that the nobility as a class was not fundamentally prosperous. For the provincial noblesse d'épée, the families of the old nobility, the period was one of economic difficulty and, for many, genuine hardship," 173.

10. Romier, *Royaume*, 1, 179, 182-184, 184, note 2.

11. De Vaissière, *Gentilshommes campagnards*, and Bitton, *The French Nobility*, v-vi, who freely acknowledges the nature and limits of his study.

175

12. De Vaissière, *Gentilshommes campagnards*, 2-3.

13. J. Russell Major, "The Crown and the Aristocracy in Renaissance France," esp. 633-634.

14. Labatut, *Les ducs et pairs de France*.

15. Meyer, *Noblesse bretonne*; Forster, *Nobility of Toulouse*; and Mohamed El Kordi, *Bayeux aux XVIIe et XVIIIe siècles*.

16. Meyer, *Noblesse bretonne*; François Bluche, *Les magistrats du Parlement de Paris au XVIIIe siècle (1715-1771)*; and Pierre Goubert, *L'ancien régime*.

17. J.-R. Bloch, *L'anoblissement en France*; and Bitton, *The French Nobility*, address themselves to this problem, as do Goubert, *Régime*, I, 145-189, and Roland Mousnier, "Introduction," 11-48.

18. Bitton, *The French Nobility*; and J.-R. Bloch, *L'anoblissement en France*, are especially good on this debate. Most royal proclamations and edicts dealing with the nobility can be found in Louis-Nicolas-Henri Cherin, *Abrégé chronologique d'édits, déclarations, règlemens, arrêts et lettres-patents des rois de France*.

19. Goubert, *Régime*, I, 17-18, 147-148.

20. Ibid., 167. See also Edmond Esmonin, *La taille en Normandie au temps de Colbert (1661-1683)*, 224-228.

21. Goubert, *Régime*, I, 81, 151.

22. For mostly Norman examples see Roland Mousnier, *La vénalité des offices sous Henri IV et Louis XIII*, 53-58, 331-343, 425-494. Nevertheless, land was still usually the most important part of an official's fortune, 458-459.

23. Madeleine Foisil, *La révolte des Nu-Pieds et les révoltes normandes de 1639*, 211-212; Meyer, *Noblesse bretonne*, I, 21-27; Jean Meyer, "Un problème mal posé: la noblesse pauvre," 161-188; Goubert, *Beauvais*, I, 212-213.

24. Bitton, *The French Nobility*, 27-41, discusses the military aspects of noble status; Romier, *Royaume*, I, 160, describes the ancient nobility as remaining "dans ses traits essentials, rustique et guerrière"; Mousnier, "Introduction," 33-35, cites contemporaries on the essentially military nature of nobility; Goubert, *Régime*, I, 167-168, notes the cult of arms nurtured by the *gentilshommes campagnards*.

25. Goubert, *Régime*, I, 148-149; Robert Mandrou, *La France aux XVIIe et XVIIIe siècles*, 155-158, esp. 156-157, discusses the myth of the noble warrior living on his estate. Also see Pierre Deyon, "A propos des rapports entre la noblesse française et la

monarchie absolue pendant la première moitié de XVIIᵉ siècle," 350, for the small proportion of nobles following a military career in the *bailliage* of Amiens in the first half of the seventeenth century. The decline of the *ban* and *arrière-ban* from an institution in which large numbers of nobles served personally in the fifteenth century to a mechanism for levying financial contributions in the late sixteenth and seventeenth centuries is outlined by Abbé P.-F. Lebeurier in the introduction to his *Rôle des taxes de l'arrière-ban du bailliage d'Evreux en 1562*, 9-64.

26. Cf. François Bluche, *Magistrats*; Meyer, *Noblesse bretonne*; Roupnel, *La ville et la campagne*; and Franklin Ford, *Robe and Sword*.

27. Meyer, *Noblesse bretonne*, II, 1,017-1,052; Goubert, *Régime*, I, 158, 179, 181-182; Esmonin, *Taille*, 230.

28. Goubert, *Régime*, I, 151-154; Mandrou, *France*, 157-158.

29. Mousnier, *Vénalité*, 58; Goubert, *Régime*, I, 151-152.

30. Goubert, *Régime*, I, 152-158; Goubert, *Beauvais*, 208.

31. Goubert, *Régime*, I, 153-158.

32. Ibid., 165; Mousnier, "Introduction," 33-35.

33. Mousnier, "Introduction," 33.

34. Goubert, *Régime*, I, 154.

35. Ibid., 153.

36. Ibid.

37. Ibid., 159.

38. Mousnier, "Introduction," 33-42, and "L'évolution des institutions monarchiques en France et ses relations avec l'état social." This general theme is also developed in Romier, *Royaume*, I, 160-216, esp. 170-182; Roupnel, *La ville et la campagne*, 234-235, 313; Drouot, *Mayenne*, I, 30-46, II, 311-316; de Vaissière, *Gentilshommes campagnards*, 2-3, 35-58, 218-231; Bitton, *The French Nobility*. My article, "The Decline of the Nobility in Sixteenth and Early Seventeenth Century France: Myth or Reality?" argues against this general interpretation.

CHAPTER I

1. Major sources on the boundaries of the *élection-vicomté* are: BN 4,620 "Dénombrement des élections et paroisses de Normandie"; E. de Laheudrie, *Recherches sur le Bessin, Histoire du Bessin des origines à la Revolution*, I, 4-6; "Rôle des fiefs du grand bailliage de Caen," (1889), 577-594, 641-658; C. Hippeau, *Dic-*

tionnaire topographique du département du Calvados; and especially Pierre Gouhier, Anne Vallez, and Jean-Marie Vallez, *Atlas historique de Normandie.*

2. Mohamed El Kordi, *Bayeux aux XVIIe et XVIIIe siècles*, 29-32.

3. Gouhier, Vallez, and Vallez, *Atlas historique*, II, no pagination.

4. El Kordi, *Bayeux*, 152.

5. Ibid., 260-266.

6. Normandy was the only province in which *noble homme* was accepted as a noble title. Pierre Goubert, *L'ancien régime*, I, 146, 154.

7. For the 1585 Norman *Coutumier* see Charles A. Bourdot de Richebourg, *Nouveau Coutumier Général*, IV, 59-92, 95. For this specific privilege see article 2.

8. Edmond Esmonin, *La Taille en Normandie au temps de Colbert*, 198, 224-231.

9. Ibid., 224-231; Goubert, *Régime*, I, 157-158.

10. Bourdot de Richebourg, *Nouveau Coutumier Général*, articles 248-249 on the exclusion of females; articles 337-340 on the right of *préciput*; and articles 335-366 on *partages*, the division of property. Also see Jean Meyer, *La noblesse bretonne au XVIIIe siècle*, I, 103-134, especially the map on 111, for an explanation of the Breton noble *partage*, which was very similar to that of Normandy.

11. Bourdot de Richebourg, *Nouveau Coutumier Général*, articles 99-212. On the *ban* and *arrière-ban*, see Abbé P.-F. Lebeurier, *Rôle des taxes de l'arrière-ban du bailliage d'Evreux en 1562*, 9-64.

12. Abbé Hulmel, "La recherche de Montfaut," 22 (1927), 629. Abbé P.-E. de la Rocque, *Recherche de Montfaut*, 3-4.

13. Hulmel, "Recherche," 22 (1927), 633.

14. Ibid.

15. Ibid.

16. Ibid., 23 (1930), 57.

17. Ibid., 22 (1927), 629; Abbé de la Rocque, *Recherche*, 4-5.

18. Hulmel, "Recherche," 22 (1927), 630. Jean-Richard Bloch, *L'anoblissement en France au temps de François Ier*, 43.

19. Hulmel, "Recherche," 22 (1927), 633.

20. Ibid., 629-630.

21. J.-R. Bloch, *L'anoblissement*, 42-43.

22. Ibid., 43-44. Abbé P.-F. Lebeurier, *Etat des anoblis en Normandie de 1545 à 1661*, vi.

23. Lebeurier, *Etat des anoblis*, vii-x.

24. Hulmel, "Recherche," 22 (1927), 630. J.-R. Bloch, *L'anoblissement*, 39-45.

25. J.-R. Bloch, *L'anoblissement*, 44-45.

26. On the general topic of the *recherches*, see: Abbé Le Mâle, "Recherche de la noblesse faite en la généralité de Caen (1598-99)," esp. the table (1918), 34; Meyer, *Noblesse bretonne*, I, 29-61; Esmonin, *Taille*, 198-224. My "La structure sociale de la noblesse dans le bailliage de Caen et ses modifications (1463-1666)," discusses the value of these sources for social history. See D. J. Sturdy's "Tax Evasion, the *Faux Nobles*, and State Fiscalism," for a detailed analysis of the operation of the *recherche* of 1634-1635 which, unfortunately, did not cover the *élection* of Bayeux.

27. These six *recherches* exist in the following forms: for 1463 Hulmel, "Recherche" (the part relating to the *élection* of Bayeux is found in 23 [1930], 102-109); and Abbé P.-E. de la Rocque, *Recherche de Montfaut*. For 1523, BN 11,924, fols. 116-155. For 1540, BMR 2,984 (Martainville 107). For 1598-1599, BN 11,929. For 1624, BMR 2,985, 2nd part (Martainville Y-16). For 1666, A. du Buisson de Courson, *Généralité de Caen*, hereafter referred to as Chamillart.

28. BMR 2,984 fol. 1V-2R.

29. Abbé Le Mâle, "Recherche de la noblesse" (1917), 184-195.

30. Chamillart, I, v-xiii, 3-7.

31. Hulmel, "Recherche," 22 (1927), 629; de la Rocque, *Recherche*, 3.

32. Abbé Le Mâle, "Recherche de la noblesse" (1916), 454; BN 11,924, fol. 167R.

33. BMR 2,984, fol. 1R; Le Mâle "Recherche de la noblesse" (1916), 457.

34. Le Mâle, "Recherche de la noblesse" (1917), 184.

35. Ibid., 184-185.

36. Ibid., (1916), 464.

37. Chamillart, I, ix, 2.

38. BMR 2,984, fols. 1R-3R.

39. Le Mâle, "Recherche de la noblesse" (1917), 188, 195-196.

40. Chamillart, I, 2.

41. The instructions for the *règlement des tailles* of 1598 given

to Roissy in Le Mâle, "Recherche de la noblesse" (1917), 187-195, give a detailed description of the types of records that were to be examined, but all the *recherches* contain references to these various types of documents.

42. Such *arrêts* and inquiries are mentioned in all the *recherches* except 1463, but the best descriptions of such documents are found in the 1540 *recherche*: BMR 2,984, fols. 6V-7R, 29V-31R, 56V-57R, 64V-65R, 71V-72R, 208V-210R.

43. BMR 2,984, fols. 29V-31V, 69R-71R, 92R-92V, 119R, 121R-122R, 131V-133R, 152R-153V.

44. For example, BN 11,929, fol. 311, 318, 320, 325.

45. BMR 2,985, fols. 25R, 57R.

46. Chamillart, II, 773, 769, 806; AN E398B, no. 48, fol. 139.

47. Hulmel, "Recherche," 22 (1927), 633.

48. BN 11,924, fol. 168V.

49. Ibid., fols. 90V-92R.

50. Ibid., fols. 143R-145R.

51. Le Mâle, "Recherche de la noblesse" (1918), 188.

52. BMR 2,985, fol. 161R.

53. Chamillart, I, viii, 2.

54. Ibid., 48, 414, II, 777.

55. BN 11,928, fol. 88.

56. BMR 2,984, fols. 56V-57R; BN 11,929, fol. 313; Chamillart, II, 808.

57. AN E 396B, no. 31, fol. 254V.

58. AN E* 397C, no. 9, fol. 69V.

59. *Règlemens rendus sur le fait des tailles . . . de Normandie* (Rouen, 1710), 55, quoted in Le Mâle, "Recherche de la noblesse" (1917), 199-200; Chamillart, II, 787, 803.

60. Chamillart, I, vii. For uses of the *noble d'ancienneté*, or its equivalent, in other *recherches* see: BN 11,924, fols. 171V, 175R; BMR 2,984, fols. 8R, 44V-46R, 200V, 204R; BN 11,929, fols. 308, 309, 315-317.

61. Le Mâle, "Recherche de la noblesse" (1917), 200.

62. Chamillart, I, viii.

63. The manuscript copies of the 1540 and 1624 *recherches* contain inventories that indicate the many kinds of documents used as proofs: BMR 2,984, 2,985. The *arrêts de conseil* given to nobles who were condemned by Chamillart in 1666, and then maintained on appeal to the royal council, give detailed descrip-

tions of both proofs and counterproofs. See, for example, AN E 395B, no. 12, E 398B, no. 48, and E 398B, no. 79.

64. BN 11,924, fols. 171V, 175V; BMR 2,984, fols. 116-193; BN 11,929, fols. 307, 310.

65. BMR 2,984, fol. 10V.

66. Ibid., fol. 8R.

67. BN 11,928, fol. 146.

68. BMR 2,984, fol. 57V.

69. Ibid., fol. 197.

70. Ibid., fols. 33V-34R.

71. Ibid., fols. 165V-166R.

72. Ibid., fols. 80R-81R.

73. Chamillart, II, 772; AN E 397C, no. 19, fol. 63V.

74. BMR 2,984, fols. 16V, 126V.

75. Ibid., fols. 50V-51R.

76. Ibid., fols. 119R, 139V-142V. Chamillart, supplement, 60-61.

77. BMR 2,984, fols. 96V, 107V.

78. Ibid., fol. 10R.

79. Ibid., fols. 5R-6V.

80. Ibid., fol. 127R; BMR 2,985, fols. 138R, 193R.

81. BN 11,929, fol. 311.

82. Ibid., fol. 309.

83. BMR 2,985, fols. 142R, 193R.

84. For example, AN E 396B, fols. 258V-259R, and E 398B, fol. 323V.

85. Hulmel, "Recherche," 22 (1927), 633.

86. BN 11,929, fol. 326.

87. Ibid., fol. 316.

88. Ibid., fol. 337.

89. BN 11,929, fol. 313; BMR 2,985, fols. 15R, 87R, 103R, 101V-102R, 143V-144R, 161R, 187V-188R; Chamillart, II, 770, 781, 790, 791, 793, 800, 806.

90. Chamillart, II, 769-770, 782-783, 787, 789-791, 797, 804, 806, 810.

91. BN 11,928, fols. 140, 196, 311; Chamillart, II, 781.

92. BMR 2,984, fol. 68V; BN 11,929, fol. 314; BMR 2,985, 190R; Chamillart, II, 766-767, 784, 811, 812.

93. BMR 2,984, fols. 8V, 116R, 158V; BN 11,929, fols. 316, 327, 336; Chamillart, II, 766-767, 795.

94. BN 11,928, fols. 160, 176, 194; Chamillart, II, 812.

95. Chamillart, II, 812; BN 11,928, fol. 176.

96. Chamillart, II, 800; BN 11,928, fol. 196.

97. For the Arragon see BMR 2,984, fol. 119R, BN 11,929, fol. 319, and BMR 2,985, fol. 25R. For the Senescal see BMR 2,984, fol. 16V and BMR 2,985, fol. 15R. See also the cases of the Marchand, BMR 2,985, fols. 81V-82R, Chamillart, II, 797; and the Leopartie, BN 11,929, fol. 327, Chamillart, II, 795.

98. BMR 2,984, fol. 197; AN E 397C, fol. 71R.

99. BMR 2,984, fols. 90R-92R, 95V-96R; Chamillart, II, 801.

100. BMR 2,984, fol. 150; BMR 2,985, fol. 193R; Chamillart, II, 768-769, 787, 791, 800, 802, 804, 810; AN E 400B, no. 5.

101. BMR 2,984, fols. 12V-13R, 23R-24V, 113R-113V, 162V-165R, 205V; Chamillart, II, 768-769, 772, 784, 804, 808; AN E 397C, fols. 63V, 70R.

102. BMR 2,984, fols. 55V-56R, 124R-125V; Chamillart, II, 769-770, 773, 775-777, 785-787.

103. Chamillart, II, 790, 803; AN E 400A, no. 55.

104. Chamillart, II, 772, 798-799; AN E 397C, fol. 63V.

105. BMR 2,984, fols. 61R-62V; BN 11,929, fols. 337, 359bis; Chamillart, II, 772, 776-777, 784, 787, 790, 792-793, 798, 803, 806; AN E 395B, no. 12, E 397A, no. 34, E 397C, no. 9, E 398B, no. 79, E 399B, no. 31, E 401, no. 81, E 403B, no. 60.

106. Chamillart, II, 806; AN E 396B, fol. 254V.

107. AN E 396B, fols. 254V-260V.

108. Ibid., fols. 254V, 257R-259R.

109. Ibid., fol. 254V.

110. AN 397A, no. 34, esp. fols. 96R, 98V-99R; Chamillart, II, 806.

111. Chamillart, II, 772. AN E 397C, no. 9, fols. 63R-66V.

112. AN E 397C, no. 9, fol. 63V.

113. Ibid.

114. Ibid., fol. 70R.

115. Ibid., fol. 71R.

116. Ibid., fols. 71V-72R.

117. Ibid., fol. 69V.

118. Fourteen of the twenty-four families who were condemned by Chamillart in 1666, then maintained by an *arret de conseil*, had incomes of 800 or more livres per year. The highest income was 10,000 livres, and seven of the fourteen were between 1,000 and 2,400 livres. These incomes were substantial—well above the

median noble family income for the *élection* as a whole; BN 11,928, fols. 3, 18, 22, 24-25, 51, 110, 244, 266, 270. Not all *maintenues*, however, had substantial incomes: six families, for example, were poor, having incomes of 500 or less livres per year; ibid., fols. 124, 244, 362. Nor did wealth always command reversal of a condemnation. Many examples could be cited: Jean Le Pantou, a former *président* in the *élection* of Bayeux, was permanently condemned as a usurper in 1666 despite an income of 10,000 livres per year; ibid., fol. 24.

119. Esmonin, *Taille*, 44, 198-224; Sturdy, "Tax Evasion," 553.
120. Esmonin, *Taille*, 222-223.
121. Meyer, *Noblesse bretonne*, I, 46-55.

CHAPTER II

1. See especially Edouard Perroy, "Social Mobility among the French Noblesse in the Later Middle Ages," 31. Pierre Goubert, *Beauvais et le Beauvaisis*, I, 220-221; Goubert, *L'ancien régime*, I, 170-171; Davis Bitton, *The French Nobility in Crisis*, 1-3, 7-18, 27-63, 77, 92-99, 115-117, 168-174; Henri Drouot, *Mayenne et la Bourgogne*, I, 30-46; II, 311-316; Lucien Romier, *Le royaume de Catherine de Médici*, I, 160-216, esp. 170-182; de Vaissière, *Gentilshommes campagnards de l'ancienne France*. Louis Henry and Claude Lévy, "Ducs et pairs sous l'ancien régime," trace the demography of the upper nobility in the eighteenth century.

2. Perroy, "Social Mobility," 32-36; L.-N.-H. Cherin, *Abrégé chronologique*, i-lvi, esp. lvi; J.-R. Bloch, *L'anoblissement en France*, and François Bluche and Pierre Durye, *L'anoblissement par charges avant 1789* on methods of ennoblement; Jean Meyer, *La noblesse bretonne au XVIIIᵉ siècle*; Roland Mousnier, "Introduction," and *La vénalité des offices*; and the works by Bitton, Goubert, Drouot, Romier, and de Vaissière mentioned in note 1, this chapter.

3. On the "inevitability" of this process, see Perroy, "Social Mobility," 31; Goubert, *Régime*, I, 170-171; and my article, "Demographic Pressure and Social Mobility among the Nobility of Early Modern France."

4. Romier, *Royaume*, I, 160-216, esp. 170-182. G. d'Avenel, *La noblesse française sous Richelieu*; Gaston Roupnel, *La ville et la campagne*, 234-235, 313; Drouot, *Mayenne*, I, 30-46, II, 311-316;

Paul Raveau, *L'agriculture et les classes paysannes*, 37-136, esp. 119-120, 244-245; de Vaissière, *Gentilshommes campagnards*, 2-3, 35-58, 218-231; Mousnier, *Les XVIe et XVIIe siècles*, IV, 106-107; Bitton, *The French Nobility*, 1-3, 7-18, 27-63, 77, 92-99, 115-117, and 168-177.

5. The unit Perroy used to count nobles in the *vicomté* of Forez; Perroy, "Social Mobility," 27.

6. Goubert, *Régime*, I, 90-91.

7. BN 11,929.

8. Assuming a total population in the area of the *élection* of Bayeux of between 80,000 and 100,000. See note 3, chapter 1.

9. On the *gentilshommes campagnards* and their *déracinement* (uprooting) to town and court in the seventeenth and eighteenth centuries, see de Vaissière, *Gentilshommes campagnards*, 1-105, 175-185.

10. Bitton, *The French Nobility*, 98-99.

11. Ibid., 1-2, 92-94, 98-99; Romier, *Royaume*, I, 181-187.

12. Disappearance from the *élection* during the periods between *recherches* did not necessarily mean that a line or family had become biologically extinct. Some lines and families disappeared because they left the area. Although it is sometimes possible to trace emigrant families, it is impossible to determine precisely the relative importance of actual extinction and emigration. Since the number of lines that disappeared and then later reappeared is quite small, for all practical purposes disappearance from the *élection*, whatever its cause, was permanent.

13. These losses are strikingly similar to those Perroy found among the Forez nobility; Perroy, "Social Mobility," 31. Goubert noted a similar phenomenon in the *élection* of Beauvais; Goubert, *Beauvais*, I, 220-221.

14. A simple example will make this clearer. Both the Fayel and Mathan noble line, each composed of two nuclear families, appeared in the 1463 *recherche*. The Mathan had disappeared by the time of the 1598 *recherche*. The Fayel, however, greatly increased their numbers: from two nuclear families in 1463 to four in 1523, six in 1540, sixteen in 1598, and eighteen in 1624. Therefore the numerical expansion of the Fayel line had more than made up for any losses entailed in the disappearance of the Mathan line. Abbé Hulmel, "La recherche de Montfaut," 23 (1930), 103, 105; BN 11,924, fols. 81R, 182; BMR 2,984, fols. 89, 90R, 160R-

162R; BN 11,929, fols. 313, 327; BMR 2,985, fols. 171V-172R. Table II.3 shows that this process took place on a very large scale in the *élection*.

15. That this could actually happen has never, as far as I can tell, been considered by historians. No previous effort to trace the descent of a large group of families across time has ever been made.

16. Contradicting the conclusions of Perroy and Goubert; Perroy, "Social Mobility," 31; Goubert, *Régime*, I, 170-171.

17. Although many contemporary observers and modern historians noted an increase in the number of new nobles in the second half of the sixteenth century, no one appreciated the full magnitude of the increase in total noble numbers.

18. Perroy, "Social Mobility," is the best example of this technique.

19. Lebeurier's *Etat des anoblis en Normandie de 1545 à 1661* was also helpful in identifying recipients of letters of ennoblement.

20. Some of these geographically mobile families were also upwardly mobile in the sense of bettering their social or economic status (through marriage or inheritance). But their movement into the *élection* and addition to the Bayeux nobility was not the result of any new creation of nobles.

21. A minority of these *anoblis* were also geographically mobile, but in terms of the internal composition of the Bayeux nobility the more important fact was that they had recently been elevated to the nobility from the Third Estate (legally or otherwise).

22. Bitton, *The French Nobility*, 98-99; Cherin, *Abrégé chronologique*, i-lvi, esp. lvi.

23. Lebeurier, *Etat*, v-x; Goubert, *Régime*, I, 170-173, 176; Meyer, *Noblesse bretonne*, II, 1,245-1,246; Perroy, "Social Mobility," 25-38; J.-R. Bloch, *L'anoblissement*, 25-31, 34-55, 211.

24. Perroy, "Social Mobility," 31.

25. Goubert, *Régime*, I, 170.

26. Bluche and Durye, *L'anoblissement*, I, 15-18.

27. J.-R. Bloch, *L'anoblissement*, 54-55; Mousnier, "Introduction," 36-37; Goubert, *Régime*, I, 176.

28. Goubert, *Regime*, I, 172.

29. Ibid.

30. Ibid., 171-172.

31. J.-R. Bloch, *L'anoblissement*, 42-45; Lebeurier, *Etat*, v-x.

32. Perroy, "Social Mobility," 34-35.
33. J.-R. Bloch, *L'anoblissement*, 25-31, 36.
34. Meyer, *Noblesse bretonne*, II, 1,245-1,246.
35. Goubert, *Régime*, I, 176.
36. J.-R. Bloch, *L'anoblissement*, 211.
37. Goubert, *Régime*, I, 173.
38. Lebeurier, *Etat*.
39. J.-R. Bloch, *L'anoblissement*; Lebeurier, *Etat*, Goubert, *Régime*, I, 172.
40. Mousnier, *Vénalité*, 528-532.
41. Goubert, *Régime*, I, 174-176.

CHAPTER III

1. The principal work on this development remains Roland Mousnier's *La vénalité des offices*.

2. See François Bluche, *Les magistrats du Parlement de Paris au XVIIIᵉ siècle*; François Bluche and Pierre Durye, *L'anoblissement par charges avant 1789*; Pierre Deyon, *Amiens: capitale provinciale*; René Fédou, *Les hommes de loi Lyonnais à la fin du Moyen Age*; Pierre Goubert, *L'ancien régime* and *Beauvais et le Beauvaisis*; Bernard Guenée, *Tribunaux et gens de justice dans le bailliage de Senlis à la fin du Moyen Age*; Jean Meyer, *La noblesse bretonne au XVIIIᵉ siècle* and "Un problème mal posé: la noblesse pauvre"; and Roland Mousnier, "Introduction," *Les XVIᵉ et XVIIᵉ siècles*, and *Vénalité*.

3. See esp. Mousnier, "Introduction," 32-35.

4. Ibid., 36-38.

5. Ibid., 33-35; Davis Bitton, *The French Nobility in Crisis*, 27-41; Lucien Romier, *Le royaume de Catherine de Médici*, I, 160; Goubert, *Régime*, I, 167-168; Robert Mandrou, *La France au XVIIᵉ et XVIIIᵉ siècles*, 155-158.

6. Copies of the 1552, 1562, 1567, 1568, 1587, 1597, and 1639 *ban* have survived. The *ban* for the *bailliage* of Caen in 1552 has been published by Emile Travers as *Rôle du ban et arrière-ban du bailliage de Caen en 1552*, for Bayeux, 9-18, 41-66, 110-115, 147-164. For the *vicomté* of Bayeux, copies of the 1562 and 1567 *ban* for the *bailliage* are in BN 24,116, fols. 1-221; parts relating to the *vicomté* of Bayeux are: for 1562 fols. 35R-66V; for 1567 fols. 155R-177R, 218V-219R. Copies of the *ban comptes* for 1568, 1587, and 1597

were made by Dom Jacques-Louis Lenoir in the eighteenth century and form part of his vast collection of notes on Normandy preserved on microfilm at the Archives nationales. The 1568 *ban* is found in AN 104 Mi 13, 281-332, the parts specifically dealing with the *vicomté* of Bayeux, 294-309; the 1587 *ban* is in AN 104 Mi 12, 371-425, for the *vicomté* of Bayeux principally 379-388; the 1597 *ban* appears in AN 104 Mi 12, 263-317, specifically 276-288. Another useful document in the Dom Lenoir collection, entitled "Taxes faites par les commissaires députés par le Roy sur aucuns gentilhommes ou bailliage de Caen qui n'ont esté au siège d'Amiens en l'an 1597," is in AN 104 Mi 71, 717-768; for the *vicomté* of Bayeux, 719-722, 728-729, 743-744, 755-756, 761. Lists of nobles and their revenues made in preparation for the *ban* in 1639-40 (which was never held), are in BN 18,942, fols. 2-207, entitled "Roolles des Nobles de Normandie. L'An 1639 et 1640. Bailliage de Caen." The part relating to the *vicomté* of Bayeux, fols. 85-112, is entitled "Estat des gentilhommes et—voeufes demoiselles employées aux Minuttes tiré de rolles des tailles Fait pour les parroisses du vicomté de Bayeux 1640."

7. Cited in note 27, chapter one.

8. Part of BN 18,942, "Extrait des noms des gentilhommes plus considerables ou en naissance ou en biens ou en gallité demeurantz dans l'estendue du bailliage de Caen, tiré sur le roolle général dudit bailliage. 1640," fols. 4-25, and for Bayeux fols. 18-25, has been useful. This document was published by L. Sandret under the title "Rôle des principaux gentilshommes de la Généralité de Caen, Accompagné de notes secrètes, Rédigées en 1640," in the *Revue Nobiliare*. Notes on Bayeux nobles appear in the ninth volume (1871), 370-380. Also useful was Abbé P.-F. Lebeurier's *Etat des anoblis*, and a document accompanying the 1666 *recherche*, BN 11,928, fols. 1-365, which recorded the offices, military records, and incomes of all the nobles and condemned false nobles appearing in the 1666 *recherche* documents. The *arrêts de conseil* from series E of the Archives nationales frequently cited in the notes of chapter one were also a good source. BN 32,581, "Éstats des deniers deubz au Roy . . . à cause de la chevallerye de Monseigneur le Dauphin, suivant la coustume de Normandie," provided some information. Finally, many genealogical and family monographs, as well as standard reference works were consulted.

9. The tables and figures presented in this chapter rest, unless

otherwise stated, on information drawn from the many documents cited in notes 6-8 above. Specific references will be made only when individual examples are given, or when a general reference to an entire document is needed. In the text the various *bans* and surveys will be referred to simply by their date.

10. BMR 2,984, fols. 11R-12V; Chamillart, I, 253.

11. BN 32,581, fol. 150; BN 18,942, fol. 100R; and G. du Bosq de Beaumont, *La Châtellenie de Beaumont-le-Richard*, 1-18.

12. BMR 2,985, fols. 23V-24R; BN 24,116, fol. 110R; and Abbé A. Alix, *Généalogie de la famille de la Rivière*.

13. BN 24,116, fol. 46V; BN 11,929, fol. 316.

14. Ibid., fol. 354bis; Chamillart, II, 784; AN E 395B, fols. 285R-295R; and F.-A. de la Chesnaye-Desbois, *Dictionnaire de la Noblesse*, VI, 433-435.

15. Travers, *Rôle du ban*, 153-154; BN 24,116, fol. 61R; AN 104 Mi 13, 308; BN 11,929, fols. 314, 324; BN 18,942, fol. 85R; BN 11,928, fol. 84; Chamillart, II, 637-638.

16. BN 11,929, fol. 308; BN 18,942, fol. 85R; Chamillart, II, 657; and La Chesnaye-Desbois, *Dictionnaire* XI, 889-891.

17. La Chesnaye-Desbois, *Dictionnaire*, 890-891; BN 11,928, fol. 4.

18. This takes exception to Mousnier's statement that it was rare for officials to take up the life of a gentleman and a military career and that only cadet branches did so; "Introduction," 36-38.

19. BMR 2,984, fol. 4; AN 104 Mi 12, 287, 386; BN 11,929, fol. 325; BN 18,942, fol. 104V; BN 11,928, fol. 293; Chamillart, II, 580; and A. du Buisson de Courson, *Notes recueillies sur la commune de Colombiers-sur-Seulles*, vii-66.

20. Travers, *Rôle du ban*, 113; BN 24,116, fol. 64V; AN 104 Mi 12, 411; BN 11,929, fol. 315; BMR 2,985, fol. 123R; Chamillart, II, 535; Lebeurier, *Etat*, 183; and G. du Bosq de Beaumont, *Monographes normandes*, which gives an interesting history of this family.

21. Travers, *Rôle du ban*, 57, 275; BN 24,116, fol. 50R; AN 104 Mi 13, 302; AN 104 Mi 12, 287; BN 11,929, fol. 318; BN 11,928, fol. 243; Chamillart, II, 671.

22. BN 11,929, fol. 326; BN 18,924, fols. 85R, 91V; BN 11,928, fols. 1, 4; Chamillart, II, 575-576; Lebeurier, *Etat*, 78.

23. BMR 2,984, fols. 139V-142V; AN 104 Mi 12, 410; BN 11,929, fol. 319; BMR 2,985, fols. 83V-84R; Chamillart, II, 565; and the article by J. Depoint and J. Vergnet, "Boran."

24. BN 11,924, fol. 180V; BMR 2,984, fol. 86R; BN 11,929, fol. 311; BMR 2,985 fols. 35V-36R; BN 18,942 fols. 100V, 102R; BN 11,928, fols. 274, 304; Chamillart, II, 558-559; Lebeurier, *Etat*, 178.

25. Lebeurier, *Etat*. This argument for assimilation of new nobles will be considerably strengthened in the next chapter, which analyzes the rate at which new nobles were marrying into older families.

26. See notes 6 and 8, this chapter. The 1666 survey is BN 11,928, fols. 1-365.

27. Abbé P.-F. Lebeurier, *Rôle des taxes de l'arrière-ban du bailliage d'Evreux en 1562*, 9-64.

28. BN 24,116, fols. 35R-66V; AN 104 Mi 13, 294-309; AN 104 Mi 12, 379-388.

29. Sandret, "Rôle des principaux gentilshommes," 1 (1862), 145.

30. BN 18,942, fols. 85-112.

31. Travers, *Rôle du ban*, 162-164.

32. Ibid., 162.

33. BN 24,116, fols. 35R-66V, BN 18,942, fols. 85-112.

34. BN 11,928, fols. 1-365.

35. Since no *recherches* were held in 1562 and 1639, the population at those dates was estimated from the *recherches* that most closely preceded and followed those dates.

36. BN 18,942, fols. 89R, 101V, 109R; BN 11,928, fols. 12, 203, 216, 258, 293; Chamillart, I, 117.

37. AN 104 Mi 12, 276-288; AN 104 Mi 71, esp. 719-722, 728-729, 743-744, 755-756, 761, AN E 395B, fols. 257R, 289V, 290V.

38. BN 11,928, fol. 320.

39. Ibid., fol. 264.

40. Ibid., fol. 164.

41. Ibid., fol. 246.

42. Ibid., fols. 266, 297.

43. Ibid., fol. 190.

44. Ibid., fols. 100, 236.

45. Ibid., fols. 1-315.

46. Ibid., fols. 1-365. Ages were also recorded in Chamillart.

47. BN 24,116, fol. 63R; AN 104 Mi 12, 287; BN 32,581, fol. 149; BN 18,942, fol. 94R; and La Chesnaye-Desbois, *Dictionnaire*, IX, 574-626, esp. 586-594.

48. BN 18,942, fol. 107; BN 11,928, fols. 214, 224-226; Chamil-

lart, I, 49-50; Sandret, "Rôle des principaux gentilshommes," 9 (1871), 374; La Chesnaye-Desbois, *Dictionnaire*, IV, 178-201; and Eugene Haag, and Emile Haag, *La France protestante*, II, 510-513.

49. BN 11,924, fol. 172V; BMR 2,984, fol. 198; Travers, *Rôle du ban*, 113; BN 24,116, fol. 64; AN 104 Mi 12, 287, 410; BN 11,929, fol. 318; BMR 2,985, fol. 57R; BN 18,942, fol. 95R; BN 11,928, fols. 6, 132; Chamillart, I, 173; and La Chesnaye-Desbois, *Dictionnaire*, XII, 279-285.

50. BN 18,942, fol. 109R; BN 11,928, fol. 317; AN 104 Mi 14, 410.

51. BN 24,116, fol. 65V; AN 104 Mi 12, 411; BN 18,942, fol. 101R; and Sandret, "Role des principaux gentilshommes," 9 (1871), 371-372.

52. BN 24,116, fol. 66; AN 104 Mi 12, 410-411.

53. BN 24,116, fol. 66R; AN 104 Mi 12, 411.

54. BN 11,928, fol. 236.

55. AN E 395B, fols. 289V, 290V-291R.

56. BN 11,928, fol. 2.

57. AN E 397A, fol. 88V.

58. AN E 396B, fols. 257R-259R.

59. BN 11,928, fol. 4.

60. The use of this income data anticipates information that is set forth in more detail at the beginning of chapter five. The income rankings given in table III.11 are based on the 1552 and 1562 *bans*, cited in note 6, chapter three and the 1639 and 1666 income surveys cited in notes 3 and 6, chapter five.

CHAPTER IV

1. See, for example, François Bluche, *Les magistrats du Parlement de Paris au XVIIIe siècle*; Marcel Couturier, *Recherches sur les structures sociales de Châteaudun, 1525-1789*; Bernard Guenée, *Tribunaux et gens de justice dans le bailliage de Senlis à la fin du Moyen Age*; Louis Henry and Charles Levy, "Ducs et pairs sous l'ancien régime"; Jean-Pierre Labatut, *Les ducs et pairs de France au XVIIe siècle*; Jean Meyer, *La noblesse bretonne au XVIIIe siècle*; and Roland Mousnier, *La vénalité des offices sous Henri IV et Louis XIII*.

2. Mousnier, "Introduction," 11-24.

3. Ibid., 33-42 and Mousnier, "L'évolution des institutions monarchiques en France et ses relations avec l'état social." These general themes are also developed in Lucien Romier, *Le royaume de Catherine de Médici*, I, 160-216, esp. 170-182; Gaston Roupnel, *La ville et la campagne au XVIIe siècle*, 234-235, 313; Henri Drouot, *Mayenne et la Bourgogne*, I, 30-46, II, 311-316; Pierre de Vaissière, *Gentilshommes campagnards de l'ancienne France*, 2-3, 35-58, 218-231; Davis Bitton, *The French Nobility in Crisis*. My article, "The Decline of the Nobility in Sixteenth and Early Seventeenth Century France: Myth or Reality?" argued against this general interpretation.

4. Cited in note 27, chapter one, and supplemented by Abbé P.-F. Lebeurier's *Etat des anoblis*. In addition, for 1666, part of Bernard de Marle's *recherche* of the *généralité* of Alençon, to which the *élection* of Falaise had been transferred, was also used: "Recherches de la noblesse de la généralité d'Alençon faite par Bernard de Marle."

5. The type of surname matching used to determine the social origins of noblemen's wives was similar in concept to techniques that have been used to reconstruct families in Beauvais, or study social mobility in Boston, but is based on information of much lower quality than either parish or modern census records. See Pierre Goubert, *Beauvais et le Beauvaisis*, and Stephen Thernstrom, *The Other Bostonians*.

6. Chamillart, I, 368, II, 757.

7. BMR 2.985, fol. 70R; Abbé Hulmel, "La recherche de Montfaut," 23 (1930) 41, 106; BN 11, 929, fol. 310.

8. Chamillart, II, 566-567, 646-647, 771; Lebeurier, *Etat*, 12-13, 33, 59; BN 11,929, fols. 304, 312, 315, 329.

9. The number of marriages per decade increased over time from an average of 35 per decade in 1430-1499, and 57 per decade in 1500-1569, to 105 per decade in 1570-1669. There were no differences in the marriage patterns of eldest and younger sons.

10. Chamillart, I, 233, 281; BMR 2,985, fols. 23V-24R; and Abbé G. A. Simon, *Généalogie de la Maison d'Aigneaux*.

11. Simon, *Maison d'Aigneaux*; Chamillart, I, 281.

12. BMR 2,985, fols. 23V-24R; Chamillart, I, 233; and Abbé F. Alix, *Généalogie de la famille de la Rivière*.

13. A x^2 test was made to determine significance. The hypothesis that the two groups' marriages were the same was rejected at

the .02 level of significance ($x^2 = 10.7$ with three degrees of freedom). Once again, there were no differences in the marriage patterns of eldest and younger sons.

14. See figure II.1.

15. Meyer, *Noblesse bretonne*, II, 961, note 2.

16. A series of x^2 tests was used to determine significance. The proposition that the patterns of the four generations were the same was rejected at the .05 level of confidence ($x^2 = 17.785$ with nine degrees of freedom). The hypothesis that the patterns of the first three generations were the same was not rejected (0.3 level of significance, $x^2 = 8.25$ with six degrees of freedom), while the proposition that the first three generations were the same as the fourth was rejected at the .05 level of confidence ($x^2 = 7.749$ with three degrees of freedom).

17. BMR 2,984, fol. 202R; BMR 2,985, Fol. 13R; BN 11, 929, fol. 317; Chamillart, II, 576-577.

18. BMR 2,984, fol. 184; BMR 2,985, fol. 123R; Chamillart, II, 523, 535; Lebeurier, *Etat*, 183; and G. du Bosq de Beaumont, *Monographes normandes*, which includes a contemporary sketch of the seigneurie of Mesnil-Vité.

19. For the Clinchamps: Hulmel, "Recherche," 105; BMR 2,984, fols. 191R, 203V; BMR 2,985, fols. 15V-16R, 37R, BN 11,924, fol. 32; BN 11,929, fol. 321; Chamillart, I, 74-75; and Joseph Noulens, *Maison de Clinchamps: histoire généalogique*. For the Garsalles: BMR 2,984, fols. 38R-43V; BMR 2,985, fols. 50V-51R; BN 11,924, fol. 6; BN 11,929, fol. 326; Chamillart, I, 380-381.

20. BMR 2,984, fols. 206R-208V; Chamillart, I, 380-381.

21. For the Fayel: Hulmel, "Recherche," 105; BMR 2,984, fols. 160R-162V; BMR 2,985, fols. 170V-172R; BN 11,924, fols. 31-32; BN 11,929, fols. 313, 329; and Chamillart, I, 113-116; for the d'Escageul: Hulmel, "Recherche," 105, 107; BMR 2,984, fols. 8R, 198V; BMR 2,985, fols. 45V-46R; BN 11,929, fols. 327, 359; Chamillart, I, 103-104. For the Guyenro: BMR 2,985, fols. 5V-6R; BN 11,924, fol. 29; BN 11,929, fol. 324; Chamillart, I, 138-140.

22. The hypothesis that marriage patterns in the first and third period, combined, were the same as the patterns in the second and fourth period, combined, was rejected at the .001 level of confidence ($x^2 = 33.3$ with three degrees of freedom).

23. On this theme see Romier, *Royaume*, I, pp. 160-216; de

Vaissière, *Gentilshommes campagnards*, 2-3, 35-58, 218-231; Bitton, *The French Nobility*; and J. Russell Major, "The Crown and the Aristocracy in Renaissance France."

CHAPTER V

1. Emile Travers, ed., *Rôle du ban et l'arrière-ban du bailliage de Caen en 1552*, 9-18, 41-66, 110-115, 147-164 for the *vicomté* of Bayeux.
2. Ibid., 10-11.
3. For the list of nobles and their incomes, see BN 18,942, fols. 2-207, entitled "Roolles des Nobles de Normandie. L'An 1639 et 1640, Bailliage de Caen." The part relating to the *vicomté* of Bayeux, fols. 85-112, is entitled "Estat des gentilshommes et voeufes damoiselles employées aux Minuttes tiré de rolles des tailles Fait pour les parroisses du vicomté de Bayeux 1640."
4. To arrive at a total income figure for all nobles it was necessary to estimate the total income of the nobles whose exact income was not given. This total could have ranged from zero (if all were totally destitute) to 94,400 livres (if all had the maximum of 400 livres). Having no other information, it was decided to split the difference and estimate each income at 200 livres, for a total of 47,200 livres.
5. BN 18,942, fols. 91R, 107R.
6. BN 11,928, fols. 1-365, entitled "Memoirs des nobles gentilshommes et le pretendants telz qui ont este assignes par devant Monseigneur de Chamillart." All further general references to the 1552 *ban* and the 1639 and 1666 income surveys are based on the documents listed in this note and notes 1 and 3, this chapter.
7. As in 1639, nobles with incomes of less than 400 livres were simply described as "poor" or by other euphemisms denoting a relatively small income. The procedure used in computing the total income of such nobles in 1639 was also used for computing the total income of poor nobles in 1666, i.e., each individual was estimated to have an income of 200 livres.
8. BN 11,928, fol. 88.
9. See Pierre Deyon, "A propos des rapports entre la noblesse française et la monarchie absolue pendant la première moitié du XVIIᵉ siècle," 349-351, for another example of using the *ban* and *arrière-ban* to determine the distribution of wealth among nobles.

10. The question may also be raised as to whether poverty within the nobility was the equivalent of poverty within the Third Estate. For example, in 1639, in the *élection* of Bayeux, a noble with an income of 400 livres was considered a poor noble. Yet as late as the mid-eighteenth century, in Brittany, an income of 300 livres was considered the beginnings of *l'aisance* (affluence) for a commoner; Jean Meyer, "Un problème mal posé: la noblesse pauvre," 184-187. Meyer thoroughly discusses the problem of the relativity of noble "poverty," 161-188.

In the middle of the seventeenth century a mason at Rouen earned about 20 *sous* a day; Madeleine Foisil, *La révolte des Nu-Pieds et les révoltes normandes de 1639*, 211. This meant that under optimum conditions he may have been able to earn a yearly income equal to the annual income of a poor nobleman. But since most noble income would have been essentially unearned, and even most poor nobles, as we shall see, owned a manor house and its accompanying lands and buildings (and therefore did not pay rent for their lodgings, raised most of their own food, and in addition were able to borrow money on the capital worth of their property), it seems simplistic to conclude that a majority of poor nobles enjoyed a standard of living only equivalent to that of urban skilled workers.

11. Pierre Goubert, *L'ancien régime*, I, 169-170.

12. BN 18,942, fol. 107V; Sandret, "Rôle des principaux gentilshommes," 9 (1871), 374.

13. BN 11,928, fol. 78.

14. ADC 2B.

15. On the *décret* process, see the section, "Titre des executions par décret," articles 546-596 of the 1585 Norman Custom; Charles A. Bourdot de Richebourg, *Nouveau Coutumier Général*, IV, 88-91. *Décrets* of Bayeux nobles are to be found in ADC 2B 1,366, 1,368-1,370, 1,487-1,489, 1,771, 1,773-1,778, 1,778bis, 1,780-1,785, 1,785bis, 1,786-1,789, 2,029-2,030, 2,032-2,034, 2,038-2,040, and 2,044-2,046. The general analysis that follows is based on these documents, and references to them will be repeated only in the case of specific examples.

16. Some of the records were water damaged, and a few volumes were totally ruined.

17. As given in BN 18,942 or 11,928.

18. ADC 2B 2,033; BN 11,928, fol. 284.

19. ADC 2B 1,489, 2,034.
20. ADC 2B 1,489; BN 11,928, fol. 311.
21. ADC 2B 1,489; BN 11,928, fol. 2.
22. ADC 2B 1,786; BN 11,928, fol. 10.
23. ADC 2B 1,783; Sandret, "Rôle des principaux gentils hommes," 9 (1871), 378.
24. ADC 2B 1,773; BN 11,928, fols. 24, 114.
25. The monetary value of claims presented in figure V.3 should be taken as an approximate rather than an exact figure. The written claims filed against each estate were not always clear: sometimes, for example, a claimant would ask for payment of the arrears of a loan or obligation without specifying the amount actually owed, or legal damages of an unspecified amount would be requested. Such cases form only a small minority of all claims, however, and do not seriously affect the general accuracy of the totals given in figure V.3.
26. A figure in which the 1675 claims against the estate of Gilles de Bricqueville, seigneur of Colombières, a very rich (20,000 livres annual income) but indebted *noble de race*, bulk large (274,997 of 389,940 livres total claims against *nobles de race*); ADC 2B 1,370. However, even without Bricqueville's case, 62 percent of the value of all claims against old nobles still came from other *nobles de race*. At least 37,660 of the 151,278 livres paid out in settlements, or 25 percent, went to claimants who were related by blood or marriage to the *décrété*.

Chapter VI

1. See articles 100-101 of the Norman custom; Charles A. Bourdot de Richebourg, *Noveau Coutumier Général*, IV, 64. Articles 99-212 of the custom, 64-70, governed fiefs and feudal rights. Articles 335-366 cover the indivisibility of fiefs and *partage d'heritage*, 77-78.
2. In the area around Paris, for example, *cens* payments frequently brought in less than 5 percent of the real value of tenures; Mousnier, "Introduction," 43; *Etat et société sous François Ier et pendant le gouvernement personnel de Louis XIV*, 323-329; and "L'Evolution des institutions monarchiques en France et ses relations avec l'état social," 67-71.
3. A census of fiefs in the *vicomté* of Bayeux made in 1640, the

most complete extant list, identifies 563 fiefs. Of these ecclesiastics held 76, leaving 487 in secular hands. The 1640 census, BN 18,942, has been published, with some notes, as "Rôle de fiefs du grand bailliage de Caen et leurs possesseurs," in *Le Bulletin Héraldique de France*. The part relating to the *vicomté* of Bayeux is 2 (1889): 577-594, 641-658. See also Abbé V. Bourrienne, "L'ancienne noblesse féodale de l'arrondissement actuel de Bayeux." In the following pages references to fiefs and fief ownership include only fiefs owned by secular persons and exclude fiefs held by the church.

4. This estimate is based on an examination of *aveux* made by fief owners in the *vicomté* of Bayeux in the late sixteenth and seventeenth centuries. An *aveux* was a written document in which a vassal acknowledged to his lord that he held a fief from him and described the physical and legal components of the fief. Collections of hundreds of *aveux* for the *vicomté* of Bayeux can be found in ADSM II B 391, 392, and 395. AN P 298¹, 298², 299², 299³, 300¹, 300², 300³, and 306ᶜ contain *aveux* for the *bailliage* of Caen. Dom Lenoir's notes contain transcripts of many *aveux* and descriptions of fiefs, most dating from before the sixteenth century; AN 104 Mi, 6-11, 34-37, 42-53, 62-66, 74. For descriptions of manors and manor life see Katherine Fedden, *Manor Life in Old France*; and Claude Blanguernon, *Gilles de Gouberville, gentilhomme de Cotentin*.

5. ADSM II B 391, fols. 1R-7R.
6. Ibid., fols. 33R-34R and the immediately preceding *aveux*, unpaginated.
7. Ibid., unpaginated, sixth *aveux* in the volume.
8. Ibid., fol. 6V-7R.
9. Ibid., fols. 33R-34R and the immediately preceding unpaginated *aveux*.
10. Ibid., unpaginated, sixth *aveux* of the volume.
11. For the incomes of the *vicomté*'s most important fiefs and seigneuries around 1680 see G. A. Prévost, ed., *Notes du Premier Président Pellot sur la Normandie*, 266-276.
12. ADSM II B 391, unpaginated *aveux* preceding fol. 33R.
13. Prévost, *Notes du Premier Président Pellot*, 275, note 2, 275.
14. ADSM II B 391, unpaginated *aveux*.
15. ADSM II B 391, fols. 53R-54R.
16. Ibid., fol. 54.
17. Prévost, *Notes du Premier Président Pellot*, 274, note 4, 274.

Jean Meyer, in *La noblesse bretonne au XVIIIe siècle*, II, 801-805, also noted that in Brittany seigneurial dues in the form of agricultural products or mill profits formed a very important part of the income of an estate.

18. Lucien Romier, *Le royaume de Catherine de Médici*, II, 182-184; Gaston Roupnel, *La ville et la campagne au XVIIe siècle*, 234-235; Davis Bitton, *The French Nobility in Crisis*; Henri Drouot, *Mayenne et la Bourgogne*, I, 40-45; Pierre de Vaissière, *Gentilshommes campagnards de l'ancienne France*, 220-221; Pierre Goubert, *Beauvais et le Beauvaisis*, I, 207-208, 214-221.

19. For the 1552 *ban* see Emile Travers, ed., *Rôle du ban et arrière-ban du bailliage de Caen*. For the 1640 census, note 3, this chapter.

20. BN NA 4,210, fols. 166-210 for the 1503 census.

21. Citations for 1552 are given in note 19 and for 1640 in note 3, this chapter. A copy of the *ban comptes* of 1597 was made by Dom Jacques-Louis Lenoir in the eighteenth century and is preserved as AN 104 Mi 12, 276-288. Fief ownership in 1562, 1567, 1568, and 1587 is revealed by the *bans* of those years, cited in note 6, chapter three. Ownership of fiefs in these additional years was analyzed but in the interests of simplicity, and because the results of the analysis supported the following conclusions about ownership trends, they have not been included.

22. See chapter three, note 6.

23. See chapter five, note 15. All information about seized property in the discussion that follows comes from ADC 2B.

24. Acres have been converted to English acres taking into account differences in the size of local measures of area in the parishes in which land was seized. On this subject see M. le commandant H. Navel, "Recherches sur les anciennes mesures agraires normands: acres, vergées, et perches."

25. The income produced by a capital sum is estimated at one-thirtieth of its value, the ratio used by Jean-Pierre Labatut in his *Les ducs et pairs de France au XVIIe siècle*.

26. ADC 2B 1,488, unnumbered and unpaginated *déclarations* dated July 30 and November 30, 1669.

27. See the sale of the *heritages* of Louis Manvieux, sieur of Tracy in 1672; ADC 2B 2,046, unnumbered *état*, fols. 1R-12R, for an excellent example of a bourgeois, Philippe Gosselin, being highest bidder at the public auction (11,400 livres for two manors and eighty-two acres of land), but then reselling his right to purchase

to three noblemen, two of whom were seigneurs in the parishes in which Manvieux's estate was located.

28. A favorable state of affairs which lasted, in the *élection* of Bayeux, at least, until the end of the old regime. See, for example, the map at the beginning of Mohamed El Kordi, *Bayeux aux XVIIᵉ et XVIIIᵉ siècles*, which dramatically underscores the landed wealth of the Bayeux nobility in the eighteenth century.

CHAPTER VII

1. See J. A. Galland, *Essai sur l'histoire du protestantisme à Caen et en Basse-Normandie*, especially the fold-out map of the diocese of Bayeux.

2. Michel Béziers, *Mémoires pour servir à l'état historique et géographique du diocèse de Bayeux*, I, 80-84, 201-205, 296-297; Eugene Haag and Emile Haag, *La France protestante*, II, 510-511.

3. BN 20,366, fols. 93-98.

4. For abjurations between March 23, 1570 and August 18, 1573 see Eugene Anquetil, "Abjurations protestantes à Bayeux," esp. 179-187.

5. AN 104 Mi 13, esp. 294-309.

6. AN 104 Mi 12, 276-288.

7. Jean Delumeau, *Naissance et affirmation de la Réforme*, 182; AN 104 Mi 71, 719-722, 728-729, 743-744, 755-756, and 761.

8. F.-A. de la Chesnaye-Desbois, *Dictionnaire de la Noblesse*, supplemented by the 1666 income survey, BN 11,928, fols. 1-365.

9. Anquetil, "Abjurations protestantes," 174-178.

10. Haag and Haag, *La France protestante*, II, 510-511.

11. The comparative income rankings are based, for 1568-73, on the 1552, 1562 and 1568 *bans*; Emile Travers, ed., *Rôle du ban et arrière-ban du bailliage de Caen*; BN 24,116, fols. 35-66; AN 104 Mi 13, 294-309; for 1639, BN 18,942, fols. 85-112; and for 1666, BN 11,928, fols. 1-365.

12. BN 11,928, fols. 1-365; see the discussion of noble incomes at the beginning of chapter five.

13. The basic source for this paragraph is family dossiers compiled from the various *recherches*.

14. References to such episodes can be found in the 1540 *recherche*; BMR 2,984, fols. 31R, 63R-65R, 77V, 83, 135V-137V, 186V, among others.

⚘ BIBLIOGRAPHY ⚘

I. MANUSCRIPT SOURCES

Archives Nationales

E 395B-460. Arrêts de Conseil.

P 298¹-300³ and 306ᵉ. Chambre des Comptes, *Aveux* of the *bailliage* of Caen.

PP 24. "Dictionnaire des Fiefs de Normandie par Brussel."

AN 104 Mi-6-13, 34-37, 42-53, 62-66, 71, 74. Collection Dom Lenoir. *Bans* of 1587 and 1597.

Bibliothèque Nationale

Manuscrits français

4,620. "Dénombrement des élections et paroisses de Normandie."

11,924. "Recherche des élus de la vicomté de Bayeux, faite en 1525, par Jacques de Bosq." Fols. 116-155.

11,928. "Memoire des nobles gentilshommes et la pretendants telz qui ont este assignes par devant Monseigneur de Chamillart" (incorrectly labeled BN Supplement français 3,159 above the title page). Fols. 1-365.

11,929. "Recherche de la noblesse, dans la Généralité de Caen, par Jean-Jacques de Mesmes, seigneur de Roissy, Michel de Repichon et Jacques de Croismare (1598-99)." Fols. 269-370.

18,942. "Roolles des Nobles de Normandie. L'An 1639 et 1640, Bailliage de Caen." "Extrait des noms des gentilhommes plus considerables ou en naissance ou en biens ou en gallité demeurantz dans l'estendue du bailliage de Caen, tiré sure le roolle général dudit bailliage. 1640." Fols. 4-25. "Estat des gentilhommes et voeufes damoiselles employées aux Minuttes tiré de rolles des tailles Fait pour les parroisses du vicomté de Bayeux 1640." Fols. 85-112. "Roole des fiefz et des possedentz iceux en la ville et vi-

199

conté de Bayeux, bailliage de Caen. 1640." Fols. 118-141.

20,366. "Extraict des registres de la Court de Parlement . . . viconte de Caen au siege de Bayeux 1568 contre . . . les nouvelle pretendue Religion." Fols. 93-98.

24,116-24,117. "Rôle de la taxe du ban et arrière-ban du bailliage de Caen, pour les années 1562 et 1567." Fols. 1-221.

32,315. "Mélanges sur la noblesse de Normandie," Second part, "Généalogies des gentilhommes de l'élection de Bayeux, par eux produites, avec les titres justificatifs de leur noblesse, en l'an 1523." Fols. 1-78.

32,581. "Estats des deniers deubz au Roy par les tenans et propriettaires des duchez, contez, marquisatz, baronnies, fiefs, terres et seigneuries nobles, rellevantz neument de sa Majesté, . . . pour le droict d'aydes chevelz deubz à Sa Majesté à cause de la chevallerye de Monseigneur le Dauphin, suivant la coustume de Normandie." (1609).

Nouvelles acquisitions

4,210. "Dénombrement des fiefs de la viconté de Bayeux en 1503." Fols. 166-210.

4,214. "Aveux de la Généralité de Caen." Second part. Fols. 1-196 (*vicomté* of Bayeux).

Bibliothèque Municipale de Rouen

2,984. (Martainville 107). "Recherche de 1540 de l'Election de Bayeux." Fols. 1-213.

2,985. (Martainville Y-16). Second part. "Recherche de 1624 (Paris) Pour l'Election de Bayeux." Fols. 1-201.

2,977. (Martainville Y-60). "Recherche de 1655 pour l'Election de Caen, Bayeux, Falaise, Vire, etc."

Archives Départementales de Calvados

1B 2,083. *Procès verbaux* of the *ban* of 1587.
1B 2,083bis. *Bans: bailliage* of Caen.
2B 1,365-2,046. *Décrets, déclarations*, and *adjudications* of *heritages* in the *vicomté* of Bayeux.

BIBLIOGRAPHY

Archives Départementales de la Seine-Maritime

II B 391, 392, and 395. Chambre des Comptes. *Aveux—Vicomté de Bayeux.*

II B 362-369. Chambre des Comptes. *Dons et Mainlevées de Gardes-nobles.*

II. PRINTED SOURCES

Anquetil, Eugene. "Abjurations protestantes à Bayeux." *Mémoires de la Société des Sciences, Arts, et Belles-Lettres de Bayeux.* 9 (1907), 129-188.

Bourdot de Richebourg, Charles A. *Nouveau Coutumier Général.* Vol. IV. Paris, 1724.

Buisson de Courson, A. du. *Généralité de Caen. Recherche de la Noblesse faite par ordre de Roi en 1666 et années suivantes, par Guy Chamillart.* 2 vols. and a supplement. Caen, 1887 and 1889.

Cherin, Louis-Nicolas-Henri. *Abrégé chronologique d'édits, declarations, réglemens, arrêts, et lettres-patents des rois de France . . . concernant le fait de noblesse, précédé d'un discours sur l'origine de la noblesse . . . et les causes de sa décadence.* Paris, 1788.

Hulmel, Abbé. "La recherche de Monfaut." *Revue de l'Avranchin.* 22 (1927), 629-640; 23 (1930), 33-57, 97-112, 641-644.

Le Mâle, Abbé. "Recherche de la noblesse faite en la généralité de Caen (1598-99) . . . Procédée d'une introduction sur les recherches de noblesse de la Basse-Normandie." *Revue catholique de Normandie.* (1916), 440-468; (1917), 184-218; (1918), 15-35.

Prévost, G. A., ed. *Notes du Premier Président Pellot sur la Normandie, 1670-1683.* Rouen, 1915.

"Recherches de la noblesse de la généralité d'Alençon faite par Bernard de Marle." *Annuaire de l'Orne pour l'année 1866.* 1866, 269-284.

Rocque, Abbé P.-E. de la *Recherche de Montfaut, contenant les noms de ceux qu'il trouva noble et de ceux qu'il imposa à la taille, quoiqu'ils se prétendissent nobles, en l'année 1465.* 2nd ed. Caen, 1818.

"Rôle de fiefs du grand bailliage de Caen et leurs possesseurs. Dressé en l'année 1640." *Le Bulletin Héraldique de France.*

New series. 2 (1889), 449-462, 513-526, 577-594, 641-658; 3 (1890), 3-18, 65-80, 129-144.

Sandret, L. "Rôle des principaux gentilshommes de la Généralité de Caen, Accompagné de notes secrètes, Rédigées en 1640." *Revue Nobiliare.* 1 (1862), 145-156, 264-272, 326-332, 514-517; 3 (1865), 351-360; 7 (1869), 255-261, 9 (1871), 370-380. Vols. 3, 7, and 9 correspond to vols. 1, 5, and 7 of the new series beginning in 1869.

Travers, Emile, ed. *Rôle du ban et arrière-ban du bailliage de Caen en 1552.* Rouen, 1901.

III. SECONDARY WORKS

Alix, Abbé A. *Généalogie de la famille de la Rivière.* Caen, 1911.

Baehrel, R. *Une-Croissance: la Basse-Provence rurale.* Paris, 1961.

Béziers, Michel. *Mémoires pour servir à l'état historique et geographique du diocèse de Bayeux.* 3 vols. Rouen, 1894-1896.

Bitton, Davis. *The French Nobility in Crisis. 1560-1640.* Stanford, 1969.

Blanguernon, Claude. *Gilles de Gouberville, gentilhomme du Cotentin, 1522-1578.* Coutances, 1969.

Bloch, Jean-Richard. *L'anoblissement en France au temps de François Ier. Essai d'une définition de la condition juridique et sociale de la noblesse au début du XVIᵉ siècle.* Paris, 1934.

Bloch, Marc. *Les caractères originaux de l'histoire rurale française.* 2 vols. Paris, 1952-1956.

Bloch, Marc, and Febvre, Lucien. "Enquêtes—Les Noblesses: Reconnaissance général du terrain." *Annales d'histoire économique et sociale.* 7 (1936), 238-242.

Bluche, François. *Les magistrats du Parlement de Paris au XVIIIᵉ siècle (1715-1771).* Paris, 1960.

Bluche, François, and Durye, Pierre. *L'anoblissement par charges avant 1789.* 2 vols. La Roche-sur-Lon, 1962.

Bosq de Beaumont, A. du. *Notes et documents pour servir à l'histoire de la recherche de Chamillart, par un membre de Conseil héraldique de France.* Caen, 1890.

Bosq de Beaumont, G. du. *La Châtellenie de Beaumont-le Richard.* N. p., n.d.

———. *Monographes normandes.* St. Lô, 1905.

Boüard, Michel, ed. *Histoire de Normandie.* Toulouse, 1970.

Bourrienne, Abbé V. "L'ancienne noblesse féodale de l'arrondissement actuel de Bayeux." *Congrès du Millénaire de la Normandie. Compte rendu des travaux.* Rouen, 1912, 182-190.

———. "La recherche des élus de Bayeux en 1523." *Société des sciences, arts et belles-lettres de Bayeux.* 10 (1908), 174-181.

Boutruche, Robert. *La crise d'une société: seigneurs et paysans du Bordelais pendant la Guerre de Cent Ans.* Paris, 1947.

Braudel, Fernand. *Civilisation matérielle et capitalisme.* Vol. I. Paris, 1967.

———. *La Méditerranée et le monde méditerranéen a l'époque de Philippe II.* Paris, 1949.

Buisson de Courson, A. du. *Notes recueillies sur la commune de Colombiers-sur-Seulles.* Caen, 1890.

Cavard, Pierre. *La Réforme et les guerres de religion à Vienne.* Vienne, 1950.

Chaussinand-Nogaret, Guy. *La noblesse au XVIIIᵉ siècle, de la féodalité aux lumières.* Paris, 1976.

Cloulas, Ivan. "Les aliénations du temporel ecclésiastique sous Charles IX et Henri III (1563-1587)." *Revue d'histoire de l'église de France.* 44 (1958), 5-56.

Colloque de l'Ecole Normale Supérieure de Saint-Cloud. *L'histoire sociale: sources et méthodes.* Paris, 1967.

Couturier, Marcel. *Recherches sur les structures sociales de Châteaudun, 1525-1789.* Paris, 1969.

D'Avenel, le vicomte G. *La noblesse française sous Richelieu.* Paris, 1901.

Delumeau, Jean. *Naissance et affirmation de la Réforme.* Paris, 1965.

Depoint, J., and Vergnet, J. "Boran." *Memoires de la société académique de l'Oise.* Vol. 24. Beauvais, 1924, i-384.

Devyver, André. *Le sang épuré: Les préjugés de race chez les gentilshommes français de l'Ancien Régime (1560-1720).* Brussels, 1973.

Deyon, Pierre. *Amiens: capitale provinciale. Etude sur la société urbaine au XVIIᵉ siècle.* Paris, 1974.

———. "A propos des rapports entre la noblesse française et la monarchie absolue pendant la première moitié du XVIIᵉ siècle." *Revue historique.* 221 (1964), 341-356.

Doucet, R. *Les institutions de la France au XVIᵉ siècle.* 2 vols. Paris, 1948.

Drouot, Henri. *Mayenne et la Bourgogne: Etude sur la Ligue (1587-1596)*. 2 vols. Paris, 1937.

Duby, Georges. "Lignage, noblesse et chevalerie au XIIᵉ siècle dans la région mâconnaise." *Annales: économies, sociétés, civilisations.* 27 (special number, July-October 1972), 803-823.

Dupâquier, Jacques. "French Population in the 17th and 18th Centuries." In Rondo Cameron, ed., *Essays in French Economic History.* Homewood, Ill., 1970, 150-199.

El Kordi, Mohamed. *Bayeux aux XVIIᵉ et XVIIIᵉ siècles.* Paris and the Hague, 1970.

Esmonin, Edmond. *La taille en Normandie au temps de Colbert (1661-1683).* Paris, 1913.

Estaintot, Robert Charles René Langlois, comte d'. *La Ligue en Normandie, 1588-1594.* Paris, 1862.

Fedden, Katherine. *Manor Life in Old France.* New York, 1933.

Fédou, René. *Les hommes de loi Lyonnais à la fin du Moyen Age.* Paris, 1964.

Foisil, Madeleine. *La révolte des Nu-Pieds et les révoltes normandes de 1639.* Paris, 1970.

Ford, Franklin L. *Robe and Sword: The Regrouping of the French Aristocracy after Louis XIV.* New York, 1953.

Forster, Robert. *The House of Saulx-Tavanes; Versailles and Burgundy, 1700-1830.* Baltimore, 1971.

———. *The Nobility of Toulouse in the Eighteenth Century.* Baltimore, 1960.

Frondeville, Henri de. *Les conseillers du Parlement de Normandie au seizième siècle 1499-1594.* Rouen, 1960.

———. *Les conseillers du Parlement du Normandie sous Henri IV et sous Louis XIII (1594-1640).* Rouen, 1964.

———. *Les présidents du Parlement de Normandie 1499-1790.* Rouen, 1953.

Frondeville, Henri de, and Frondeville, Odette de. *Les conseillers du Parlement de Normandie de 1641 à 1715.* Rouen, 1970.

Galland, J. A. *Essai sur l'histoire du protestantisme à Caen et en Basse-Normandie (1598-1791).* Paris, 1898.

Goubert, Pierre, *L'ancien régime.* 2 vols. Paris, 1969.

———. *Beauvais et le Beauvaisis de 1600 à 1730.* 2 vols. Paris, 1960.

Gouhier, Pierre. *Port-en-Bessin (1597-1742). Etude d'histoire démographique.* Caen, Cahiers des Annales de Normandie, no. 1, 1962.

Gouhier, Pierre, Vallez, Anne, and Vallez, Jean-Marie. *Atlas historique de normandie*. 2 vols. Caen, 1967-1972.

Guenée, Bernard. *Tribunaux et gens de justice dans le bailliage de Senlis à la fin du Moyen Age (vers 1380-vers 1550)*. Paris, 1963.

Haag, Eugene, and Haag, Emile. *La France protestante*. 10 vols. Geneva, 1966.

Heers, Jacques. *L'occident aux XIVe et XVe siècles: aspects économiques et sociaux*. Paris, 1970.

Henry, Louis, and Lévy, Claude. "Ducs et pairs sous l'ancien régime: caractéristiques démographiques d'une caste." *Population*. 15 (1960), 807-829.

Hippeau, C. *Dictionnaire topographique du département du Calvados*. Paris, 1883.

Hufton, Olwen H. *Bayeux in the Late Eighteenth Century: A Social Study*. Oxford, 1967.

Huppert, George. *Les Bourgeois Gentilshommes. An Essay on the Definition of Elites in Renaissance France*. Chicago, 1977.

Kymadec, R. T. de. *Les lettres d'anoblissement sous les règnes de Henri IV et Louis XIII*. Paris, 1954.

Labatut, Jean-Pierre. *Les ducs et pairs de France au XVIIe siècle*. Paris, 1972.

La Chesnaye-Desbois, F. A. Aubert de. *Dictionnaire de la Noblesse*. 3rd ed. 19 vols. Paris, 1863-1876.

Laheudrie, Edmond de. *Recherches sur le Bessin, Histoire du Bessin des origines à la Revolution*. 2 vols. Caen and Bayeux, 1930.

Lapeyre, Henri. *Les monarchies européenes de XVIe siècles: les relations internationales*. Paris, 1967.

Lebeurier, Abbé P.-F. *Etat des anoblis en Normandie de 1545 à 1661. Avec un supplément de 1398 à 1687*. Evreux, 1866.

―――. *Rôle des taxes de l'arrière-ban du bailliage d'Evreux en 1562. Avec une Introduction sur l'histoire et l'organisation du ban et l'arrière-ban*, Paris, 1861.

Le Roy-Ladurie, Emmanuel, *Les Paysans de Languedoc*. 2 vols. Paris, 1966.

―――. "Système de la coutume. Structures familiales et coutume d'heritage en France au XVIe siècle." *Annales: économies, sociétés, civilisations*. 27 (special number, July-October 1972), 825-840.

Logie, Paul. *La Fronde en Normandie*. 3 vols. Amiens, 1951-1952.

Major, J. Russell. "The Crown and the Aristocracy in Renaissance France." *American Historical Review.* 69 (1964), 631-645.

Mandrou, Robert. *La France aux XVIIe et XVIIIe siècles.* Paris, 1970.

Mauro, Frederic. *Le XVIe siècle européen: aspects économiques.* Paris, 1970.

Merle, Louis. *La métairie et l'évolution agraire de la Gâtine Poitevine.* Paris, 1958.

Méthivier, H. *L'ancien régime.* Paris, 1961.

Meyer, Jean. *La noblesse bretonne au XVIIIe siècle.* 2 vols. Paris, 1966.

——. *Noblesses et pouvoirs dans l'Europe de l'ancien régime.* Paris, 1973.

——. "Un problème, mal posé: la noblesse pauvre. L'exemple breton au XVIIIe siècle." *Revue d'histoire moderne et contemporaine.* 18 (1971), 151-188.

Mousnier, Roland. *Etat et société sous François Ier et pendant le gouvernement personnel de Louis XIV.* Paris, n.d.

——. "L'évolution des institutions monarchiques en France et ses relations avec l'état social." *XVIIe Siècle.* 58-59 (1963) 57-72.

——. "Introduction." In Roland Mousnier, J.-P. Labatut, and Y. Durand, *Problèmes de stratification sociale. Deux cahiers de la noblesse pour les Etats Généraux de 1649-1651.* Paris, 1965.

——. *Les XVIe et XVIIe siècles.* Vol. IV: *Histoire générale des civilisations.* 5th ed. Paris, 1967.

——. *La vénalité des offices sous Henri IV et Louis XIII.* Rouen, n.d.

Navel, M. le commandant H. "Recherches sur les anciennes mesures agraires normands: acres, vergées, et perches." *Bulletin de la Société des Antiquaries de Normandie.* 40 (1932), 29-183.

Neufbourg, comte de. "Project d'une enquête sur la noblesse française." *Annales d'histoire économique et sociale.* 8 (1936), 243-255.

Noulens, Joseph. *Maison de Clinchamps: histoire généalogique.* Paris, 1884.

Perroy, Edouard. "Social Mobility among the French Noblesse in the Later Middle Ages." *Past and Present.* 21 (1962), 25-38.

Plaisse, A. *La baronnie du Neubourg.* Paris, 1960.

Procacci, Giuliano. *Classi sociale e monarchia assoluta nella Francia della prima mèta del secolo XVI.* N.p., 1955.

Puy de Clinchamps, Phillippe du. *La noblesse.* Paris, 1959.

Raveau, Paul. *L'agriculture et les classes paysannes. La transformation de la propriété dans le Haut Poitou au XVe siècle.* Paris, 1926.

Romier, Lucien. *Le royaume de Catherine de Médici.* 2 vols. Paris, 1922.

Roupnel, Gaston. *La ville et la campagne au XVIIe siècle. Etude sur les populations du pays dijonnais.* Paris, 1955.

Saffroy, Gaston. *Bibliographie généalogique, héraldique et nobiliaire de la France.* 2 vols. Paris, 1968-1970.

Sagnac, Philippe. *La formation de la société française moderne.* 2 vols. Paris, 1945-1946.

Salmon, J. H. M. *Society in Crisis. France in the Sixteenth Century.* New York, 1975.

See, Henri. *Histoire économique de la France.* Vol. 1: *Moyen Age et l'ancien régime.* Paris, 1939.

Simon, Abbé G. A. *Les études généalogiques en Normandie.* Caen, 1926.

———. *Généalogie de la Maison d'Aigneaux.*

Sturdy, D. J. "Tax Evasion, the *Faux Nobles*, and State Fiscalism: The Example of the *Généralité* of Caen, 1634-35." *French Historical Studies.* 9 (1976), 549-572.

Teall, Elizabeth Salmon. "The Renaissance Seigneur: Advocate or Oppressor?" *Journal of Modern History.* 37 (1965), 131-150.

Thernstrom, Stephen. *The Other Bostonians. Poverty and Progress in the American Metropolis.* Cambridge, Mass., 1973.

Vaissière, Pierre de. *Gentilshommes campagnards de l'ancienne France.* Paris, 1925.

Venard, M. *Bourgeois et paysans au XVIIe siècle. Recherche sur le rôle des bourgeois parisiens dans la vie agricole au sud de Paris au XVIIe siècle.* Paris, 1957.

Wiley, W. L. *The Gentlemen of Renaissance France.* Cambridge, Mass., 1954.

Wood, James B. "The Decline of the Nobility in Sixteenth and Early Seventeenth Century France: Myth or Reality?" *Journal of Modern History.* 48 (1976), iii.

———. "Demographic Pressure and Social Mobility among the

Nobility of Early Modern France." *Sixteenth Century Journal.* 8 (1977), 3-16.

———. "Endogamy and *Mésalliance*, the Marriage Patterns of the Nobility of the *Élection* of Bayeux, 1430-1669." *French Historical Studies.* 10 (1978), 375-392.

———. "La structure sociale de la noblesse dans le bailliage de Caen et ses modifications (1463-1666)." *Annales de Normandie.* 22 (1972), 331-335.

Yver, Jean. *Essai de géographie coutumière.* Paris, 1966.

Bankrupt nobles (*cont.*)
of, 130-31. *See also* Bankruptcies; Indebtedness
Banville, fief of, 31, 143-44
Bastards, 36-37
Baucquet, Henry, 94
Baudre, Marie de, 112
Bayeux, *bailliage* of, 129
Bayeux, city of, 22, 27, 153;
attacked by Calvinists, 160;
noble residence in, 47; population of, 22; sack of cathedral,
160
Bayeux, *élection-vicomté* of, 3;
boundaries and description,
21-22; population of, 22
Behavior of nobles: alternate
socioeconomic explanation of,
157; explanations of, need for
revision, 118-19; misunder-
standing of effect of social
structure on, 157-58; socio-
economic roots of, 4-5, 10,
17-19. *See also* Activism; Inter-
pretations of the nobility; De-
cline of the nobility
Bertrand, Pierre, 134
Bessin, 9, 22
Beuvron, Duke of, 79, 92
Bishop of Bayeux, 139
Bitton, Davis, 7-8
Blais, Gilles, 79
Bloch, J. R., 60, 62, 64-65
Bocage, 22
Boisdelles, Pierre, 88
bons menagers, 127
Bourbon, Constable, 8
Bourran, 79
Bourran, Francois, 79
Bourran, Geoffrey, 79
Bourran, Guillaume, 79
Bourran, Philippe, 79
Brebeuf, 103-04
Brebeuf, fief of, 143
Brebeuf, Margueritte du, 103

Bret, Francois, 6, 31-32
Bricqueville, 91
Bricqueville, Francois de, 91, 160,
163
Bricqueville, Gabriel de, 91, 121,
129
Brittany, 60; letters of ennoble-
ment in, 64; nobility of, 6, 9,
41, 61
Bunel, 79
Burgundy, nobility of, 7

Cabazac, 112
Cabazac, Jean, 112
Cabazac, Pierre de, 112
Cabazac, Thomas, 113
Caen, *bailliage* of, 22
Caen, city of, 22, 67, 107, 153
Caen, *élection* of, 103
Caen, *généralité* of, 21-22, 102
Calvinism, 5, 9, 17, 160-61. *See
also* Calvinist nobility; Prot-
estant nobility; Protestantism
Calvinist nobility: *Arrêt* against,
160; antiquity of, 101-63; size
of, 160-63; socioeconomic iden-
tity, 159. *See also* Protestant
nobility
Canivet, Jacques, 134
Careers, and antiquity, 95
Carentan, *élection* of, 103
Catholic League, 84, 92
Cauvet, Gilles, 134
Challenges of proofs, 31-33. *See
also* Condemnations; Proofs of
nobility; *Recherches*
Chamillart, Guy, 26-28, 30, 41
Chamillart, Michel, 26
Charles IX, 24
Chartier, Charles, 88
Chartre des francs-fiefs, 24-25, 32,
61, 167; as origin of Bayeux
nobles, 61
Chastel, 28
Chastel, Alonce du, 28

INDEX

Chastel, Thomas du, 28
Châtillon, Admiral de, 77
Civil disturbances and disorders, 17-19; role of nobility in, 5. *See also* Activism; Opposition to the crown
Claimants, identity of, 135-37; payments to, 137-39. *See also* Bankruptcies; Claims; Creditors; Indebtedness
Claims: payments of, 137; settlement of, importance of nobility in, 139. *See also* Bankruptcies; Claimants; Indebtedness
Clinchamps, 115
Colbert, 26
Coligny, Admiral, 160
Commoners, marriages with nobles, 104-06
Computer, 102
Condemnations, 35-36; protests against, 39-40; reasons for, 36-39. *See also* Challenges of proofs; Prescriptions; Proofs of nobility; *Recherches*; Usurpation
Conflict, between nobles: *See* Internal divisions
Cossey, Guillaume de, 107
Cossey, Jacqueline de, 107
Country gentlemen, 71-72, 94-95, 133-34; and Protestantism, 163
Cour des Aides, 32, 38, 41; *arrêt* against Calvinists, 160; *arrêts* of, 27, 30, 63
Courtelais, Jacques, 36
Courtelais, Philippe, 34
Courtelais, Pierre, 34
Coutances, city of, 107
Coutances, *élection* of, 103
Creditors: importance of nobles as, 135-37; of nobility, 130; payments to, 137-39; *See also* Claimants

Crisis, sense of, 47; *See also* Decline of nobility
Croixmare, Jacques de, 26
Croq, Claude du, 113
Croq, Henry du, 113
Crown: causes of opposition to, 168; noble opposition to, 159. *See also* Modern state; Monarchy; Regulation of nobility by the crown
Customary definition of nobility, 42
Customary laws of Normandy, 22
Cuves, Jean de, 103
Cyresme, Anthoine, 78
Cyresme, Christophe, 78
Cyresme, Jacques de, 143-44
Cyresme, Jean-Baptiste, 78

Damigny, castellany of, 143
Damigny, fief of, 142-43
damoiselle, 103
Daneau, Herve, 78
Davy, Renée, 106
Decline of the nobility, 5-6, 7-10, 17, 19, 44, 122, 144-45, 154-55, 157, 166, 170; lack of evidence for, 8-9. *See also* Economic condition of the nobility; Interpretations of the nobility
Décrétants, social identity of, 131-32; *See also* Claimants; Creditors; *Décrets des heritages*
Décrets des heritages, 129-31, 133, 135, 149; *See also* Bankruptcies; Claimants; Creditors, *Décrétants*
défalcations, 138-39
Definition of nobility, 10-15
Degrees of nobility, 29-30
Derogation, 25-26, 36-37, 39
Dérogeance: See Derogation
Dieppe, 67
Dieu, or Le Dieu, 103
Dieu, or Le Dieu, Marie, 103

distribution of, 146-47; and
noble status in Normandy, 61;
ownership of, 142; and
prescription, 59-61; rents in
kind, 143-44; size of, 142-43;
value of, 143 44. *See also*
Fiefownership; Landowner-
ship; Manors
Fiefownership, 145-47; military
mystique of, 142; and military
service, 82; net changes in,
147-49; and operation of social
mobility, 148-49; prestige of,
142; rights and prerogatives,
141-42; significance of changes
in, 144-45, 147-49; success of
nobility, 148-49. *See also* Fiefs;
Landownership
Fontenay le Pesnel, fief of, 31
Forestier, Antoine, 35
Forez, nobility of, 58, 60-61
Forster, Robert, 6, 9
Foullognes, 91-92
Foullognes, Jean de, 134
franc-fief, 24, 61
Francs-fiefs et nouveaux acquêts,
commissioners of, 24
French nobility: as dying class,
43; stability and flexibility of,
119; importance of nobility,
4-5, 19. *See also* Interpretations
of the nobility
Frolet, 34
Fronde, 65, 104, 117, 127
Fumée, 115

Gallon, 30-31
Gallon, Guillaume, 31
Gallon, Jean, 31
Gallon, Richard, 31
Garsalles, 115
Gascoing, Fleurie de, 113
Gascoing, Jean de, 113
Gaubot, Marin, 134
Genealogies, 30-33, 47. *See also*

Proofs of nobility; *Recherches*
Generations of nobility, and
officeholding, 79-80
Gentilhommerie, 76
gentilshommes, as principal
beneficiaries of noble bank-
ruptcies, 137-39
Gentilshommes campagnards, 47
Geographical mobility, 44, 54,
58, 62; of old nobles, 55;
effect on membership of
nobility, 56-58. *See also* Im-
migration of old nobles;
Social mobility
Godefroy, 41, 94
Godefroy, Laurens, 39
Godefroy, Pierre, 39
Goubert, Pierre, 12, 58, 60-62
Gouye, Marie, 107
Gradualistic ennoblement, 68.
See also Ennoblement; Prescrip-
tion
Grand conseil, 35
Grand recherche of Colbert, 42
Grandval, Jean de, 32
Grimouville, 115
Grimouville, Etienne de, 142
Grimouville, Richard, 32
Growth of the nobility, 54-55;
effect on membership of
nobility, 47; effect on social
structure, 46-47. *See also*
Expansion of the nobility;
Population
Guerente, Jacques, 32
Gueroult, Charles, 135
Guyenro, 115
Gygnel, Margueritte, 33

Hamel, 78
Hamel, Charles du, 134
Haye, Jean de la, 33
Haye, Pierre de la, 33
Hebert, Hervieu, 87
Helyes, Jean, 34

Helyes, Nicolas, 34
Helyes, Pierre, 34
Henry IV, 70, 91, 161
High robe, 67-68, 75
Historical interpretations of the
nobility: *See* Interpretations of
the nobility
homage, 141
Horizontal mobility, 54
Hostility between *anoblis* and
gentilshommes, lack of, 117-18
Hotot, 76, 115
Hotot, Charles, 76
Hotot, Jean, 76
Hotot, Noel, 76
Hudebert, Guillaume de, 34
Hue, Cleophus, 85
Hue, Mathurin, 104
Huguenots, 5, 17-19, 84. *See
also* Calvinism; Protestantism

Ideology, role of, 159
Immigration of old nobles, 55,
63. *See also* Geographical
mobility; Social mobility
Impoverishment of nobility, 7-8,
16, 122. *See also* Decline of the
nobility; Poverty
Incomes, 7, 16, 120-122; degree
of inequality of, 123; distribution of, 120-24, 126-27; from
fiefs, 120-122; increases in,
127; and indebtedness, 130-34;
and new nobles, 123-24; and
old nobles, 123-24; of Protestant nobles, 164-66; surveys of,
121-22; and careers, 95-96.
See also Poor nobles; Poverty
Indebtedness of nobles, 16-17,
128-33; identities of indebted
nobles, 130-31; and income,
130-34; sources for, 129. *See
also* Bankruptcies; Bankrupt
nobles; Claimants; Claims;
Décrets des heritages

Inflation, 127
Informants, 28-29
Intermarriage: lack of exclusion
of new nobles, 112-13; among
new nobles, 71; between nobles,
107-08; with nobles of Lower
Normandy, 104-06; between
old and new nobles, 115-16;
between old and new nobles,
periodicity of, 116-17; between
old and new nobles, theories
of, 101; periodicity of, 111;
regional nature of, 102-03.
See also Assimilation; Marriage
patterns
Internal divisions of the nobility,
11, 13-15, 95, 99, 156-57; along
class lines, unimportance of,
118-19; conflicts between old
and new nobles, 69; conflicts,
explanation of, 159; literary
evidence for, 15; role of wealth
in, 95; tension between groups,
101. *See also* Activism; Membership of the nobility
Interpretations of the nobility,
3-10, 17-18; criticisms of, 157;
implications of revision for
French history, 170-71; need
for revision, 156-57, 169-71.
See also Decline of the nobility; Methodology
Investigations of the nobility:
See Recherches

Joan of Arc, 35

King's council: *See* Royal council
Kinship groups: *See* Family
groups

L'Archier, Jean, 87
Labatut, Jean-Pierre, 6, 9
labor obligations, 144

Marriage patterns (*cont.*)
nobles, 109-10; of provincial
nobility, 100; tendency towards
endogamy, 100, 104-06; theories
of, 100-01. *See also* Endogamy;
Intermarriage
Matignon, 78, 91, 94, 163
Matignon, Jacques, 91
Matignon, Odet, 91
Membership of the nobility, 10,
20, 43-44, 54, 62; calculation of
continuity of, 47; changes in,
49, 51-53, 56-58; domination by
old nobles, 58; expansion in,
53; regulation of, 62. *See also*
Expansion of the nobility;
Internal divisions of the
nobility; Population; Social
mobility
Ménardiere, Helene de la, 113
Ménardiere, Marc de la, 113
Mésalliance, by *noblesse de race,*
113-16. *See also* Intermarriage;
Marriage patterns
Mesmes, Jacques de, 26-28, 34
Mesnil, Francois, 88
Messager, 34
Methodology, used in this study,
3, 4, 14-19; advantages of,
157. *See also* Interpretations
of the nobility
Meyer, Jean, 6, 9, 41, 60-61, 64-65
"Middle class," of nobility, 127
Military: *See* Military activity;
Military capability; Military ex-
perience; Military hierarchy;
Military leaders; Military nobil-
ity; Military obligations;
Military service; *Noblesse
d'épée*
Military activity, importance for
nobles, 88; level of, 82-85
Military capability, surveys of,
81-82, 84-85
Military careers, 81; and

antiquity, 73; and Protestantism, 163-64; regularity of, 72;
and wealth, 73
Military experience, noteworthy,
87-88
Military hierarchy: effect of
social mobility on, 90; and new
nobles, 93; and old nobility,
90-92; structure of, 90. *See
also* Military leaders
Military leaders, 72-73, 83, 90;
antiquity of, 90-91. *See also*
Military hierarchy
Military nobility, 99; and Bayeux
nobles, 88-89; importance of,
85; total size, 86-87. *See also
Noblesse d'épée*
Military obligations, attempts to
expand, 81-82, 84-85
Military service, 71-72, 120; by
age cohort, 88-90; and *anoblis,*
73; and assimilation, 72-73; attempts to increase, 81-82; exemptions from, 82; extent of,
87, 89-90; lack of, 88-90;
length of, 88-89, 93-94; and
new nobles, 94-95; surveys of,
81-82; types of, 87-88
Modern state, development of,
5-8; and mobility, 170
Moigne, Noel le, 34
Monarchy, 4-6; and nobility,
170; role in creation of new
nobles, 65. *See also* Crown;
Modern state; Regulation of
nobility by the crown
Monnier, Jean, 37
Montfaut, Raymond de, 23, 26,
27-28
Montfriart, Joachim, 42
Montpensier, Duke of, 78
Mousnier, Roland, 68

Name-matching, 102-03; accuracy

Real social mobility, 58, 63.
See also Social mobility
Recherches, 13-15, 20-23, 25-44,
48-50, 55, 60, 103-04, 121, 145,
161, 167-68; complaints against,
36, 168; completeness of, 46;
conventions used by commissions, 54; decisions of, 35-36;
direction of, 25, 41-42; effectiveness of, 28; in the élection
of Bayeux, 25; family units
represented in, 45; as historical
source, 25, 51, 54, 65-67, 73;
and marriage records, 101-02;
methods of operation, 23, 27-
36, 41-42; motives behind,
22-23, 25, 37-38, 42; reliability
of, 41-42; reversals of adverse
decisions, 40-42; rigorousness
of, 36, 40-42, 61; suppression
by Louis XI, 23; value of, 47;
value in measuring social
mobility, 54. See also Condemnations; Regulation of
nobility by crown; Usurpation
Reformation, 5
Reformations of the nobility:
See Recherches
Regulation of nobility by crown,
40, 42, 61; legalistic nature
of, 168; by letters of ennoblement, 64-65; in Middle Ages,
60; origins, 22-25; and Protes-
tantism, 167-69. See also
Recherches
Religious behavior. See Activism;
Behavior of nobles
Religious conviction, 166
Repichon, Michel de, 26
Research, need for, 169-70
Reviers, 28
Reviers, Anthoine de, 134
Reviers, Nicolas, 28
Rich nobles, antiquity of, 124-25
Riuray, Jesse de, 28

Riuray, Pierre de, 28
Rivière, de la, 76-77, 107
Rivière, Francois de la, 77, 107
Rivière, Guillaume de la, 77
Rivière, Jean de la, 77
Roissy. See Mesmes, Jacques de
Romier, Lucien, 7-8
Rouen, 67
Roupnel, Gaston, 7
Royal council, 41, 67-68, 74
Royal household, 68
Royville, Jean de, 29
Ruined nobles, stereotype of, 130

Saint Bartholomew's Day Mas-
sacre, 160-61
Saint-Gilles, 115
Saint Lô, 27, 107, 163
Saint-Ouen, Tanneguy, 88
Sale of titles, crown's reasons
for, 44
Saon, Henry, 88
Secretaries of the king, 68
Seigneurial rights, 141-42
Seigneurial titles, 96
Seized property, 129-30; im-
portance of nobles as pur-
chasers, 153-54; extent and
value of, 129, 149-52; identity
of purchasers, 151-54; pro-
cedures, 135; sale at auction
of, 129, 149, 151. See also
Bankruptcies; Décrets des
heritages; Indebtedness
Seizures of property. See Seized
property
Self-identity, of nobles as military
class, 71-72
Social cohesiveness, 118
Social conflict. See Internal
divisions of nobility
Social divisions. See Internal
divisions of nobility
Social history, adequacy of
sources, 20

LIBRARY OF CONGRESS CATALOGING IN PUBLICATION DATA

Wood, James B   1946-
   The nobility of the election of Bayeux, 1463-1666.

   Bibliography: p.
   Includes index.
     1. Bayeux, France—Nobility—History.   2. Bayeux,
France—Nobility—History—16th century.   3. Bayeux,
France—Nobility—History—17th century.   4. Bayeux,
France—Social conditions.   I. Title.
HT653.F7W66   301.44'2   79-3235
ISBN 0-691-05294-8